Fianna Fáil and Irish Labour

Fianna Fáil and Irish Labour

1926 to the Present

Kieran Allen

Pluto Press

LONDON · CHICAGO, ILLINOIS

First published 1997 by Pluto Press
345 Archway Road, London N6 5AA
and 1436 West Randolph,
Chicago, Illinois 60607, USA

British Library Cataloguing-in-Publication Data
A catalogue record for this book is available from the British Library

ISBN 0 7453 0865 1 hbk

Library of Congress Cataloging in Publication Data
Allen, Kieran, 1954–
    Fianna Fáil and Irish labour: 1926 to the present/Kieran Allen.
      p.   cm.
    ISBN 0–7453–0865–1
    1. Ireland—Politics and government—1922– 2. Working class–
  –Ireland—Political activity—History—20th century. 3. Political
  parties—Ireland—History—20th century. 4. Labor movement–
  –Ireland—History—20th century. 5. Fianna Fáil—History.
  I. Title.
  DA963.A6   1997
  941.5082—dc21   96–50123
                                                                CIP

Designed and produced for Pluto Press by
Chase Production Services, Chadlington, OX7 3LN
Typeset from disk by Stanford DTP Services, Milton Keynes
Printed in Great Britain

Contents

List of Tables

Abbreviations

ACA	Army Comrades Association
ATGWU	Amalgamated Transport and General Workers Union
CIE	Coras Iompair Eireann (Irish State Transport Company)
CIO	Commission on Industrial Organisation
CIU	Congress of Irish Unions
CSO	Central Statistics Office
DATA	Draughtsmen's and Allied Technicians' Association
ESB	Electricity Supply Board
FIM	Federation of Irish Manufacturers
FRW	Federation of Rural Workers
FUE	Federated Union of Employers
GAA	Gaelic Athletic Association
GNP	Gross National product
ICTU	Irish Congress of Trade Unions
IDA	Industrial Development Authority
ILP	Irish Labour Party
IMETU	Irish Municipal Employees Trade Union
IRA	Irish Republican Army
ITA	Irish Telephonists Association
ITGWU	Irish Transport and General Workers Union
ITUC	Irish Trade Union Congress
JLC	Joint Labour Committees
NCCL	National Council of Civil Liberties
NIC	Newly industrialised country
NICRA	Northern Ireland Civil Rights Association
NILP	Northern Ireland Labour Party
NLP	National Labour Party
OPW	Office of Public Works
PAYE	Pay as you earn
RTE	Radio Telefis Eireann (Irish Radio and Television)
RUC	Royal Ulster Constabulary
SDLP	Social Democratic and Labour Party
SPO	State Papers Office
TD	Teachta Dála (Member of the Dáil)
WUI	Workers Union of Ireland

Preface

Although Fianna Fáil is the largest political party in the Republic of Ireland, there are certain obstacles in the way of studying its development. Until recently, for example, the party did not keep its archives in any real order. Access to what records existed was often obtained by the most informal of arrangements. The party's founder Eamon de Valera kept detailed papers on his activities but lodged them with the Franciscan Order in Dun Laoghaire, Dublin, where only a section has become available.

By contrast, the official labour movement maintains the most detailed of public records. Copious annual reports are produced by large unions and central bodies such as the Irish Congress of Trade Unions (ICTU) and its predecessors, the Irish Trade Union Congress (ITUC) and the Congress of Irish Unions (CIU). These records, however, give access to the official echelons of the movement. They are often written in an overformal style and only give a little of the flavour of the day-to-day struggle and sacrifices that the workers who make up this movement experienced.

These are significant limitations on any study that examines the relationship of Fianna Fáil to the organised working class. I have, however, done my best to piece together the most accurate picture possible from the available sources. These include Labour Party annual reports; the agenda and resolutions of the Fianna Fáil annual conferences; minutes of the Fianna Fáil parliamentary party, 1927–46; minutes of the Fianna Fáil national executive for much of the 1950s; the Eamon de Valera papers; scripts of speeches by Ministers of Labour from 1966 to 1990; minutes of the executive committee of ITUC, CIU, ICTU from the 1930s to 1970s; and ITGWU annual conference reports. Most of the individuals who gave me access to this material will disagree vehemently with the conclusions I have drawn from the material. My thanks, however, are due to them.

I was fortunate also to commence this study just after ICTU donated an immense collection of its files to the National Archives. These are an invaluable source of material for anyone studying the direction taken by the Irish labour movement. They add considerably to the body of material found in a variety of institutions around Dublin. My thanks are also due to the staff of: the National

Archives, University College of Dublin Archives; Trinity College Library, and the National Library of Ireland.

The study commenced as a piece of research that was undertaken under the auspices of the Trinity College Sociology Department. Hilary Tovey played an important role in forcing me to clarify my ideas by challenging confusions and muddles through espousing a different perspective to my own. Willie Cumming, Dave McDonagh, Kevin Wingfield, and Conor Kostick all read various drafts of this book. Marnie Holborow spent considerable time in redrafting certain sections and in arguing for a sharper form of analysis. Less obviously, my involvement in the Socialist Workers Party has given me insights and ideas into the realities of class conflict in Ireland. And that, in the final analysis, is what prompted me to look at the thorny subject of the relationship between Fianna Fáil and Irish labour.

Introduction

Fianna Fáil used to have a proud boast: it was not a 'mere political party' like the others but was rather a 'national movement'.[1] This was a claim that was not entirely without foundation. Alongside the Catholic Church it has probably done more than any other institution to shape the society of the Republic of Ireland. Until the seventies, it occupied government office for longer than most other parties in Western Europe, with the significant exception of the Unionist Party in Northern Ireland. Between 1932 and 1973, for example, it was only out of office on two occasions totalling seven years. Fianna Fáil's tentacles seemed to reach into almost every area of Irish life. In its heyday the party membership was numbered at around 100,000 in a country whose total population was less than 3.5 million adults and children. Everywhere one looked there was a trace of its influence. If you took part in the Gaelic Athletic Association, the country's main sporting organisation, you were likely to find Fianna Fáil activists running the local committee. If you wanted a job or a local authority house, it was sometimes wise to approach a Fianna Fáil councillor. Even when organisations claimed to be non-political, as the primary teachers' union did, it so happened that their political nominee to the Senate was a Fianna Fáil member.

By contrast, the Irish labour movement presents something of an enigma. It has strong roots in Irish society, with the unions organising half of the workforce. Two of its founders – James Connolly and James Larkin – are legendary figures, almost canonised by an establishment that has named schools, railway stations, and hospitals after them. This did not simply reflect a nostalgic harking back to the past. Despite the country's sometimes conservative image, trade unionism in Ireland is respected and popular. Few disputes have ever been resolved by strike breaking and many have gained immense sympathy and support. The shrill complaint from those 'who have done well' that there exists a deep sense of 'begrudgery' in the country is not without foundation. Amongst much of the population there is a profound ambivalence about those who usher in redundancies and low pay to claim their place among the pantheon of entrepreneurs.

Yet the strength of organised labour fails to find a political expression. The Irish left was once compared to the pinch of salt that is thrown in to make bread: it adds a little flavour but hardly any substance. In the past, it certainly seemed to be marginal and even irrelevant. For most of its history, the Irish Labour Party has been formally linked to the unions – but it has failed to win the votes of those members. The party has become a pale shadow of its European counterparts, marginalised in electoral terms and held up as an object of contempt by Fianna Fáil supporters, who veer between denouncing it as the haven of 'smoked salmon socialists' and an anachronism that belongs to the dated class politics of Britain. As the Labour Party never gained more than a fifth of the popular vote, the only time it has seen government office has been in administrations where right-wing politicians were dominant.

The reality is that Fianna Fáil won the support of Labour's 'natural constituency'. As a catch-all party, its singular achievement was to win nearly equal shares of votes from all classes in Irish society and it has normally never achieved less than 40 per cent of the votes of the skilled and unskilled working class. The party's influence, however, goes deeper than these electoral figures would suggest. Unfortunately, many political scientists focus mainly on the manifestos, policies and arguments during election campaigns, rather than on the deeper roots that a party like Fianna Fáil sank throughout Irish society. Fianna Fáil built a tradition where thousands of working-class people saw it as their main hope for advancement. They may not have looked at the party in class terms but they still supported Fianna Fáil because they believed that it promised 'social ascent as a universal possibility', as one writer described populist movements.[2]

The glaring paradox is that the stated objectives which Fianna Fáil was established to achieve remain as distant as ever. It pledged to restore the Irish language as the main medium of conversation. Yet after more than six decades of state effort, only 3 per cent of the population regularly speaks the language and many of the rest of the population are barely competent in it.[3] It solemnly promised to remove partition and win a united Ireland. Yet this is rarely mentioned in the party's electoral addresses, and if there is a strategy for achieving this end, it remains a secret even from its supporters. One former Fianna Fáil cabinet minister, Kevin Boland, probably articulated a suspicion which many hold when he claimed that the party which had been founded to remove partition has become its greatest bulwark.[4] The party certainly seems more at home running the 26-county state rather than involving itself in the messy business of 'solving the national question'.

Where then does Fianna Fáil's uniqueness originate? John Whyte claims that Ireland diverges from the pattern in the rest of Europe, because its politics, mysteriously, have no social basis.[5] Yet it is just this view that Fianna Fáil has played on to secure, so successfully, its own hegemony. Social class would seem to have little or no influence on voting patterns *because* Fianna Fáil has been dominant. In this process, the normal representations of working-class politics have been pushed aside and the traditional left–right divide has failed to take place in Ireland. How this occurred is the main subject of this book.

Explanations

The paradoxical nature of Fianna Fáil seems to have struck awe into many researchers. The party has yet to see a full-length history written about its activities. Where explanations of its activities are offered, they often refer to irrational sources of power. One of the few books on Fianna Fáil, by the prominent journalist Dick Walsh, relies heavily on the notion that Fianna Fáil has almost a sixth sense for keeping uniquely in touch with the wellsprings of the nation. At the heart of its organisation is, apparently, a 'blazing mystique [which had] no social content'. The party is able to invoke the deepest instincts of all classes of Irish people because, '[it] looked neither left nor right but steadfastly to the past and drew on the spirit of the nation, almost but not quite as Thomas Davis and the Young Irelanders had dreamed of it'.[6]

This, of course, coincides almost exactly with how the party would like to see itself. Nationalist movements have a habit of claiming to derive their strength from a mystical communal past rather than from representing the interests of particular groups and classes. Instead of an explanation, therefore, this simply offers another version of the party's own ideology.

Walsh's approach is by no means unusual. J.P. Carroll concluded about Eamon de Valera that the strength of the party founder's politics 'lay in the fact that it drew on much of what was beyond the rational'.[7] Jeffrey Praeger even goes so far as to argue that when it was formed in 1926, Fianna Fáil represented the cultural form of 'Gaelic Romanticism', and that after it won office in 1932, '"hot" politics was the new order; technical or formal rationality in decision making divorced from transcendent meanings could no longer disguise the cultural interests involved in policy making'.[8] This focus on the 'hot', irrational basis for Irish republican politics belongs to a long tradition that dates back to Matthew Arnold. Arnold believed that he had discovered the very secret of the inner essence of 'the Celt' when he found they were 'truly sentimental – always ready to react against the despotism of fact'.[9] This grating cultural stereotype simply hampers any serious inquiry.

Other, more serious academic analyses of the party have tended to polarise between intuitive explanations that focus on Ireland's political culture and overmechanical explanations which see the party clientelist practices as the key to its success. In the former case, the most influential writer has been Basil Chubb who argued that Ireland's political culture was the product of a unique intermeshing of the Westminister state apparatus with Irish peasant life. From Britain there arrived the values of parliamentary democracy and from the peasantry there came a propensity to nationalism, pre-industrial ideologies, Catholicism, anti-intellectualism and authoritarianism. The peasants wanted access to the formal structures of the new Irish state through a series of intermediaries who embodied their culture and gave a more personal service. The party most suited for this was Fianna Fáil as it focused on these primary values.[10]

This notion that Fianna Fáil's success rested on a rural past dominating an urban present has been given a sharper and more polemical edge by Tom Garvin. Garvin believes Ireland has a 'pre-industrial ideology' which was 'devised for the needs of de-tribalised and stateless peasants'. This culture was formed primarily in the more rural, western periphery of the country and then transmitted into the cities by Fianna Fáil who engaged in 'an invasion of commercialised and urban Ireland'. This culture continues to see the real Irish occupying a peripheral position in relation to Britain and it retains its influence because of the continuing Anglo-Irish impasse.[11]

The belief that Fianna Fáil derived its strength from a largely peasant-based, Catholic culture has been popular for a number of reasons. It reinforces the prevailing conservative forms of sociology and political science which seek to explain society by reference to more general norms and values rather than material forces. The writers can assume that they themselves have risen above this particular culture but nevertheless value its contribution to upholding consensus and cohesion. In this outlook, classes may exist as purely economic categories, but they have little bearing on real social life, which is shaped primarily by a common culture. This approach, which regards traditional and modern culture as polar opposites, obviates the need for any serious analysis of how societies change.

Moreover, the explanation that sees the strength of Fianna Fáil deriving from an older rural-based political culture makes little sense. It ignores the fact that the party won as many votes in Dublin as in rural areas from a very early stage. It fails to explain why the culture of the west of Ireland was so successful in invading the cities rather than the other way round. The reference to Fianna Fáil's system of organisation being based on a 'leaders–local activists grassroots system' is unconvincing. It is voluntaristic and simply ignores how the party's specific policies clearly held some appeal for particular urban classes. Writers who focus on the rural imagery and discourse of Fianna Fáil fail to appreciate that urban classes can often draw on idioms of the rural past to express current interests. De Valera's famous statement about 'comely maidens dancing on the crossroads' need not be taken solely as a vision for a future society – but rather as an ideology that gave a romantic gloss to the hardships imposed by his party's attempt to forge a native capitalism through protectionism and isolation.

The other main academic approach to Fianna Fáil looks at the pattern of clientelism and seems at first more convincing. After all, Irish politics has developed the rather unique institution of 'the clinic' where almost every politician, from government minister to aspiring country councillor, will sit in a room above a pub, or even an undertaker's, to hear constituents' individual problems. Local studies by a number of sociologists in different areas have revealed extensive clientelist networks where politicians expect votes for favours delivered.[12] Originally these investigations were undertaken from within the theoretical perspective of the political culture school. Later, however, the focus on clientelism was given a more radical veneer as writers such as Hazelhorn, Higgins and Gibbon saw it as a product of a particular form of 'dependent capitalism'.[13] These writers challenged the emphasis on political culture and claimed to have a more rigorous and materialist analysis which took account of the conflicts in Irish society. From this perspective, Fianna Fáil's long hold on office gave it a privileged opportunity to build up clientelist practices which bought individual loyalties and functioned as a political strategy to divide the working class.

Again, however, this approach has its own pitfalls. The image of a patron–client relationship conjures up an extraordinary level of dependency for the services on offer. Fianna Fáil might have been able to tell individuals that they were getting a local authority house, but there was no guarantee they would vote for the party at the next election. Higgins and Gibbon's assumption that near 'feudal relations' persist in the present mode of capitalist production seems, at best, exaggerated. Contrary to the sometimes impressionistic local studies, there is some evidence to suggest that clientelist networks are not nearly as widespread as was assumed. The Institute for Public Administration, for example, found that 80 per cent of the electorate never even approached a politician individually for a favour.[14] The focus on clientelism tends to assume an unduly cynical approach to politics. It forgets that, particularly in the past, many people supported political parties because they believed in their actual politics and tradition. More seriously, it assumes that the working class are atomised and disorganised. They become the object and not the subject of history. The record, however, shows that far from Fianna Fáil having to deal with a disorganised working class, it had to make strenuous efforts to relate to a very organised labour movement.

The main exception to this type of academic literature has been the writings of Bew, Patterson and Dunphy.[15] These have developed a common perspective where they analyse Fianna Fáil in class terms. They argue that the party was concerned both to foster capitalist development and to maintain its hegemony over the working class. Their writings often focus on the internal divisions that this contradictory approach imposed on the party. While this theoretical framework has generated many insights it has suffered from one crucial oversight – there is little reference to workers' own actions. Instead, the working class appear mainly as dupes of the rather complex manoeuvres that take place in the upper echelons of Fianna Fáil. These writers consequently look to parties such as the Labour Party or Democratic Left to develop hegemonic strategies which can displace Fianna Fáil. Dunphy, for example, claims that the challenge facing the Labour Party is to 'exploit the contradictions inherent in Fianna Fáil's support base by setting an agenda of economic, social and political reforms which Fianna Fáil can respond to only at its peril'.[16] This only begs the question of whether the record of Irish social democracy inspires any confidence that they are indeed capable of pressing even for substantial reforms. Fianna Fáil has tended to make gains precisely when Labour enters coalition governments and then attacks its own supporters rather than delivering major change.

Alibis: the Left and Fianna Fáil

The Irish left has always been uneasy about Fianna Fáil. Mesmerised by the party's strength, there are some who can barely imagine how this great monolith will be cracked. Some of the explanations offered about the strength of Fianna Fáil have become alibis for the failures of particular strategies on the left.

One alibi has been to make reference to what one writer called 'the durability of inherited allegiances'.[17] Fianna Fáil has a 'traditional vote' that is passed down through the generations almost like a family heirloom. This is usually connected with an argument about a missed opportunity in 1918 when the Labour Party, in a gesture of foolish magnanimity, stood aside from the general election to allow Sinn Féin to express the general will of the Irish people for independence. The cleavage that later occurred among the elected representatives laid the basis for the civil war and the formation of Fianna Fáil and Fine Gael. The left, it seems, were ever after excluded from traditional voting allegiances.

There are a number of problems with this view. For one thing, it conveniently glosses over Labour's reasons for abstaining in 1918. The decision not to participate was symptomatic of a more general failure to advance a distinct and coherent class response in the fight against the British Empire.[18] The Labour Party showed a similar shyness during 'the troubles' in Northern Ireland after 1968 and was unable to produce a coherent working-class perspective. Confusions and divisions that have surfaced within the Labour Party whenever the 'national question' has moved to the foreground. This prevarication has done little to increase the party's credibility. More importantly, the theory of the Missed Opportunity looks on Irish politics as if they have been preserved in aspic. All major conflicts after 1923 are simply a replay of civil war clashes. This ignores how Fianna Fáil had to fight for its hegemony over workers and how the 1918 election was only one of many occasions when the Labour Party missed outstanding opportunities to mount a sustained challenge. Fianna Fáil, if nothing else, was certainly clear that its predominant position in Irish politics was never guaranteed by the past. This is why it so actively intervened to try to shape the labour movement in its image.

A second alibi invokes the country's underdevelopment and claims that the left could not grow amidst a largely rural population. There is obviously an important grain of truth in this, and the advent of industrialisation has created openings for a far wider layer of workers to become responsive to socialist ideas. However, there has been a tendency to magnify the insight out of all proportion. The Workers Party, for example, adopted a rigid 'stages' approach whereby the duty of the left was first to promote an industrial revolution – against a 'lazy' native bourgeoisie – before the fight for socialism could begin. This theory arose from a form of mechanical materialism that failed to appreciate how workers can still be the key agents for change by virtue of their collective class consciousness rather than simply by their sheer size. Economic backwardness alone cannot explain just how weak the Irish left was. Significant forms of class struggle took place right throughout the history of Southern Ireland – yet the left made few gains from these. Moreover, the striking fact about Labour Party TDs up until the late 1960s was that they were more likely to resemble a 'collection of rural personalities' than products of an urban-based movement. The Labour Party did not just lose out in Irish society in general, but also in equal measure among urban Irish workers.

Yet another alibi relates to the domination of nationalist politics in Ireland. Michael Gallagher probably summed up much of the common sense of both the republican and social democratic left when he wrote that,

> For as long as Ireland is politically divided Fianna Fáil will have something to stand for, a cause far more inspiring than either of the other main parties can offer, and will continue to win votes which in other circumstances would go to Labour.[19]

However, if Fianna Fáil has robbed Labour's natural constituency through its use of an anti-partition rhetoric, it must have performed the political equivalent of a three-card trick. Its rhetoric on partition has certainly not been matched by any degree of success. Fianna Fáil did little about the border because it did not want to upset the stability of capitalist social relations on the island. It often rhetorically attacked British influence, but once it established that the South was a sovereign independent state, it was more than willing to work with the British ruling class. Gallagher's view misunderstands the central kernel of Fianna Fáil's nationalism. The potency of Fianna Fáil's green rhetoric came from the way in which it was connected to the economic development of the South. Fianna Fáil translated the language of national achievement into that of capitalist growth and promised that there would be real benefits for all. This is why many of its election manifestos barely mentioned the North but focused on promises to increase industrial growth and to provide housing, social welfare and education benefits for all.

This is not to argue that the North has been irrelevant to the concerns of Southern workers – only to claim that Fianna Fáil's occasional rhetoric on the issue never guaranteed it a base. Even when the national question intruded more directly into the political life of the South, as it did on a number of occasions, this did not always work to the benefit of Fianna Fáil. When the Northern conflict broke out in 1969, for example, it initially contributed to the growth of left-wing ideas in the South. When the H Block crisis emerged in 1981, it contributed significantly to the failure of Charles J. Haughey to form a majority government.

The more general problem with Gallagher's argument is its assumption that nationalism is almost a spiritual force, more passionate and interesting than mundane class struggle, and able to seize people's hearts totally and permanently. In reality, it is far more contradictory.[20] Workers have often experienced a glaring gap between Fianna Fáil's talk of a 'national community' and the reality of class conflict in the South. If there existed a left which stood wholeheartedly on the side of workers it could have pointed to why Fianna Fáil had not only failed on partition, but also why the problems that Southern workers faced no longer stemmed from a colonial establishment but a nationalist elite.

Such a left, of course, has hardly existed in Ireland up to recent times. The past failures of the Irish left, therefore, revolve primarily around the failure of the Irish Labour Party. It is not necessary to adopt an 'if only' approach to Irish politics to appreciate the depth of the party's historic failure. We can grant that in many instances the objective conditions were unfavourable to the growth of the Labour Party. Where workers suffered major defeats and where protectionism offered some prospect of growth – as it did in the 1930s, for example – it is not surprising that Fianna Fáil was dominant. We can equally appreciate that at the start of the 1960s Fianna Fáil received a new impetus from its alliance with multinationals.

But to focus on objective circumstances alone is to look for an alibi. It means ignoring the political weakness of the Labour Party itself. Instead of looking simply at individual episodes of abstention or betrayal, it is important to grasp that there is a pattern to the failure of the Irish Labour Party. The social democratic tradition is everywhere based on a separation of economic and political struggles. Social democracy sees real politics as being focused on parliament and tends to ignore the importance of the day-to-day struggles of workers. It has a disdain for class struggle and a tendency to shore up the state, which it sees as the main vehicle for reform. In the Irish context, this has meant that it has willingly thrown away opportunities to challenge Fianna Fáil at its weakest point. When workers engage in major struggles, particularly in those involving confrontation with their own state, they are more likely to question the sort of traditional allegiances which in the past have tied them to Fianna Fáil. The Labour Party, however, rarely supports this type of conflict and in some instances will even attack such struggles for undermining the legitimacy of parliament. In doing so it helps to relegate itself to a minor role in Irish politics. That too is a central theme of this book.

Approaching Fianna Fáil

What follows is an attempt to analyse the relationship between Fianna Fáil and organised workers from a Marxist perspective. For some this may appear an unusual exercise. As the classic catch-all party, Fianna Fáil seems to transcend class divisions, which may appear to make it not amenable to this approach. However, the fact that a political movement decries any talk of class division and loudly proclaims its allegiance to 'the people', does not mean that it does not serve particular interests. As Ian Roxborough puts it, in a Latin American context: 'a movement which claims to be classless may well be composed of classes or at least identifiable in terms of classes and class interests'.[21] In Ireland, where almost all official politics are based on denial of class conflict and yet where poverty and oppression are rampant, a Marxist approach is all the more necessary.

In its early period Fianna Fáil espoused a form of populist politics that shared some similarities with many such movements in Latin America. The first four chapters examine the rise and fall of this particular method of establishing hegemony over the workers' movement. Populism is clearly a very loose, slippery term that covers a multitude of political formations. A succinct definition of populism has been offered by di Tella:

> A political movement which enjoys the support of the mass of the urban working class and/or peasantry but which does not result from the autonomous organisational power of either. It is also supported by non-working class sectors unpholding an anti-status quo ideology.[22]

Although somewhat broad, this definition can serve as a useful starting point for examining the early Fianna Fáil. It highlights how the party both sought the support of workers while constantly depreciating their ability to move forward as a distinct class. It used a radical anti-status quo rhetoric but one that was careful never to question the basis of capitalism itself.

According to many conventional sociologists, populist movements form when there is a charismatic leader who emerges in a time of social crisis. This approach is derived from Weber who took the term 'charisma' from the vocabulary of early Christianity where it meant an individual possessing 'the gift of grace'.[23] This almost mystical perspective on political developments reveals the inadequacy of this form of sociology when it comes to explaining social change. It makes no attempt to see why social groups give backing to these movements, but simply sees people as manipulated emotionally. Its focus on leadership qualities leads to the image of a Pied Piper leading the 'gullible and discontented along devious routes to power'.[24] Applied to Fianna Fáil, the emphasis on charisma borders on the absurd. How could Eamon de Valera possibly be regarded as a 'charismatic' leader if no account is taken of the social and economic conditions that raised this rather dull orator to the level of a national hero?

In Latin America where populist movements have been more common, a number of Marxist writers have offered a different explanation. Ianni, for example, argued that one of the effects of colonialism was that the ruling elite had greater difficulties consolidating itself as a united class.[25] More traditional sections, often based more around a landed oligarchy, sought to supply primary produce to the old metropolis. Others wanted to take the road of industrial development and opposed the form of neocolonialism that held back their countries. This conflict within the elite was often only resolved when the latter group mobilised support from the lower classes to bring about a change in the control of the state. A 'pro-industrial alliance' was often established which promoted an ideology of national development where all classes were promised gains.[26] In order to hold the movement together the very idea of class conflict was attacked and attributed to foreign intervention that distorted the natural and harmonious development of the national community.

But why did workers support such movements? In countries such as Argentina, Mexico or Ireland various forms of syndicalist militancy which encouraged a distrust of middle-class politicians were deeply ingrained in the traditions of the working class before the rise of populism. Many reasons help to account for how this changed. Underdeveloped countries do not provide as stable patterns of employment as the more advanced. There are large pockets of casual labour, underemployment and unemployment which surround the core of the organised working class. Lacking a wider political framework, a layer of workers can sometimes come to believe that industrial development is directly in their interests. More particularly, their union leaders see it as a condition for establishing more stable trade union organisations.

This tendency is often exacerbated by major defeats in the class struggle. Syndicalism can thrive on solidarity and militancy when a working class feels its strength. In periods of defeat, however, it falls back on meagre political resources to survive difficulty and can sometimes melt away as quickly as it emerges. However, none of these tendencies can be divorced from the issue that organised left-wing parties are arguing. Petras has shown, for example, in Argentina that because both the Communist Party and the socialist parties were tied to the concerns of the Cold War rivals, Peronism became the vehicle by which anger and radicalism was expressed.[27] A study of Fianna Fáil's relation to Irish workers must therefore in turn include a discussion of how left-wing parties reponded to Fianna Fáil.

This approach to populism emphasises that there are both structural and ideological processes at work. In the Irish case, the neocolonial link with Britain provides a vital context for understanding the growth of Fianna Fáil in its early period. The party challenged the domination of the agro-export model and so helped to create the space in which native industrial capitalism could start to expand. It set out to establish sovereignty and to promote the national development of the 26-county state. While partition was officially opposed, it remained at the level of a national grievance, a symbol that might one day be righted – but not an item of pressing importance. Chapters 1 to 4 trace the transition that Fianna Fáil made from a radical sounding populist movement to a party that used a virulent form of Catholic nationalism to consolidate its hold over the South.

The populist politics of Fianna Fáil entered a dead end in the bleak 1950s. The saliency of the conflict with Britain seemed to have receded and yet full-scale independence for the Irish Republic had brought few gains for workers. Chapters 5, 6 and 7 attempt to show how Fianna Fáil used the '1958 turn', which opened up Ireland to the multinationals, to reconstitute its hegemony. Ireland has traditionally combined elements of the First World and Third World societies. After 1958, however, the former became more predominant and Fianna Fáil attempted to maintain its hegemony over workers through social partnership arrangements with the union leaders. Starting in the early 1960s, union leaders became involved in a variety of tripartite committees and commissions which began to tie them into supporting the main priorities of Irish capitalism. By the end of the 1980s Ireland had a very dense form of social partnership in which the union leaders promoted wage restraint as part of a political exchange to achieve formal rights of consultation on most aspects of social policy.

Niamh Hardiman has argued that 'strong corporatist' arrangements were not feasible in Ireland because there did not exist the political conditions that could produce a 'positive sum' game of class compromise.[28] This, however, misreads the purpose of these arrangements; they are not seriously designed to produce gains for both sides. Instead, they have become the means by which employers have gained the freedom to raise productivity while workers are tied to both wage restraint and 'no strike' agreements. In brief, social partnership is a strategy for domination over workers. It appeals mainly to the union bureaucracy, which can see the benefits of organisational stability that flow from the agreements. Streeck has shown, for example, in West Germany that corporatist arrangements have led to a growing 'professionalisation' of the unions where the number and influence of full-timers grow and key areas of decision making become more 'sealed off' from the rank and file.[29] The political conditions for these arrangements were long established in the friendly relations that Irish union leaders traditionally had with Fianna Fáil.

Between both periods of the party's domination, however, there lies a common thread. Fianna Fáil has succeeded when it has delivered on promise of expansion and growth. The famous remark by Lemass that a national tide lifts all boats deliberately ignored the inequalities between the social classes. Nevertheless, when he spoke either as Minister for Industry and Commerce in the 1930s or as Taoiseach in the 1960s, he could still point to a tide. When it goes out, Fianna Fáil could be in trouble – particularly if there is an alternative that roots itself in the struggles of workers. This book is part of a contribution to building that alternative.

CHAPTER 1

Fianna Fáil: The Radical Years, 1926–1932

On 16 May 1926 the inaugural meeting of Fianna Fáil was held at the La Scala Theatre in Dublin. The party was born from a split within the Sinn Féin movement and was formed in an atmosphere of defeat. Six months before, the 26-county parliament had voted to give assent to the boundary agreement which confirmed the partition of Ireland. At grassroots level, republicans faced hardship and many experienced victimisation. They were often blacklisted from state jobs after their defeat in the Civil War and many of their friends and supporters were forced to join the emigrant ship. It was clear to many republicans that a new turn was needed and de Valera had first tried to bring about a change within Sinn Féin. As president of the party, he called an extraordinary Ard Fheis to argue that the party should enter parliament if the oath of allegiance to the British monarchy was removed. By a margin of five votes, de Valera was defeated on abstentionism and he immediately led his followers out to form Fianna Fáil.[1]

Once the new party was formed, it became clear that other changes were in store. After the Civil War the republican movement had been content to claim the high ground of spiritual nationalism. Politics was regarded with disdain and only the armed struggle was seen as productive. A culture of sacrifice and moral uprightness permeated the whole movement and there was little interest in economic conditions. This was encapsulated in its attitudes to emigrants where its paper, *An Phoblacht*, argued that 'men and women who emigrate when, with a little or much hardship, they might stay at home are acting unpatriotically. ... they will not prove good citizens to whatever country they go'.[2]

This was not the first time Sinn Féin had displayed disdain for the realities of poverty. Many of the Sinn Féin leaders such as Austin Stack or Art O'Connor had helped to suppress the seizures of land during the War of Independence. It left them with an abiding fear of any class conflict which might destroy their lofty ideals of an Irish Ireland. 'We will oppose any and every proposal which is for the interest of a class instead of the nation', proclaimed their paper.[3]

14

De Valera shared many of these conservative instincts. But he recognised the dangers of republicanism becoming marginalised if did not address more immediate and pressing economic conditions. If this involved an ambiguous appeal to 'the poor' or 'the workers and small farmers', he was flexible enough to make it. The inaugural meeting of Fianna Fáil in La Scala was therefore characterised by a new concern for 'the social and economic side' and it was de Valera who gave the lead. He told his listeners that political freedom was only a means to a greater end and that he had come to 'sympathise fully with James Connolly's passionate protest', which he then quoted at length:

> Ireland as distinct from her people is nothing to me and the man who is bubbling over with love and enthusiasm for Ireland and can yet pass unmoved through our streets and witness all the wrong and suffering, the shame and degradation brought on the people of Ireland – aye, brought by Irishmen upon Irishmen and Irish women – without burning to end it is, in my opinion, a fraud and a liar in his heart, no matter how he loves that combination of chemical elements he is pleased to call Ireland.[4]

The association of the new party, Fianna Fáil, with James Connolly was particularly evocative. Despite the hardships of the War of Independence and the subsequent Civil War, political independence in the 26 counties had brought little change in the living conditions of the majority. In 1927, for example, the *Irish Times* could report that a near famine had broken out in Erris in North Mayo. People only managed to survive because of the plentiful supply of carrigeen moss in the area.[5] De Valera's aim was to appeal to those for whom the Free State brought little improvement and he pledged that Fianna Fáil would 'take an effective part in improving the social and material conditions of the people'.[6]

But how? Fianna Fáil's founding documents declared that 'the resources and wealth of Ireland are subservient to the needs and welfare of all the people'.[7] The party promised to 'break up the large grazier's ranches and distribute them as economic farms among farmers and agricultural labourers'.[8] It favoured a national legal minimum wage and the regulation of the conditions of employment.[9] But the core of the whole programme lay elsewhere. And, rather surprisingly, it did not lie in a major concern about ending partition. True, the party was pledged to a 32-county Ireland and was appalled at the Boundary Commission report which made partition a permanent feature of Irish life. But the issue of the border was not highlighted prominently in the party's literature. There was certainly little discussion about strategies for how it might be removed. The unification of the country was seen as a vague aspiration, and partition was almost a symbol of a national wrong rather than an immediate obstacle that was to be removed.

From the very outset, the core of Fianna Fáil policies lay in a form of economic nationalism. Once again, de Valera enunciated the subtle shift in emphasis:

> If we put into effect the programme we have with respect to building up our industries and make this part of Ireland a part that human beings will be glad to live in and if we have a policy of social life here that will be far superior to the life they live up there, then England will find it hard to make people up there their tools.[10]

The 'people up there' were, of course, Northern Protestants and the indirect appeal to unity was made from within a Catholic 26-county framework.

The overriding aim of the party's economic programme which was launched in 1926 was simply to 'encourage native industries that minister to the needs of the people and to protect them by adequate tariffs'.[11] Native industries would, it was argued, operate differently from foreign capitalists. They would be more humane and there would be a 'ruralisation' programme to help them locate in small towns and so escape all the evils associated with industrialisation in Britain.[12] They would provide the means by which the nationalist goal of 'self-sufficiency' could be achieved. At this stage the party was quite hostile to foreign capital. According to Sean McEntee, foreign capital had been a 'menace to the peaceful development and advancement of other countries'.[13] Fianna Fáil only favoured the entry of foreign investment into Ireland under a leasing system whereby the government was left with an option to buy it out. Alongside protectionism, the party favoured a very mild tax regime for native capitalists. One spokesperson, Hugo Flynn, even called for the abolition of all income tax on money invested in the employment of Irish labour.[14] But the general demand was for extremely reduced levels of taxation on Irish manufacturing.

At the start there seemed to be little contradiction between this desire to create an Irish business class and a more radical sentiment for social justice. Resolutions to the first conference of the party from the newly formed Fianna Fáil branches showed a marked sympathy with the underdog. A resolution from the Micheal O' Mheallain Cumman, for example, condemned the wage cuts imposed on workers who were building the Shannon Electrification Scheme. The resolution promised that if the party won power it would ensure there was 'a wage that will permit the labourer to live under conditions commensurate with his dignity as a human being'.[15] The Fintan Lawlor Cumman demanded steps 'to make profiteering an offence punishable by imprisonment'.[16] At the following year's Ard Fheis various branches called for a levy on capital to provide jobs for the unemployed, a 40-hour week and the provision of proper housing for 'the ordinary labourer'.[17] This combination of radical rhetoric and a promotion of Irish business interests was not altogether new within Irish republicanism.

Irish republicanism was born among the radical industrialists of Belfast and Dublin in the late eighteenth century. It was a revolutionary doctrine that drew its inspiration from the French Revolution. Its founder Wolfe Tone had been able to convince erstwhile liberal Protestants to oppose Catholic discrimination and to see British rule as a basic impediment both to their freedom and, not insignificantly, to their commerce.[18] When it came to the need to wage a revolutionary war against the British Empire, Wolfe Tone had no compunction about turning to 'the men of no property'. This particular phrase helped to create a later myth that republicanism was established to promote the interests of the propertyless. Far from it. The leadership of the United Irishmen was overwhelmingly drawn from the industrialists and the professional middle class.[19] While it appealed to the artisans and the peasantry, it watched their more radical instincts with a wary eye. It sought French military help not only as an added bulwark against British forces, but also to help impose discipline in their own ranks.[20]

The first Sinn Féin party was formed in 1905 by Arthur Griffith who made no secret of his desire to establish an Irish Stock Exchange and even an Irish empire, if that were possible.[21] But the party still sought to win a political base by expressing a concern about the social conditions amongst Dublin's workers. For a brief period between 1908 and 1911 it was highly successful in doing so. Leading trade unionists such as P.T. Daly joined the party and one prominent Sinn Féin representative even claimed that 'Sinn Féin is wide enough and all-embracing enough to take in the best of socialism'.[22] Griffith's synthesis of radical pro-capitalist nationalism and working-class support only fell apart with the growth of militant trade unionism after 1911.

During the War of Independence, republicans also felt there was a need to advance a specific programme for workers and small farmers. The Democratic Programme of the First Dáil promised very radical changes and was originally written by the Labour Party leader, Tom Johnson, at the time when the influence of the Russian Revolution was enormous. Although the original draft was toned down, it was still designed to win workers to the side of 'the Republic'. But for all the radicalism of aspiration, they advocated in practice that 'Labour should wait'.[23]

In the midst of the Civil War, there emerged a tradition of 'social republicanism' around Liam Mellows. Faced with the defeat of the anti-Treaty forces, Mellows wrote two documents where he once again called for a programme 'to keep Irish Labour for the Republic'.[24] He argued that the 'stake in the country people' would only support republicans after they won power. He promised more state control over the economy and favoured the break-up of the lands of the 'aristocracy'.[25] Yet he never broke from the idea that these changes had to be bestowed upon the poor by the republicans. His radicalism took the form of a bargain struck with the dispossessed that in return for supporting 'the cause' they would be rewarded after victory. Any thought that the working class or the small farmers could act as agents of their own liberation remained foreign to Mellows. During the War of Independence the republicans had established land courts to prevent small farmers in the west of Ireland breaking up the estates of the landlords themselves.[26]

While in prison after the Civil War, de Valera must have reflected on this ambiguous tradition. In one of the letters which were smuggled out, he noted that 'the more we lean on the economic side the better it will be for the political side'.[27] But an interest in economic matters did not mean that republicans had to abandon the notion that all Irish people had a common interest. De Valera insisted that they raise 'a national programme for the common good not a class programme'.[28] Moreover, he was acutely aware that if republicans could not articulate economic grievances in nationalist terms, there was a real possibility of Irish politics splitting on class lines:

> It is vital that the Free State be shaken at the next general election, for if the opportunity is given to it to consolidate itself further as an institution – if the present Free State members are replaced by farmers and labourers and other class interests, the national interest as a whole will be submerged in the clashing of rival economic groups. It seems to be a case of now or never – at least in our time.[29]

An Outgarden of Britain

Fianna Fáil was able to combine a rhetoric about social justice with a policy of promoting Irish business because it could argue that the cause of Irish poverty was the British Empire. The Treaty granted political independence to the 26 counties but within such narrow constraints that the *Sunday Times* could comment that: 'The English victory is plain. Everything that left the question of the imperial connection in doubt in the Irish draft has been positively and successfully replaced.'[30] Sovereignty was limited even within the 26 counties. Dáil deputies were obliged to take an oath of loyalty to the British monarch. The British navy retained three bases in Irish territory. The universities were granted six seats in the Dáil. In the Senate, supporters of the former regime were over represented and were able to use that body to impose delays on legislation from the Dáil. But it was mainly the economic arrangements which added credence to Fianna Fáil claims that the link with Britain was the cause of poverty.

In 1926, the Ultimate Financial Settlement was signed between the Free State and the Empire. It contained a secret treaty whose content was revealed by the former government TD, Colonel Maurice Moore.[31] Moore showed that the treaty meant a yearly imposition of £5 million on the Irish people. The figure was made up of £3 million derived from land annuities and the remainder from an agreement to pay 75 per cent of Royal Irish Constabulary pensions, compensation for damage done to government buildings during the War of Independence, and a pledge to pay a share of the deficit of the Unemployment Fund in the United Kingdom.[32] Yet these financial commitments were only a small part of the neocolonial arrangement that persisted between the Empire and the fledgling Irish Free State. Fianna Fáil presented itself as the most determined opponent of these economic links. In his first major speech on economic policy in Dáil Eirinn, de Valera claimed that Ireland was simply 'an outgarden for the British'.[33]

It was a singularly apt description. Few industrial jobs were created in the first years of independence and the surplus population was forced to emigrate. Between 1921 and 1931, it is estimated that 33,000 people left the country annually.[34] The dependency of the economy on Britain was shown in the country's trade figures. In 1926, for example, 97 per cent of all exports went to Britain.[35] The Department of Industry and Commerce at the time, divided the trade figures into three categories but in all three, agricultural products were predominant. Category 1 was composed of live animals and represented 18 per cent of exports. Category 2 was food, drink and tobacco and made up 48 per cent of exports. Category 3, which made up 34 per cent of the total, was officially composed of 'other raw materials' and manufactured goods; in reality, it was mainly made up of leather, hide and wool products.[36]

The primary objective of the Cumman na nGaedheal government was to bolster the interests of the strong farmers who exported to Britain. Here they faced a problem because, by the mid-1920s, agricultural prices were falling steeply. The Commission on Agriculture which was established in 1922 had recommended against any direct subsidies to the farming population. The alternative course was to reduce taxes by cutting back on government spending and to push down the costs, particularly the cost of hired labour for the wealthier farmers. Just a year after the Civil War ended the Free State government had already embarked on this policy when it supported big farmers in their fight to cut the wages of agricultural workers.[37] The other element of this strategy was to preserve near free-trade conditions between Ireland and Britain. The protectionist policy advocated by Arthur Griffith was quietly dropped, much to the annoyance of sections of the Irish capitalist class. At the Fiscal Inquiry Committee in 1923 several industries argued the case against British imports. But by 1931, only 68 articles were subject to tariffs at an average rate of 9 per cent.[38]

The other area where Ireland's dependency on Britain was most acute was in the financial markets. As a result of the boom in agricultural prices during the First World War, there were, initially, large deposits in the Irish banking system. However, by the mid-1920s a considerable part of these assets was being invested in Britain. The Minister for Industry and Commerce estimated that income derived by Irish Free State residents in the year 1926/27 from foreign investments was £12 million.[39] This suggests that they held overseas assets of £200 million which was a very substantial sum for a small country. The Currency Act of 1927 maintained the parity with sterling and continued the practice of extremely lax exchange controls.This ensured that interest rates remained high as they were kept 1 per cent above the British rate to stem the flow of funds to Britain.[40]

Here, then, were the classic features of a neocolony. The formal political independence barely hid a much deeper reliance on British imperialism. Production in Ireland was one-sided and orientated to traditional sectors. Exports were exclusively directed to Britain and were almost entirely in primary produce. Capital was drained out of the country for circulation in British markets. The costs of this arrangement were borne primarily by the urban poor and the mass of small farmers. High levels of unemployment, pitiful social welfare, poor investment in housing and education, and appalling levels of emigration were all exacerbated by the underdevelopment of Irish capitalism. But if these groups bore most of the costs, sections of the emerging capitalist class also opposed these neocolonial structures. They saw the arrangements with Britain as stifling their expansion and wanted the Irish state to play a more active role in assisting their growth. This was the base from which Fianna Fáil sought to develop a populist project which united workers and capitalists.

Fianna Fáil's Politics

Between 1926 and its accession to power in 1932, Fianna Fáil used the most radical of rhetoric to win an electoral base. It could not have succeeded otherwise. As the world economy entered a major slump from 1929 onwards, there were many who wanted social change. But for all the radicalism of its rhetoric, Fianna Fáil had little to do with left-wing politics. De Valera could tell workers that 'they should not merely be wage slaves or simply spending their lives to make money for somebody or other'.[41] But he was never specific on what the alternative to wage slavery was. There was a vague suggestion that one day they might be working for themselves, possibly in rural Ireland, where the sturdy self-sufficient farmer was held up as the ideal. How Ireland was meant both to industrialise and to maintain this rural idyll was never explained. Instead Fianna Fáil concentrated on a series of themes which gave the party a distinct 'social flavour' without necessarily endangering support for free enterprise.

The Banks and Financial Plunder

Populist parties often focus on the banks as the primary causes of poverty and underdevelopment. A contrast is drawn between the healthy, productive manufacturing sector and the avaricious, greedy and parasitical financial network. Banks are seen as making illegitimate profits that bear no relation to manual labour. It is almost as if real capitalism can play a socially useful role if it is freed from the clutches of financial interests.

The attack on banking was quite central to Fianna Fáil in this period. In 1927, the party launched *The Nation* and members were encouraged actively to promote it. Its pages are littered with attacks on the Irish banking network. It claimed the banks were 'satellites of the Bank of England'.[42] It associated them with the commercial classes who added little of value to the economy. The aim of Fianna Fáil was to 'free the country from exploitation by dealers in needless imports and by bankers who are little better than agents for British finance'.[43] It saw them as the principle cause of poverty. *The Nation* argued that it was the 'pro-British financiers who control our economic system and visit us with all those sorrows, wanton and without cause'.[44]

Sean McEntee, one of Fianna Fáil's main spokespersons on economic matters and usually regarded as belonging to the more conservative wing of the party, shared these criticisms:

> The banks, which have been bleeding the Irish farmer, crushing Irish industry, investing Irish money abroad, jeopardising it in British securities, want to retain the present government in office for their purposes ... A Fianna Fáil government would not be tied up with the old Unionist Party and the banks.[45]

One of the prominent writers in *The Nation*, Sean O'Muinneachain, advocated an alternative to the banking network based on a system of 'national credit'. Here there would be a state bank with a network of credit societies which acted as its agents. The primary aim of this system was not profit making but rather the revitalisation of the country's industries and agriculture.[46] The former Chief of Staff of the IRA and prominent Fianna Fáil leader, Frank Aiken, agreed: 'Banks should not exist to amass profits but should perform such functions as they were performing in France where they managed credit and issued money for the benefit of ordinary people.'[47]

The focus on the banks and the payment of land annuities to Britain allowed Fianna Fáil to project an inherent unity between those groups involved in real production: the workers, the small farmers and the native entrepreneurs. It also allowed the party to engage in a fierce rhetoric without attacking the profit system as such. In 1929, for example, *The Nation* attacked Finance Minister Ernest Blythe's budget as 'A Surrender to the Rich'. But it then described the subject of its headline as 'that section of the wealthy which is least patriotic and of least use to Ireland', and went on to call for more support for Irish industrialists.[48]

A Free Ireland means Cheap Government

The demand for cheap government was a common theme of radicals from the time of the French Revolution. It was also a demand taken up by many populist movements in the twentieth century. Fianna Fáil's novelty was to link the cost of the state structures to the legacy of imperialism. Cumman na nGaedheal were accused of trying to run Ireland on a 'grand imperial scale'.[49] A Fianna Fáil election leaflet in 1928 aptly summarised the party's charge:

> Fianna Fáil is opposed to imperialism in Ireland not only because it must mean the denial of Ireland's rights and therefore endless unrest but also because it means extravagant and wasteful government ... The Free State are trying to run Ireland as an empire on the income of a small nation. As a result of that policy they are driving people deeper and deeper into poverty.[50]

By contrast Fianna Fáil held up the value of frugality which was associated with freedom and pride. In one of his more famous analogies, de Valera claimed that Ireland could either act like 'the servant in the mansion' or a 'man in the cottage'. Freedom from servitude meant 'giving up the idea of having cushions and ... the various things that might come to him from the table of the lord'.[51] Ostentation and comfort were the marks of an imperial mind-set.

This focus on wasteful government fed into Fianna Fáil's radicalism in a powerful way. De Valera's dictum was that no man was worth more than £1,000 a year. He called for cuts in the pay of civil servants who earned above that figure, arguing that 'the top hats may have to be cut off and done without'.[52] It gave the party a strong anti-establishment image. A Fianna Fáil leaflet entitled 'Prosperity' printed a list of Free State expenses which detailed the salaries of the higher civil servants and incidentals such as 'the uniforms for the President's chauffeurs'. It ended by claiming that these officials talk of 'prosperity' while 'people are starving and emigrating'.[53] Fianna Fáil claimed that it could attack the cost of government by abolishing the Senate, reducing the Dáil to 100 TDs, and cutting the number of civil servants,[54] but it focused on two targets in particular.

The first was the office of the Governor General. This post was legally established under the treaty and opposition to it allowed Fianna Fáil to display both its republicanism and its indignation about poverty. De Valera claimed that the office was 'a symbol of our defeat and a badge of our slavery'.[55] He denounced the spending of £27,000 annually on it and argued that the same sum could sustain a thousand unemployed people who were on the verge of starvation.[56] The second target was the repressive institutions of the state. Rather surprisingly in view of its later concern for law and order, Fianna Fáil favoured the abolition of the standing army and the cutting down of the police force to 'a fraction of their present size'.[57] The standing army was seen as an imperialist invention whereas the republicans favoured a citizens' militia. Sean Lemass argued that the defence of Ireland would not be carried out by 'highly drilled troops organised around the model of the British army but by organising the manhood of Ireland on a volunteer basis and getting men who are willing to serve in the defence of their country without reward'.[58]

Catholic Social Justice

Fianna Fáil argued that Ireland could create a unique society that was built on the social principles of Catholicism. Despite incurring the wrath of the bishops during the Civil War, the party was imbued with a strong Catholic ethos. A year after entering the Dáil, for example, it urged the government to take parliamentary holidays on Catholic feast days.[59] It believed that the fusion of Catholicism and Irish nationalism could produce a unique society constructed around social justice. Thus, when rejecting any imputation of communism in Fianna Fáil, de Valera stated:

There was an Irish solution that had no reference to any other country; a solution that came from our traditional attitude to life that was Irish and Catholic. That was the solution they were going to stand for as long as they were Catholics.[60]

A key figure in elaborating the practical implications was the front-bench spokesperson, Joseph Connolly. He rejected the 'so-called prosperity of the US' and sought to establish a 'new civilisation in life, industry and the control of human beings'.[61] In a notable speech in 1931, entitled 'The Economics of a Christian Social State', he claimed that the 'absence of Christianity is the root cause of all our social problems and misery'.[62] Christian social philosophy, according to Fianna Fáil, favoured state intervention to mitigate the evils of unbridled capitalism. Connolly argued that this intervention was 'inevitable if the exploitation of the masses is to be prevented'.[63]

Fianna Fáil also argued that 'it is the duty of the State to provide work'.[64] Lemass claimed that unemployment could be made 'an evil memory within 5 years' of a Fianna Fáil government.[65] The compassion and support that Fianna Fáil gave to the dignity of the unemployed was contrasted sharply with the attitude of Cumman na nGaedheal. One of the party's most popular leaflets was a highly effective juxtaposition of a quote from the Cumman na nGaedheal Minister for Industry and Commerce, P.J. McGilligan,

> It is not the function of the Dáil to provide work and the sooner this is realised the better … people may have to die in this country of starvation.

with one from Eamonn de Valera where he stated that,

> I hold it is the primary duty of a modern state to ensure that every man who is able and willing to work will have work, so that he may earn his daily bread.[66]

The Appeal to Workers

While staking a claim to represent the downtrodden with its radical populism, Fianna Fáil also made a distinct appeal to organised labour. *The Nation* claimed that 'although not technically a workers' party, they were mainly so'.[67] The party argued that workers suffered most from foreign domination because exploitation and poverty were worse when foreign masters were in control. As Irish political independence was only a fig leaf to hide continuing domination by colonial rulers, Fianna Fáil's claim to represent workers followed naturally from its role as the leading fighter against imperialism. Once again de Valera used Connolly in support of this argument, claiming that he had told him,

> to secure national freedom as the first step in order to get workers of Ireland the living they were entitled to in their own

country. Because he said, 'As long as a foreign imperial power holds this country, the workers are the people who are principally exploited'.[68]

Fianna Fáil attacked the Labour Party for having departed from this tradition and becoming an 'imperialist Labour Party'.[69] It pointed to the manner in which its leader, Tom Johnson, had won praise for his parliamentary performance from the *Irish Independent* when the owner of that paper had supported calls for the execution of James Connolly.

Fianna Fáil's critique also went much deeper than simply the performance of Tom Johnson. It prefigured what has loosely come to be known as 'the stages theory' advanced by latter-day republicans. Here it is argued that class politics can only really emerge after the fight against imperialism has been finally won. Full national freedom involved both the removal of partition and the attainment of 'economic independence'. Looked at from this point of view, the very existence of a Labour Party was an anachronism for Fianna Fáil and was seen to have drawn its inspiration from an imported, British model of politics. When the Labour Party formally emerged as an independent entity from the Irish Trade Union Congress in 1930, *The Nation* proclaimed: 'Our conclusion in simple words is that whereas in the circumstances a political Labour party without a national policy would be ridiculous, a political Labour party with either of the two alternative national parties would simply be redundant.'[70]

At this stage Fianna Fáil claimed to be a supporter of trade unions and, in certain circumstances, favoured strike action by workers. Before coming to power in 1932, it endorsed a whole series of trade union demands. It supported calls for a 48-hour week for bread delivery workers in the Dáil.[71] In September 1929, when the Dublin Tram company cut wages, provoking a serious confrontation with its staff, Fianna Fáil supported the workers. *The Nation* denounced the company as being 'scandalous in their fight for dividends' and congratulated the workers for standing up to their employers.[72] In 1931, the National Union of Railwayworkers wrote to Fianna Fáil for support against proposals by the Railway Wages Board to reduce wages. De Valera replied that not only were they against the cuts but they also wanted the road and rail transport industry brought under public control.[73] The party's reasoning was that wage cuts reduced the purchasing power of workers and were therefore detrimental to the growth of industries dependent on the home market.

However, even in its most radical phase Fianna Fáil support for workers' struggles was by no means unqualified. Its enthusiasm tended to be reserved for struggles against British companies or those run by the old Unionist elite, and where strikes occurred in firms run by 'patriotic Irish industrialists' its reaction was quite different. Pierce's Foundry in Wexford, for example, which had a long history of labour disputes was a case in point. Its owner, Phillip B. Pierce, became one of the first directors of the party's paper, the *Irish Press*, and when there was a strike in his workplace in January 1928, the party placed its main emphasis on the need for mediation. There was no declared support for the workers and, instead, the Fianna Fáil TD, Dr Allen, was praised for his efforts to reach a settlement. *The Nation* also gave one of the first hints of a theme that would later become popular in Fianna Fáil circles when it stated that the strike would not have taken place if the workers in Pierce's had all been members of an Irish union.[74]

Yet the party's hostility to British unions and British employers, did not mean that it ignored the models of industrial relations being established in the 'old enemy'. Just as the party was being formed in 1926, British workers were engaging in a nine-day general strike which ended in abject defeat. One outcome of this was the formation of a commission by Sir Alfred Mond which issued new recommendations on the conduct of industrial relations. These mainly centred around the formation of a stringent arbitration system to avoid strikes. For all its opposition to the imperialists, *The Nation* favoured Mond's recommendations as an example for Irish workers.[75]

Workers in Retreat

By 1932, Fianna Fáil had won hegemony over a significant section of the Irish working class through the articulation of these policies. In the process it marginalised the social democratic politics of the Labour Party. This victory was by no means a foregone conclusion, as Irish workers had in the past displayed the most militant forms of class consciousness. The largest union, the Irish Transport and General Workers, was originally led by socialists such as Connolly and Larkin. These had little respect for what Gramsci called the compromise of 'industrial legality' whereby, in return for recognition and the benefits of collective bargaining procedures, the union became responsible for disciplining and imposing agreements on its members.[76] Instead, Connolly and Larkin shared a militant syndicalist outlook which looked to workers' own struggles to attain gains. The weakness of this tradition, however, was that political questions tended to be relegated to the realm of Sunday afternoon speeches with no serious effort being made to establish a party of activists who shared the same ideological outlook.

Syndicalism can often take hold when there is an upturn in workers' struggles, and its Irish variant, commonly known as 'Larkinism', grew rapidly in the period from 1907 to 1913. With the high levels of class conflict, the *Irish Worker*, the paper edited by Larkin, was easily able to outsell republican newspapers. During the period from 1918 to 1923, syndicalism also played an important role as workers fought on both the economic and national fronts, but it had little to offer when it came to providing a distinct class outlook on the fight against the British Empire.

However, when the tide of industrial militancy runs out syndicalism tends to lose its appeal. Its call to rely on solidarity between different groups of workers does not seem as feasible as before when unemployment saps workers' confidence. Having failed to establish a minority network of ideologically committed socialists in the upturn, militant movements which blossom in periods of great struggle shrivel and die in periods of defeat. This was certainly the experience of syndicalism in Britain at the turn of the century and in Italy in the early 1920s.

This is precisely what happened in Ireland in the 1920s also. The establishment of the Irish Free State, coincided with a marked decline in union influence and activity. Table 1.1 illustrates the fall in union membership in the 1920s.

Table 1.1 Trade union membership, 1924–30

Year	Membership
1924	126,522
1925	98,986
1926	95,002
1927	89,696
1928	87,696
1929	86,615
1930	70,573

Source: Department of Industry and Commerce, *Statistical Abstract* (1932).

The fall in trade union membership brought about a change in the structure of the organised working class, with the greatest losses occurring in transport where the tradition of Larkinism was strongest. Between 1924 and 1930, this sector lost 49,659 members, or 60 per cent of its total, while the decline in other sectors was not so dramatic.[77] There was thus a change in the relative weight of different sections inside the labour movement with groups who had a more moderate history now beginning to predominate. Unions in public administration and food manufacturing, for example, suffered fewer losses, and as a result, the movement as a whole now tended to be organised in smaller workplaces. The

average firm in railways and transport employed 924 workers
compared to an overall average firm size of 36 workers.[78]

With the changing composition of the labour movement in this
period, there was also a significant decline in strike activity. In the
early 1920s, over 15,000 workers per year were engaged in strike
action. By the end of the decade, the figure had declined to 3,000,
with strikes also tending to last longer as employers put up a stiffer
resistance. Table 1.2 illustrates the decline in strike activity.

Table 1.2 Number of disputes, workers involved, and workdays
lost

	1923	1924	1925	1926	1927	1928	1929	1930
Number of strikes	131	104	86	57	53	52	53	83
Workers involved (000s)	20.6	16.4	6.9	3.5	2.3	2.2	4.5	3.4
Workdays lost (000s)	120.6	301.7	293.8	85.3	64.0	54.2	101.4	77.4

Source: Department of Industry and Commerce, *Statistical Abstract* 1931–32.

By the end of the 1920s, some of the most common battles were
over wage cuts and they often ended in defeat for the workers. The
incident which symbolised the general retreat was the struggle at
the Shannon Electrification Scheme in 1925/26. When contractors
on this scheme set the wages for building workers at a mere £1.60
a week the ITGWU argued that they were violating the fair wages
clause in government contracts and called a work stoppage and
general boycott of the scheme. However, by January 1926 the
boycott had collapsed as local unemployed workers took up the jobs
at the low rates.

The downturn in activity by organised labour meant that networks
of older militants were broken up as the movement as a whole lost
its former confidence. Unable to rely effectively on their own
activity to win, many workers were encouraged to look beyond
themselves for a political party that promised decisive change. In
a period of spiralling unemployment, the minds of many workers
also tended to focus on jobs and development rather than class
struggle. Their fears on this score combined with the nationalist
ethos led many workers to look again at the issues of protectionism
and self-sufficiency. In brief, the period was relatively favourable
for Fianna Fáil to establish its hegemony. The shift in support to
Fianna Fáil was not, however, guaranteed. The party's attempts
to balance the interests of native capital and Irish workers often
came under scrutiny, even in its own ranks. The Erskine Childers

Cumman, for example, attacked the party's TDs for promoting business interests in the Dáil. It asked,

> Why bother about the sympathy of an insignificant section of the people? The Irish business people have always opposed movements of Irish national freedom ... Why does Fianna Fáil fight the battles of the manufacturing class and not give guarantees to Irish workers that they would fight against any attempt by the manufacturing class to trail for low wages and long hours?[79]

These political tensions and contradictions in Fianna Fáil were not highlighted, however, due to the weakness of its political opponents.

Labour's Political Shift

One of the reasons for this was that a decisive shift was taking place in the politics of the organised labour movement at this time. Between 1918 and the establishment of the Irish Free State, the leading figures in Irish labour – Tom Johnson, William O'Brien and Cathal O'Shannon – were seen as militant socialists; all three belonged to the Socialist Party of Ireland which had been founded by Connolly.[80] However, as Emmet O'Connor has pointed out, even at this time there was an enormous gap between their revolutionary oratory and their more passive political practice. The ITUC report for 1923 admitted as much when it stated that: 'were it not for the modifying influence of Labour leaders and officials, the present situation would be infinitely worse.'[81]

The first public break from Connolly's revolutionary positions was only articulated clearly in 1925 when Tom Johnson provoked a crisis by resigning as leader of the party. It was a short-lived resignation but Johnson used the incident to start a major discussion by writing an important letter to the Executive of the ITUC and Labour Party. Its contents expressed what Charles McCarthy called, 'the settled position of many trade union and labour leaders that followed ... a sensitive, mild, parliamentary socialism'.[82] Johnson claimed that his resignation arose from the fact that he was in a contradictory position trying to promote a moderate social democratic outlook within a movement which still proclaimed its verbal support for the more revolutionary positions of Connolly. He opposed,

> the proposition that the workers can rely solely on their economic power to attain their ends – the theory that by organising their strength in the field of industry and using it to bring the economic machinery to a full stop, can workers' ideals be realised.[83]

In place of this strategy, Johnson argued for a reliance on parliament and the state. These democratic institutions, he stated, were the custodians for the fundamental rights of labour and opened the prospect of gradual amelioration provided labour was willing to identify with, and defend, them. He linked his support for parliament with a claim that the values of the 'community' and the nation had to supersede sectional demands of the unions. In rather clumsy phraseology, Johnson proclaimed that, 'I am a community-ist, a nation-ist before I am a trade unionist.'[84] His conclusion provides an important clue to the general shift in the attitude of the Labour Party. He argued:

> We must preach the gospel of faithful service – for the uplifting of the nation – materially and spiritually. We must insist on maintaining the rights won through suffering but the power to maintain our rights is increased tenfold when we also do our duty faithfully and fulfil our obligations.[85]

Johnson was following a pattern that had become evident elsewhere. Labour parties often broke older conservative political allegiances by being identified with workers' struggles. But as trade unions and labour parties grew, a conservative bureaucracy emerged which viewed the prospect of continuing struggle with some dread. The interests of the organisation, the headquarters, the full-time staff offered a continuity that went beyond what Gramsci referred to as 'the fickle eddy of moods and currents that are typical of great tumultuous masses'.[86] In this situation, influencing the state became an alternative route for advance. Writers such as Bernstein and Kautsky provided the theoretical justification for this shift by arguing that the state was a neutral instrument which stood above classes, but the full implications of the new approach still needed to be elaborated in terms of political practice. In particular, the key issue was establishing a definite separation between political and economic struggles. Modern capitalist societies rest on a framework whereby economic struggles are categorised narrowly as 'industrial relations problems' that are governed by the procedural rules of collective bargaining, and 'real' politics is structured around debates in parliament. On no account must the potential power of workers, which was often demonstrated in strikes, be used for political ends. Johnson's letter had the merit of spelling out these implications fully.

The labour movement, however, cannot simply grow close to the state for purely tactical reasons. As Johnson indicated, there also has to be a shift in its overall value system, with loyalty to the national state becoming a dominant sentiment. The birth of a new Irish state greatly facilitated this shift as it fostered the growth of nationalism – not the more dangerous nationalism that was associated with republican turmoil in the past, but a more moderate, cautious kind that stressed the importance of national economic development.

In line with the new strategy outlined by Johnson, the Labour Party began to embrace this form of nationalism. In 1926, for example, it proposed the establishment of a National Economic Council which would lay the basis for a social partnership designed to raise productivity.[87] In the 1927 general election, it called for the encouragement of Irish industries through national credit, cheap loans, preferential railway rates and subsidised energy. It argued that industrial development was possible if 'the intelligence and organising ability of patriotic men at the disposal of the government were directed to that end'.[88] The political shift in Labour's politics brought it on to the same terrain as Fianna Fáil and sometimes it became difficult to distinguish between them. Labour no longer talked about the innate evils of capitalism but concentrated instead on how its particular national capitalism could be protected and strengthened. It followed a pattern whereby social democracy across Europe dropped its radical rhetoric in favour of peace with capitalism.

All of this meant that a rapprochement between the Labour Party and Fianna Fáil was firmly on the cards. There were, however, difficulties to be overcome, as the Labour Party was firmly committed to the Treaty. The two parties only began seriously to work together when Cumman na nGaedheal introduced the Public Safety Bill in 1927 after the assassination of Kevin O'Higgins, the Minister for Justice. This demanded that all candidates for election had to pledge to take up their seats in the Dáil. By outlawing abstentionism it forced Fianna Fáil's hand and eventually Fianna Fáil reached an agreement with Labour to enter the Dáil and back Johnson for Taoiseach in return for certain changes to the oath of allegiance. This move was narrowly defeated but the basis for a new alignment was established.

Once Fianna Fáil were in the Dáil, Johnson focused his attention on their economic policies. He supported de Valera's assertion that the state had a duty to provide work for the unemployed and noted that when a potential government accepted this principle, it became Labour's duty to 'co-operate in finding out how to make the best use of the labour of those seeking work'.[89] *The Irishman*, the paper of the ITUC and Labour Party, also took a more benign view of Fianna Fáil. It argued that:

> The main cleavage in the immediate future will be between those who are content for this country to be an appendage to the economic system of Great Britain and those who wish at any rate to make an effort to give this country an economic vitality on its own.[90]

It complimented de Valera for beginning to think of 'nationality in terms of economics' because the role of the nation state was not to wage useless fights with Britain over sentimental issues such as the oath, but rather to become a powerful instrument for economic development.[91] *The Irishman* tended to combine a slightly patronising line to Fianna Fáil for being inexperienced parliamentarians with a recognition of its 'progressive' political content. On 23 November 1929, the paper informed its readers that 'there is no doubt of the attitude of deputy de Valera to towards the trade unions. He is and has been fully sympathetic.'[92] Its successor, *The Watchword* was even more explicit in stressing a common agreement: 'Lately [Fianna Fáil] are willing to take state control of certain industries in the event of private enterprise being unable to bring about needed development. They will be advocating the labour programme before long.'[93] When T.J. O'Connell became leader of the Labour Party, support for nationalist policies became even more pronounced. In 1931, a new party programme was produced entitled 'The Nation'. Introducing it, O'Connell argued that Labour saw the nation state as an organised community where each section was dependent on another. 'Their movement was not a class movement', he announced.[94]

However, once it began to compete on the same terrain as Fianna Fáil, Labour faced obvious difficulties. It was seen as a defender of the institutions of the Free State and this meant that many Labour Party TDs benefited from voting transfers of Cumman na nGaedheal supporters. The process of distancing the party from the government and establishing itself as consistently nationalist was, however, highly problematic. This became evident in 1931 when Cumman na nGaedheal launched a witchhunt against the growing left-wing influence in republican circles. It introduced the Constitution (Amendment Number 17) Bill which gave it power to ban organisations and to establish a military tribunal with the right to impose the death penalty. The Labour Party officially opposed the measure as unnecessary but two of its long-standing deputies – Morrissey from South Tipperary and Anthony from Cork City – supported it. They were expelled from the party, but considerable damage had been done.

Labour was also outflanked by Fianna Fáil on the issue of land annuities. This had become a symbolic issue for the whole country when Fianna Fáil joined the left-wing republican Peadar O'Donnell and Colonel Maurice Moore in advocating a campaign of non-payment to Britain. In the general election in September 1926, the Labour Party did not even include the issue in their programme despite the best efforts of Moore to persuade Johnson.[95] Later, in August 1928, Johnson wrote a series of articles on the issue in which his tone was legalistic in the extreme. He argued that, 'the purchasing tenants have no justification in law or morality in repudiating their liability to pay annuities on the grounds that they are paid into British funds'.[96] Widespread sympathy for non-payment, it seems, was irrelevant. Loyalty to state institutions came first, even if, paradoxically, this forfeited electoral gain. Johnson noted that if the Labour Party, 'were to adopt the strategy of the communists and aim at disturbing and disintegrating the social fabric, this would be a promising agitation to pursue'.[97]

All of this meant that the Labour Party could be presented by Fianna Fáil as a cowardly organisation that took the side of the British Empire against the rural population. As the difficulties for Labour grew it could not even remain united. When Fianna Fáil moved a Dáil resolution to abolish land annuities in 1928, five Labour TDs voted for, while seven voted against. Johnson noted in despair that strictly speaking 'there was not a Labour Party in the Free State because of the party's 13 TDs and 5 Senators, no two of them agree even on fundamentals'.[98]

Labour's failure in the face of growing Fianna Fáil influence did not result from the fact, as is sometimes claimed, that it argued socialist politics in a conservative country. Quite the opposite. As we have seen, its class message became ever more diluted in the haze of economic nationalism where its own inconsistencies meant that it was seen as a much paler version of Fianna Fáil. That party had little occasion to accuse the Labour Party of extremism – the strength of its accusation was that it was too moderate and too timorous. Gerry Boland even urged Labour to adopt a more independent and audacious position and reminded them that 'as England despises those who run after her, so does Capital despise those who run after it'.[99] Sean Lemass summed up the public contempt Fianna Fáil felt for its rivals:

> I have already said that the outstanding characteristic of the Labour party is that it is the most respectable party in the state … So long as they cannot be accused of being even pale pink in politics they seem to think they have fulfilled their function towards the Irish people.[100]

Conclusion

Between 1926 and 1932, Fianna Fáil built the most powerful political organisation in the 26 counties on the basis of populist policies. Its arguments and political themes bear a striking similiarity to those raised by Cardenas in Mexico in the late 1930s, by Peron in Argentina in the 1940s, and, in a more complicated fashion, by Varga in Brazil in the 1940s. All these movements were concerned with national development and opposed the dominant agro-export model whereby their countries were reduced to supplying primary produce for metropolitan countries. Populist movements became the political instruments by which a shift was made from agricultural interests to the promotion of manufacturing interests.

The populist parties shared the same objectives as other middle-class elites concerned about national development – but they adopted a different approach. In many African and Asian countries after the Second World War, there emerged an urban intelligentsia who were appalled by their country's backwardness. They despised the native bourgeoise for too willingly accepting a 'comprador role' where they functioned as merchants of underdevelopment, but they had little sympathy with the 'sectional interests' of workers. Whether it was Nasser in Egypt, Nkrumah in Ghana, or, for that matter, Castro in Cuba, they looked to the model that the Soviet Union had provided for development. In brief, they favoured a form of state capitalism.[101] In many instances, this was accompanied by the required ideological package of Stalinism. But the wrapping was entirely secondary: the real aim was national economic development through a withdrawal from the world economy and tighter control of the local economy by state control.

The populist parties of Latin America took a different route. They did not see the native bourgeoisie as an enemy, but rather as a historically disadvantaged grouping that needed state support. They undertook a struggle to break the grip of the oligarchy over the state machine. Once that grip was broken, they used the state to intervene more directly in the economy – but as far as possible they sought to do so in alliance with sections of the industrial bourgeoisie.

Fianna Fáil displayed some early sympathy for the state capitalist model, with some in the party praising aspects of Stalinist Russia. Gerry Boland, for example, argued: 'In Russia, they treat Labour on a human basis not as a commodity to be bartered about.'[102] *The Nation* likewise refused to join in the attacks on the Soviet Union, arguing that there was a 'press campaign for a new world war now being directed by frightened capitalists and Russian Czarists'.[103] What was admired in Russia was not the peculiar version of 'Marxism–Leninism' promoted by Stalin, but rather the seeming vigour by which the state tackled underdevelopment. The political coloration of the exercise mattered little. While these expressions of sympathy were being made, it was equally possible for de Valera, in one of his wilder flights of rhetoric to promise that 'Fianna Fáil could do for Ireland what fascism did for Italy'.[104]

Nevertheless, whatever its attractions, the state capitalist option was never seriously considered. The particular relationship between Ireland and the British Empire meant that the indigenous capitalist class was far more entrenched and carried far more independent weight than its counterparts in other parts of the colonised world. In addition, the particular agrarian structure of Ireland ruled out any widespread collectivisation to divert surplus resources into industry. Irish farmers had just won possession of their land; they were highly organised politically and parties like Fianna Fáil recruited a significant proportion of their membership from their ranks. O'Muinneachain, the party's foremost writer in *The Nation* could therefore express profound admiration for Stalin's Five-Year Plan, but then indicate his regret that 'while capitalism had enslaved the city workers, it was left to communism to enslave the peasant'.[105]

Fianna Fáil's route to national development was therefore geared to promoting the interests of the indigenous capitalist class. It was determined to shift the resources of the state away from assisting the strong commercial farmers who exported to Britain and towards promoting manufacturing. Like its Latin American counterparts, it needed to construct an 'industrial bloc' that linked workers and native employers together to a movement that focused on national development. Conditions were certainly in favour of Fianna Fáil achieving this alliance. The defeats that the labour movement had suffered in the mid-1920s, brought about a recomposition in its ranks to the detriment of the tradition of militant syndicalism. Lacking confidence in their own ability to fight, workers were more than willing to give an ear to a radical force that promised both to stand up to British imperialism and also to provide jobs and improved conditions. When they looked at the Labour Party, the more they became convinced that Fianna Fáil held the original copyright. Labour's turn to 'national economics' could not remove its Free State links, and its legalistic approach gave it an overwhelming weak and moderate image. Labour was displaced by Fianna Fáil not because it was too radical but because it was not radical enough.

CHAPTER 2

The Triumph of Fianna Fáil, 1932–1939

In 1932, just six years after its formation, Fianna Fáil came to government. Its rivals had little to offer and could only resort to the absurd charge that it was influenced by communism. Fianna Fáil characteristically replied with a profession of their Catholicism and argued that the freemasons who held key government posts under Cumman na nGaedheal were a far greater threat.[1] The party fought the election campaign on a promise to bring improvements in economic conditions. In the North Dublin constituency, for example, only one candidate, Oscar Traynor, the former Dublin leader of the IRA, even mentioned partition in his literature.[2] Although it failed to secure an overall majority, the results represented a major triumph for Fianna Fáil. In June 1927 in its first election it won 299,626 votes and took 44 seats. By 1932, this had almost doubled, with the achievement of 566,475 votes and 72 seats. One of the main losers was the Labour Party whose vote declined dramatically. Table 2.1 illustrates the manner in which Fianna Fáil defeated the Labour Party in constituencies where the urban working class were concentrated.

Table 2.1 Percentage of total votes for Fianna Fáil and Labour in selected urban constituencies in 1927 and 1932

| | 1927 (June) | | 1932 | |
	Fianna Fáil	Labour Party	Fianna Fáil	Labour Party
Cork Borough	14	19	36	11
Dublin City North	22	7	35	5
Dublin City South	29	10	41	6
Limerick	30	14	46	7

Source: Percentages derived from data in Fianna Fáil, *An Chead Threimse* (n.d.).

Fianna Fáil's hegemony extended well beyond these crude voting figures. The flour mills may be taken as an illustration of how deep the party's influence extended amongst workers. Like many groups, the mill workers were deeply concerned about job losses and saw protectionism as a way forward. They argued that a decision by the Tariff Commission not to allow duties on flour was 'a complete victory for the foreigner' which would allow him to 'continue his system of strangling Irish industry and enterprise'.[3] They openly supported Fianna Fáil efforts to press for tariff barriers. One of their representatives claimed that the Dáil debates on protectionism gave 'the working masses a true insight into the consistency of those who preach the doctrine of building up the economic power and resources of the state and providing a solution to the unemployment problem'.[4] He went on to note that 'until the Labour party has declared as openly as Mr de Valera's party ... we cannot acclaim the party as sincere to its tradition as we would otherwise like to'.[5] It was from sentiments such as these that Fianna Fáil built its base among workers.

When Fianna Fáil took office on 9 March 1932, it already had the goodwill of organised labour. The movement's paper, *The Watchword*, stated that 'we agree with the mass opinion that Fianna Fáil should get its chance now',[6] and the minority Fianna Fáil government received the backing of the Labour Party. During its first days of office Fianna Fáil strengthened its image as a radical force when de Valera and other ministers immediately took a cut in salary. Their decision to release republican prisoners was hugely popular, with 20,000 people turning up to an IRA procession to celebrate. In addition, Fianna Fáil lifted the ban on the IRA and allowed *An Phoblacht* to reappear. However, as Fanning has noted, these measures were less significant in the longer term than the fact that the Public Safety Act was still retained.[7]

Support for the Fianna Fáil government was further enhanced by the outbreak of the Economic War on 1 July 1932. The immediate cause was a decision to stop paying the half-yearly instalment on land annuities which was due to the British government. They in turn replied by imposing a retaliatory duty of 20 per cent on Irish imports. Fianna Fáil then introduced an Emergency Imposition of Duties Act which enabled them to impose new tariffs by statutory order. In effect, they used the conflict to implement their policy of protectionism, and within a number of years almost 2,000 goods were covered by tariffs.[8] As the Economic War escalated, mass street meetings were called in support of the government. The message at such meetings was one of equality between the classes in which all suffered in order to stand up for Ireland's sovereignty. De Valera proclaimed: 'we are all brothers in this ... no one can suffer for any length of time without that suffering reflecting on the rest of us.'[9] One group, however, were excluded for this national community. Cumman na nGaedheal was seen as belonging firmly to the camp of the imperialists. McEntee accused them of being 'the Hindenberg line of foreign exploiters in this country', while Derrig claimed that they were a 'White Army – John Bull's White hopes'.[10]

The Labour Party not only supported Fianna Fáil in the Economic War, but went further and claimed also that the party was not fully committed to capitalism. Its strategy was simply 'to push Fianna Fáil to the left'.[11] In order to assist in this, the Labour Party leader, William Norton, adopted a much more nationalist tone than any of his predecessors. He supported de Valera's nomination to office claiming that he wanted a break with the previous policies of 'relying on nature's bountiful supply of grass as the chief source of livelihood for our people'.[12] He dispensed with Johnson's legalism and denounced the oath of allegiance as 'a relic of feudalism'.[13] He continually presented Fianna Fáil as a party that was at odds with the rich. On one occasion he claimed that employers who imposed wage cuts were seeking to undermine 'a government which is not a rich man's government'.[14] Norton even predicted that as a result of the Economic War,

> the far seeing members of Fianna Fáil party who are not wedded to capitalism as the only method of industrial activity will ... advocate an industrial policy along the lines of state ownership, and state control of basic industries.[15]

Norton was not the only figure to see Fianna Fáil as a potentially left-wing force. The ITUC president, Louie Bennet, claimed that the party 'was sincerely sympathetic with labour ideals in many directions'.[16] The legendary labour leader Jim Larkin also offered some endorsement to Fianna Fáil. At various stages since 1927, he had cooperated with the party and when they introduced their first budget in 1932, he stated that 'he was heartily in accord with the government policy on tariffs. His only regret was that they did not go far enough.'[17]

This was the period when a powerful myth developed on the Irish left that Fianna Fáil was a 'progressive' party. There was a belief that the party was highly pragmatic and, if it thought it sufficiently popular, would even embrace milder forms of socialism. Both the Labour and Stalinist traditions tended to define socialism exclusively in terms of state ownership, rather than in terms of worker control. The actual power which workers had over state-owned industries was of little concern. So when Fianna Fáil set up large state companies such as Aer Lingus, Bord na Mona, the Irish Sugar Company and Irish Life in the 1930s this was taken as evidence of its tendency to lean to the left. The idea that 'republicanism in politics may well be expected to develop into socialism in economic affairs' gained a currency that has remained since.[18] Yet, in reality, Fianna Fáil's project had nothing to do with any sort of socialism. It had three main objectives in this period: to expand the native capitalist class through state subsidies; to restructure the machinery of state in order to make it more suitable for its supporters; and to seek an alliance with the bishops that would help impose order and discipline on the 26 counties. Far from leaning to the left, they were forming a rock-solid conservative force. We shall look at each of these objectives in turn.

Building Native Capitalism

Fianna Fáil was determined to use the situation created by the Economic War to clear the home market of as many foreign goods as possible in order to create new opportunities for Irish business. Behind the wall of protectionism, it aimed to give maximum support to Irish employers. As the Minister for Finance, Sean McEntee, put it, their aim was to allow the small businessman 'to cast his bread on the water with the hope that it was going to come back to him a hundred fold'.[19]

The chief measures used by Fianna Fáil were the Control of Manufacturers Acts which were introduced in 1932 and 1934. These established a system of licensing to prevent foreign companies endangering the survival of Irish manufacturers. Foreign capital was not allowed to hold more than a 50 per cent stake in firms and a majority of a company's directors had to be Irish. The aim of the Acts was to stop foreign companies setting up businesses in Ireland to get around the tariff barriers. Other inducements, for Irish capital principally, took the form of tax reductions and easy access to credit. The Finance Act of 1932 created a preferential rate of income tax for Irish firms, and Fianna Fáil also increased indirect taxation as a way of reducing tax on industry. The Industrial Credit Corporation was formed to provide financial support for native capitalists. A special Industrial Development Branch was set up within the Department of Industry and Commerce to give employers greater access to state officials. In some sectors, such as cement, virtual monopolies were established for Irish firms through the use of the licensing system.

In one area there was a considerable gap between the rhetoric of opposition and the practice of office. Fianna Fáil had claimed that the banks were crushing native industry by siphoning off funds abroad, but these attacks were soon dropped. Initially a small 3 per cent stamp duty was imposed on bank notes, but even this was abolished within a decade.[20] Instead, the party set up a Banking Commission which was staffed by conservative elements. When its report was finally issued it was more concerned to regulate government spending rather than to restrict banks' profits or force them to invest in native industries. The logic of the market allowed no simple distinction between the productive industry and the financial sector and those with capital had to be allowed to invest where they pleased.

Despite these measures, Fianna Fáil continued to be charged by its Cumman na nGaedheal opponents with introducing 'an inverted style of communism that is just as undesirable as communism itself'.[21] This incredible accusation arose mainly because Fianna Fáil sought to develop state enterprises. Yet these companies were only established in areas where private capital was not operating and were used to build up an infrastructure for its expansion. Fianna Fáil's greater use of the state was a common feature of many economies in the 1930s as they tried to recover from the Wall Street crash. Far from having the slightest trace of communism, inverted or otherwise, Fianna Fáil was creating a thriving private enterprise system. Table 2.2 shows the dramatic rise in the formation of share capital in companies after Fianna Fáil took office. In 1933, there was a prodigious rise in the amount of nominal capital registered for companies. Thereafter, there was an expansion in both the number of companies formed each year and the share capital employed. Even allowing for the effects of the Wall Street crash, the number of companies established and the capital invested was still smaller under Cumman na nGaedheal governments, as Table 2.2 reveals.

Table 2.2 Total number and total nominal capital of companies registered each year between 1926 and 1939

Year	Number of companies	Total nominal capital (£s)
1926	115	1,548,598
1927	100	1,472,985
1928	145	1,341,601
1929	130	741,950
1930	108	835,400
1931	137	670,200
1932	160	1,773,850
1933	227	8,440,140
1934	242	3,523,615
1935	247	3,582,403
1936	237	6,726,650
1937	204	3,247,075
1938	180	2,636,610
1939	177	1,932,350

Source: Department of Industry and Commerce, *Statistical Abstracts* (relevant years).

Fianna Fáil made a special effort to create openings for the new business class in areas such as clothing and footwear where it was easier to enter without inordinate sums of capital. Between 1932 and 1935, the hosiery industry grew from 1,388 workers to 3,768, while boot and shoe manufacturing increased from 1,714 to 4,591.[22] Another area of relatively easy access was building, where Fianna Fáil's housing programme left its mark. In 1926, 9,852 workers were employed in the building trade, while a decade later it had nearly doubled to 18,207.[23] Table 2.3 shows the gains in output and employment in labour intensive industries in the first years of the Fianna Fáil government.

Table 2.3 Percentage increase in net output and persons employed in selected industries 1931–36

	Net output	Persons employed
Boot and Shoe	321	370
Hosiery	297	224
Fellmongery and leather	246	208
Sugar/confectionery	186	71
Linen, cotton, hemp	165	188
Paper making	163	128
Clothing	166	100

Source: Department of Industry and Commerce, *Census of Industrial Production* (1936).

However, despite all the early rhetoric, the industrialisation programme was developed at the workers' expense. In their rush into business, Ireland's nationalist bosses did not differ from their counterparts elsewhere in their desire to find cheap labour. Their success stories were found precisely in those areas where juveniles were employed in greater proportions. In 1931, juveniles made up 21 per cent of the boot and shoe industry and 18 per cent of the hosiery, yet by 1936 the figures were 37 per cent and 26 per cent respectively.[24] Overall the proportion of the workforce who were under 18 grew from 6 per cent in 1926 to 10 per cent in 1936.[25] Wage levels were also very low, as Table 2.4 indicates. The fact that 80 per cent of juveniles earned less than £1 a week may help to account for their popularity with employers, but wage rates generally were poor in this period. In 1937, the average agricultural labourer's earnings stood at £2.50 a week.[26] This may be taken as a useful indicator of a low wage as the farmers were never renowned for their generosity to their employees and, in any event, the wage was traditionally supplemented by board and meals. Yet the plain fact was that 37 per cent of men and 86 per cent of women earned less than this figure. It gave a whole new meaning to de Valera's advocacy of frugality.

Table 2.4 Percentage of wage earners by weekly rates of earnings in 1937

Weekly rate of earning	Under 18		Over 18	
	Male	Female	Male	Female
Less 50p	18	23	1	1
50p–£1	60	23	4	16
£1–£1.50	19	18	12	33
£1.50–£2	3	2	20	36
£2–£2.50	–	–	14	10
£2.50–£3	–	–	13	2
£3–£4	–	–	21	1
£4–£5	–	–	12	–
£5+	–	–	3	–

Source: Department of Industry and Commerce, *Census of Industrial Production* (1937).

Overall, Fianna Fáil was relatively successful in its aim of promoting native capitalism. True, the Irish economy still remained largely dependent on Britain in terms of exports. The ending of the Economic War though a series of coal–cattle pacts from 1935 onwards represented a recognition of this. Nor was Irish agriculture transformed, and the vision of replacing the beef with tillage was quietly dropped. Yet within the limited horizons of establishing native firms there was considerable success. Key Irish companies of today such as Cement Roadstone and Jefferson Smurfit date their origins from this period. In areas where small capital could establish more easily, imports were cut significantly. As a result industrial employment rose from 110,600 in 1931 to 166,100 in 1938.[27] Although Irish capitalism remained weak, Fianna Fáil had put the maximum effort into using the state to develop it.

Restructuring the State

Once in office, Fianna Fáil appropriated Michael Collins's strategy of using the Treaty as a stepping stone to establish sovereignty. There was, however, one proviso: the sovereignty of the 26-county state was the issue. McEntee conceded privately that in regard to partition, 'we never had a considered policy. It has always been an affair of hasty improvisation.'[28] Certainly, there is no great evidence of an abiding Fianna Fáil concern to retake the six counties. The party's aim was to turn the Free State into a republic and it took a number of decisive measures to do this. The office of Governor General was severely curtailed and the salary, which was granted to a de Valera supporter, Donal O'Buachalla, was cut from £28,000 a year to £2,000. Later the post itself was eliminated. In 1933 the right to appeal Irish law to the British Privy Council was removed. In 1936 the Senate was abolished after its Cumman na nGaedheal majority obstructed a number of Fianna Fáil proposals for reform. Later that year, the abdication crisis of Edward VIII was used to remove references to the king from the Free State constitution.

Alongside the legal and constitutional changes, Fianna Fáil made significant changes within the state machine itself. The broad general structures of the state which were inherited from the British Empire were not interfered with. The formal separation between parliament and judiciary, the procedures by which civil servants intervened in the formation of law, the organisation of the army and the police force posed no obstacle to the central task Fianna Fáil set itself, that of building Irish capitalism. Earlier calls to abolish the standing army were, for example, quietly dropped. But the party was still concerned about the personnel who staffed the state.

Munger has argued that the stability of Irish politics owes much to the manner in which Fianna Fáil accepted the state structures bequeathed to them after the Civil War.[29] Internal discussions within the party, however, show that this was not actually the case: the party was intent on placing loyal supporters in key positions and using the state as a source of patronage. In July 1932, for example, Sean Moylan moved a resolution at the parliamentary meeting calling for the placing of ex-IRA men 'in and under various departments' to ensure loyalty to Fianna Fáil policies.[30] In the same month, Fianna Fáil TDs called for utmost speed in the reappointment of civil servants who were victimised by the former regime.[31] In May 1933, a meeting of deputies again called for preference in appointments to public posts to be given to those 'with a good national record'.[32]

The rise of the Blueshirts made the issue of changes of personnel more vital. As early as July 1932, de Valera approached the prominent IRA member, Tom Barry, and spoke of the need to create a new volunteer force for 'national defence'.[33] When it was finally formed in 1934, de Valera claimed it would be 'the backbone for the advance of our national rights'.[34] In reality, it became a vehicle by which former IRA men were absorbed into the police and army.

Nevertheless, dissatisfaction with the speed of internal changes continued in Fianna Fáil. At length in April 1935, the parliamentary party agreed to appoint a representative who would handle grievances from TDs about appointments.[35]

The restructuring of the state was also designed to place the TDs in a position to dispense favours. In 1934, the party voted in a Military Pension Act which gave pensions to republicans who fought against the Treaty. It was designed both to erode the base of the surviving IRA and to provide a form of patronage. The party set out to establish the Fianna Fáil deputy as the key intermediary between the state and their constituents. In 1933, Deputy Killea moved a resolution at the parliamentary party meeting to instruct ministers not to give interviews to anyone purporting to represent local public bodies unless such interviews were arranged by the local deputy. Deputies were also to be informed by ministers of incidents when deputations approached them 'behind the back' of the local TD.[36] The long hold that Fianna Fáil eventually won on office meant that this strategy was extensively realised. Although control of patronage has been exaggerated by a number of writers as a factor in the maintenance of the Fianna Fáil base, the party had an acute appreciation of how the state could be used in an underdeveloped society.

A Catholic State for a Catholic People

Even before coming to office, Fianna Fáil was anxious to build bridges with the Catholic hierarchy. During the Civil War, many of its founding members were condemned by the bishops for disobeying a lawful government, but the republican tradition always distinguished between particular bishops who served the imperialist camp and the broad institution of the Catholic Church. With the exception of a brief period at the end of the eighteenth century, Irish republicanism never developed the secular, anti-clerical ethos that, for example, characterised French republicanism. Now the party went out of its way to prove that it was more truly Catholic than the Cumman na nGaedheal. Even before they took office in 1932, Fianna Fáil had already endorsed the policy of a Catholic state for a Catholic people. In one celebrated case, de Valera supported the decision of the Mayo County Council not to appoint Letitia Dunbar Harrison, a graduate from Trinity College and a Protestant, to the county library.[37] De Valera argued that the post had a 'propagandist education character' and as ' over 98 per cent of the population is Catholic [they] are justified in insisting on a Catholic librarian'.[38]

In government, Fianna Fáil showed no hesitation in strengthening the legal and cultural ethos of a Catholic state. It immediately provided a lavish state reception for the Eucharistic Congress in 1932 and a few weeks after the event, de Valera informed the newly appointed papal legate that 'our people [were] ever firm in their allegiance to our ancestral faith'.[39] In his St Patrick's Day broadcast in 1935, de Valera simply noted: 'Since the coming of St Patrick fifteen hundred years ago, Ireland has been a Christian and a Catholic nation ... she remains a Catholic nation.'[40] The party leadership made a point of attending Catholic functions and having bishops open new factories or housing estates. However, their zeal for strengthening a Catholic state was tempered by the fact that many of the legal foundations were already in place, laid by the former British authorities and the Cumman na nGaedheal government. It was Westminster, for example, which had set up the Irish system of denominational education whereby no publicly funded secular form of education was available. Nonetheless, Fianna Fáil stood ready to add any extra confessional measure that the bishops periodically requested. So, for example, in 1935 they outlawed the sale, advertisement and importation of contraceptives. Similarly, they responded to the bishops' obsession with the evils of dance by passing the Public Dance Halls Act, which required a judge to issue a licence for these 'occasions of sin'.

Many of the links between Fianna Fáil and the bishops, however, operated at an informal level where a strong culture of secrecy prevailed. The formal ethos of republicanism, after all, was supposed to promote a unity of 'Catholic, Protestant and Dissenter', and so a certain etiquette was required. The bishops were also well used to operating in the secret labyrinths of power and preferred to avoid committing any specific requests to paper. Instead they used informal meetings with key figures in government and intermediaries to make their views known. That, at least, is the conclusion that must arise from even the most cursory examination of the de Valera–McQuaid correspondence which is lodged, appropriately enough, in the Franciscan library in Dun Laoghaire. This contains a record one of the most extraordinary partnerships in twentieth-century Ireland. When Fianna Fáil came to power, Charles McQuaid was simply the headmaster of a Dublin secondary school, Blackrock College. It happened, however, to be the school which de Valera himself attended and where he sent his own sons. These personal connections meant that McQuaid became the key intermediary in conveying requests from the hierarchy to de Valera and vice versa during the early period of Fianna Fáil's tenure in office. Afterwards in 1940, when McQuaid was appointed Archbishop of Dublin at the age of 45 in a highly unusual fashion, the messenger became the master.

While he was a school principal, McQuaid's correspondence with de Valera was extremely detailed and precise. The letters written in 1934 give some samples of the tone. On one occasion he noted that Catholic students in the University College Dublin medical school did not have access to a teaching hospital as prestigious as the Protestant-run Rotunda hospital. He advised the leader of the Irish Free State that the 'Hospital Commission should take into consideration the Catholic position which is paramount' and upgrade the National Maternity Hospital in Holles Street. Despite its name, this was to be run on strictly Catholic lines.[41] In the same year, he gleefully noted how the 'Protestant medical interests' were having difficulty building a children's hospital in Harcourt Street. He noted that 'they seem to themselves to be blocked in some unaccountable way! ... I am sure Sean T.O'Kelly is holding firm.'[42] When the director of National Broadcasting was about to be appointed, he requested a meeting with de Valera to discuss the matter informally.[43] These are just some of the very specific and detailed requests that flowed between the Catholic Church and de Valera through the good offices of its lowly servant, John Charles McQuaid.

However, communication between Church officials and the Fianna Fáil government was by no means all one way. As Fianna Fáil acceded to the requests of the hierarchy, they also demanded that the clergy play a positive role in upholding the new republican state and distance themselves from their previous alliance with Cumman na nGaedheal. In 1935, for example, when Bishop Dermot Cohalan attacked the government for the seizure of cattle from big farmers who had refused to pay rates as a protest against the Economic War, de Valera wrote to the papal nuncio to complain. The terms of his argument reflect the precise relationship Fianna Fáil sought to establish with the Church. He argued that the nuncio should

> endeavour to prevent certain members of the clergy from making use of their high office to undermine the authority of the government but to secure their active co-operation in inculcating in the people that respect for lawful authority without which the continuance in their country of a Christian church and a Christian state would soon become impossible.[44]

Here then was the essence of the Fianna Fáil position: the Church and state had a shared responsibility to inculcate a sense of discipline. They had to cooperate to ensure that there was respect for both the spiritual and temporal authorities. It was a case of rendering unto Caesar and Catholicism things mutually beneficial to both.

The culmination of this alliance was the 1937 constitution which recognised the 'special position' of the Catholic Church. This was not just a rhetorical flourish, for Catholic social teaching was embodied in the key legal document of the land. Divorce was banned and the main articles on the status of women suggested an exclusive role as carers in the home. Private property was deemed a 'natural right' which the state could not interfere with. The preamble claimed that 'the most holy trinity' was the source of all authority in law making. Sean McEntee described the central thrust of the constitution very accurately when he claimed that it was 'almost unique in the world today to adopt ... the fundamental teachings of the Holy Father in regard to the Family'.[45] Years after it was passed John Charles McQuaid, now an archbishop, wrote to de Valera: 'My chief feeling is one of gratitude that you have been able to put into effect as the natural law so many clauses on which we laboured very much and into the small hours of the night.'[46] The framework of a Catholic state for a Catholic people was well and truly in place.

Fianna Fáil and Labour

Building a strong conservative edifice in the South did not however mean that Fianna Fáil suddenly dropped their desire to keep a base among workers. They were determined to maintain and indeed strengthen their relationship with the unions. The new Minister of Industry and Commerce, Sean Lemass, began a regular correspondence with the ITUC and briefing sessions were organised. Where before the union leaders had been treated as virtual pariahs they were now sought out for advice. The effect of this change should not be underestimated as the union organisations rested on a small number of activists. The largest union, the ITGWU, for example, had only 36 delegates at its conference in 1932 and so it was possible to bring key opinion makers closer to the state quite quickly.[47]

Alongside their more direct contacts with the union leaders, Fianna Fáil brought about changes in the institutions which governed worker–employer relations. They extended the number of industries covered by Trade Boards which fixed a minimum wage and allowed the ICTU to represent unorganised workers on them. They also established Joint Industrial Councils where union and employer representatives met under the auspices of an official of the Department of Labour. Critics like Helena Molloy of the Irish Women Workers Union, however, claimed that these bodies set very low rates and were only a means whereby, 'female and juvenile labour was going to be swept into a slave class to swell the profits of the so-called patriots'.[48]

These changes in the relationship between the state and the unions culminated in the Conditions of Employment Act in 1935. The *Fianna Fáil Bulletin* claimed that this was a 'great Social Charter' which proved that the party would 'ensure a fair deal for workers in the new industrial revival'.[49] The Act limited the number of hours of work for adults to 48 and for juveniles to 40. It also provided for the registration and legal enforcement of agreements arrived at through collective bargaining. Its underlying philosophy was to wean the unions away from militancy and towards a greater reliance on the state. Lemass claimed that 'the effectiveness of trade unions was limited', particularly when there were rival unions appealing for the loyalty of workers. The new Act, he argued was a compensation because it 'represents a decision on the part of the state to co-operate with [trade unionists] in improving the conditions of workers'.[50]

Their approach was, however, highly selective. Cooperation between the state and its own direct employees in the public sector, for example, was not much in evidence. As soon as they took office, Fianna Fáil ministers adopted a policy of refusing to negotiate directly with full-time officials of civil service unions, even when the pay of their members was being cut.[51] The party deemed it the patriotic duty of these employees to make sacrifices and no 'outside' negotiator could interfere in the unique relationship between ministers and their own staff. It also insisted that workers on relief schemes receive rates of pay below agricultural workers.[52] One Fianna Fáil TD who justified this measure was sure that 'the workers of the country are not so unpatriotic as to refuse to make a small sacrifice when called upon'.[53]

An even deeper challenge to Fianna Fáil's image as the friend of trade unionism came with the revival of strike activity. Between 1926 and 1930, the number of workdays lost exceeded 100,000 just once. After 1933, however, it was consistently above that figure. The very success of Fianna Fáil's industrialisation programme contributed to a rise in union militancy as it lent a new confidence to workers who felt more needed in their jobs. Table 2.5 illustrates the sharp revival in strike activity after Fianna Fáil came to office.

Table 2.5 Number of work people involved in disputes and workdays lost, 1930–38

	Number of work people involved	Workdays lost
1930	3,410	77,417
1931	5,431	310,199
1932	4,222	42,152
1933	9,059	200,126
1934	9,288	180,080
1935	9,513	288,077
1936	9,443	185,623
1937	26,734	1,754,940
1938	3,736	208,784

Source: Department of Industry and Commerce, *Statistical Abstract* (1939).

A strike at Dublin Trams in 1935, which the ITGWU described as the most stubbornly fought in 20 years, gave a signal that the relationship between Fianna Fáil and the union militants had reached breaking point.[54] The strike began over a demand for a wage increase but Fianna Fáil saw it as setting a headline for others to follow. Lemass quickly denounced the strikers, and the cabinet appointed a special subcommittee, which eventually decided to send in the army. De Valera, in a piece of ingenious logic, denied the charge of strikebreaking by claiming that 'it could only have that effect if the men on strike were counting on inconveniencing the public as a means of settling the dispute'.[55] When the IRA intervened rather clumsily, Fianna Fáil arrested 47 republicans and immediately transferred them to the Curragh military detention centre. However, the repression was not confined only to political activists. Detectives broke into a strike meeting that was held in a union hall and dispersed the meeting while they searched the premises. The ITGWU in its annual report noted that they 'seemed to be fighting the combined forces of the Company, the Minister concerned and the whole apparatus of the state'.[56] Fianna Fáil's intervention called forth a huge wave of solidarity as 10,000 trade unionists marched through the streets of Dublin in support of the tram workers. The strike itself dragged on until the middle of May when the workers secured a small victory with the winning of a wage increase.

As the 1930s progressed, the bravado about Fianna Fáil, the 'workers' party', began rapidly to fade. Internal debates in the party showed a sharp shift to the right as Fianna Fáil TDs began to press for more vigorous action against the unions. At one stage, Lemass toyed with the idea of compulsory arbitration for disputes, only to drop it as too dangerous. After the strikes reached a crescendo in 1937, Fianna Fáil TDs became even more vociferous in their demands for action. Government ministers took a more aggressive attitude to any talk of militancy from their staffs. The Department of Post and Telegraphy, for example, warned of disciplinary action towards the Post and Telegraph Workers Union for daring to debate the issue of industrial action at their annual conference.[57]

However, these conflicts between Fianna Fáil and workers who had once supported it did not find a stable political expression which could have uprooted the party's dominance. Disillusionment with Fianna Fáil was certainly a primary factor in the formation of the Republican Congress. This body was set up in 1934 to bring together socialists and disillusioned republicans in a fight against both British imperialism and Irish capitalism. It pushed the republican tradition from which it grew to its very limit and, for a brief period, seemed to represent a serious threat to the status quo. The first issue of its newspaper both expressed a harsher attitude to Fianna Fáil and pointed to the previous weakness of republican politics.

> We failed to state the Fianna Fáil position in terms of its Griffith teachings and confront Fianna Fáil with the vision of James Connolly. We failed to see that a Fianna Fáil government could only serve Irish capitalism and kept calling on it to restore the ranches to the landlords, to plan industry, to serve the masses instead of the factory owners and re-declare a republic.[58]

The new organisation which was led by IRA veterans such as Peadar O'Donnell and George Gilmore attracted significant support from workers. According to one of its general secretaries it had between 6,000 and 10,000 paid-up members at its height.[59] Even allowing for some exaggeration, the fact remains that 14 trade unions and trade councils were represented at its first conference, which was chaired by the ITGWU vice-president, William McMullen. Significantly, Republican Congress made it a priority to intervene in the industrial struggles, establishing congress groups in some unions and workplaces.

Nevertheless there was a serious political flaw at the heart of the Republican Congress which meant that it survived for only two years. This was the inability to agree on the nature of Fianna Fáil and the prospect of orientating to its rank and file. One group led by James Connolly's son Roddy and a section of Belfast Protestant workers saw little hope in trying to share a common political language with the grassroots of Fianna Fáil. They believed that the Congress had to declare openly that 'they do not stand for de Valera's sort of Republic but for the definite issue of the Workers Republic'.[60] They advocated the formation of a new party which would fight for socialism as its immediate goal. This, however, was rejected by a majority who were led by Peadar O'Donnell and the small Communist Party, who wanted a looser alliance and regarded the slogan of the 'Workers Republic' as too ultra-left. The justification was that they believed that many Fianna Fáil supporters would identify with a fight to win the 'true republic' but not socialism, and so, according to O'Donnell,

> We dare not jump through a stage in the fight, now raising the slogan of a 'Workers Republic' and leaving Fianna Fáil to say that they were standing for one kind of republic and we stand for a different one.[61]

Yet the very republic that Fianna Fáil stood for was one which benefited native employers and offered little to either Southern workers or to Protestant workers who might look for an alternative to Unionism. This critical division of opinion led to a split and the eventual demise of the Republican Congress. The only challenge to Fianna Fáil remained the relatively weak Labour Party who made a brief foray into radical rhetoric and then quickly withdrew following some strictures from the bishops.

Despite the conflicts of the mid-1930s, Fianna Fáil managed to gain and cultivate an ambiguous sympathy from a potentially left-wing audience. Here a crucial factor was the contrast between its approach to Irish capitalism and that of its main rival in Cumman na nGaedheal. Fianna Fáil built on the idea that its rival represented a major threat to the workers' movement and that therefore, despite some disagreements and conflict, it was deserving of support. A key factor here was the manner in which the perspectives of the leaders of organised labour came to coincide with Fianna Fáil on a variety of issues.

The Fascist Threat

The first issue which drew the official labour movement closer to Fianna Fáil was the threat posed by fascism. Irish fascism won support from large farmers who were particularly badly hit by the Economic War. Between 1931 and 1934, cattle exports fell by a third and the ranchers had little option but to have their cattle slaughtered under a subsidised scheme which aimed at reducing numbers by 200,000.[62] Driven wild with anger, many of these farmers joined with other groups who had lost out because of the new economic policies to push Cumman na nGaedheal towards fascism.

An early signal of this development was the extreme hysteria with which they attacked Fianna Fáil when it assumed office in 1932. The *United Irishman*, the Cumman na nGaedheal paper, claimed that de Valera was leading the country into 'Bolshevik servitude' and that his financial policy would cause 'despoilatory taxation, which rounded off with a dose of inflation, may be trusted to dispose of our Irish Kulak'.[63] Such language was not the stuff of normal bourgeois politics and was a direct reflection of the contradictions that had opened up within the dominant class. There was an intense division between different factions about the direction in which Irish capitalism should go. Control of the state was seen as crucial for the economic salvation of either the larger farmers or the new manufacturing class. As a result, the conflict could not be contained within the precincts of parliamentary democracy. Cumman na nGaedheal supporters simply could not see how their particular interests could be safeguarded by obeying the rules of polite debate in Dáil chambers. Hence the move towards fascist methods.

The first positive indication of a change in direction was the formation of the Army Comrades Association (ACA) in February

1932. Its original aim was to promote the interests of ex-national army personnel who feared victimisation from the new republican government, but, despite its own disclaimers, it had a distinct political identity from the outset. It was led by the Cumman na nGaedheal TD, T.F. O'Higgins, a brother of Kevin O'Higgins, and was pledged to fight communism. O'Higgins, who later became a Supreme Court judge, had never disguised his authoritarian views, declaring at one stage that 'no country in the world needs order knocked into it as much as Ireland'.[64] Until 1933 there remained the hope that Fianna Fáil could be disposed of by legitimate electoral means, but after it returned with an overall majority, its opponents were forced to conclude that other means were necessary. Supporters of Cumman na nGaedheal turned to the ACA as a focus for extra-parliamentary activities, and on 14 February 1933 the ACA adopted a distinct badge and a uniform and dropped all claims to be non-political. From then on the *United Irishman* described the new organisation, the Blueshirts, as a 'civilian corps d'elite'.[65] In fact, it had all the trappings of a fascist outfit. In July, it elected as its leader the former police chief Eoin O'Duffy, who made no secret of his distaste for the parliamentary system,

> The present parliamentary system was English. The system he championed was close to the old Irish method of government. After it had been tried for, say, ten years he would give people an opportunity of voting for or against its acceptance.[66]

Membership reached approximately 30,000 with only those 'Christians of Irish birth' allowed to join and a series of rallies accompanied by fascist style salutes were held around the country. So great was the confidence of the Blueshirts that they planned a march on the Dáil in August which bore every similarity to Mussolini's march on Rome.

The Fianna Fáil government was now fighting for life. A few months earlier Hitler had come to power and showed that no opposition to fascist rule was tolerated. De Valera invoked the old Public Safety Act which had originally been introduced by Liam Cosgrove to ban the Army Comrades Association and set up military tribunals. The Blueshirts were forced to retreat but they regrouped to launch a new organisation, Fine Gael, which was formed through the fusion of Cumman na nGaedheal, the old ACA and the smaller Centre Party. The fact that Ireland's second major party grew directly from an association with fascism has long been a cause of some embarrassment to those academics who argue that Irish politics has been established around a shared commitment to democracy. The main historian of the Blueshirts, Maurice Manning, a political scientist and a Fine Gael senator, has simply dismissed the notion that they were a fascist force.[67] Joseph

Lee has also agreed with this assessment with the strange justification that fascism was too intellectually demanding for the buffoonery of the Blueshirts.[68] Like the soft Irish weather, it is sometimes felt that Irish politics naturally abhors continental extremism.

This is simply ideological wishful thinking. It seeks to infuse the past with the new harmony that has been established within the present Irish bourgeoisie, and it certainly does not fit with how the leaders of Fine Gael described themselves at the time. Thus John A. Costello, who later became a Fine Gael Taoiseach, made absolutely clear his fascist credentials when he told the Dáil that just as 'the Blackshirts were victorious in Italy, the Brownshirts were victorious in Germany ... the Blueshirts will be victorious in Ireland'.[69] Even after the failed March on Dublin, Fine Gael continued to preach open defiance of the authority of Dáil Eireann by launching an extensive non-payment of rates campaign in protest at the Economic War. This led to confrontations between the party's supporters and the gardai when attempts were made to seize cattle in recompense for the rates.

The leaders of the Irish labour movement were in little doubt about the fascist threat presented by the Blueshirts. In its report for 1934, the National Executive of the ITUC noted that, 'the future existence of the trade union and labour movement was in grave danger from the political party, Fine Gael, their propaganda being a facsimile of the ideology of the fascist dictators on the Continent'.[70] Much of the conference address of the ITUC president for that year, Senator Duffy, was also devoted to the problem of 'the importation of fascism in the Blueshirt movement'.[71] The ITUC also organised a big demonstration against the Blueshirts in Dublin on 6 May 1934 where an impressive crowd of 10,000 people gathered.The union leaders had good reason for concern as the Blueshirt leaders had every intention of abolishing independent trade unions if they ever came to power. The constitution of the Blueshirts promised 'to promote the formation of co-ordinated national organisations of employers and employed which, with the aid of judicial tribunals, will effectively prevent strikes and lockouts and harmoniously compose industrial differences'.[72]

Soon two opposing views emerged within the ranks of organised labour on how to fight the fascists and the debate between them had important repercussions for the movement's future relations with Fianna Fáil. On one side lay the official leaders, who looked to de Valera and the power of the 26-county state to crush the Blueshirts. On the other, were a smaller grouping on the left who wanted to prevent the fascists organising by mass mobilisation and confrontion with them whenever they met or marched. Attacks on Blueshirt rallies had, in fact, begun fairly spontaneously. There were major riots against the Blueshirts in Tralee, Kilmalock, Sligo,

Limerick and Dublin which involved very disparate groups, ranging from Fianna Fáil supporters to socialists. It has been charged, particularly by Fine Gael supporters, that these attacks were simply orchestrated by the IRA. However, the leading republican Seamus Twomey presented a different picture of the anti-fascist mobilisations:

> The organisation is spontaneous and these attacks are very largely made by members of the Fianna Fáil organisation and active Fianna Fáil supporters.As a matter of fact we ordered our volunteers not to take part as units in those attacks, while saying that if there is opposition they should of course join with others who resent the preaching of treason and surrender.[73]

The Fianna Fáil leadership, however, were implacably opposed to these confrontations, and viewed disorder on the streets as a symptom of a general weakening of state authority. They decided to use the Public Safety Act not only to crack down on the Blueshirts, but also to arrest and detain their anti-fascist opponents.

The issue of how to fight the fascists – by reliance on the state or by confrontation on the streets – became a prominent focus for debate at the Labour Party Congress in 1934 when a resolution appeared on the agenda condemning the increase in state power as posing a danger to the labour movement itself. One delegate stated that 'only for the protection of the police, there would be no Blueshirt movement'.[74] Another leading figure of the left, Roddy Connolly, who had left the Republican Congress immediately after it rejected his strategy, argued that 'workers should depend upon their own organisation and the Labour Party to enable them to tackle the menace of fascism and other movements without falling back on the Military Tribunals'.[75] These views were anathema to the official leadership who shared Fianna Fáil's belief that a militant fight against fascism could spill over into new attacks on those sections of the upper class who endorsed the Blueshirts. They regarded the street confrontations as threatening the very parameters set by parliamentary democracy. William Norton claimed that he 'was willing to give any powers to the government to defeat any party setting up a military dictatorship'.[76] The former Labour Party leader Tom Johnson went so far as to deplore the anti-fascists who fought on the streets as 'thugs and rioters'.[77]

In the end, their demands to respect legality and put their trust in the gardai won out over those who, in the tradition of socialists elsewhere, advocated 'No free speech for fascists'. In the event, Irish fascism was defeated primarily because of the weakness of its social base. The precondition for success for a fascist movement was that they should win the urban middle class to a programme which rhetorically opposed 'big business' and 'big labour organisations'.

In Ireland, however, the social crisis that spawned the fascist organisation primarily affected the larger farmers. In the main, the urban middle class supported the Economic War, and indeed stood to gain if the country embarked on a programme of industrialisation. Moreover, unlike parts of Italy, the larger farmers did not have the same powers of patronage over agricultural labourers to enable them to sponsor significant fascist bands in the countryside. The numbers of labourers had declined dramatically with the change over to native ownership of the land.

One of the more lasting effects of the rise and fall of Irish fascism was a closer alliance between the labour leaders and Fianna Fáil. For decades afterwards, Fine Gael was presented as the 'real right-wing force' in Irish society. Even after they discarded O'Duffy and the Blueshirts, Fine Gael were identified as both appeasers of the British Empire and opponents of organised labour. The union leaders saw Fianna Fáil's willingness to face the Blueshirts down as a confirmation of their progressive image. By distancing themselves completely from their own left-wing critics, who advocated that fascism be smashed through the action of the workers themselves, the labour leaders also showed their loyalty to the institutions of the Southern state. More broadly, Fianna Fáil's growing right-wing policies were somewhat disguised by the extremes of its main opponent. The experience therefore became a strong stimulus for an unofficial partnership that blossomed in the 1940s.

Anti-Communism

Fascism was a real threat in Ireland for a short period in the 1930s, but its great rival, communism, was more an imaginary bogeyman. Active communists never numbered more than a few dozen, yet their very existence was an affront to a belligerent form of Irish Catholicism. Virulent opposition to communism became a significant strand in Southern nationalism in this period, functioning as a great cover to promote an enthusiasm for Catholic social teaching. The official labour movement was by no means immune to this hysteria and, in many ways, its response to the supposed threat became another important factor in helping to cement its unofficial partnership with Fianna Fáil.

A public announcement on 6 November 1932 that a Communist Party was about to be formed brought an indignant call for action by the *Catholic Standard*. It declared that 'we must take care that no Communist Party will ever be founded or allowed to function in Catholic Ireland'.[78] This was followed by a series of Lenten pastorals in 1933 which called for action against the plague. Much of the impetus for the Red Scare came from the ranks of the Army

Comrades Association and later the Blueshirts. However, the hysteria went well beyond their ranks, and both Fianna Fáil and labour organisations were called to account for any trace of communist influence in their midst. The manner in which they responded was very similar: both protected themselves by profession of a devout Catholicism.

The *Irish Press* mocked the charge of communism thrown against Fianna Fáil by stating that the party 'has behind it over a half a million Catholic voters [and its] personnel is almost exclusively Catholic'.[79] It own record showed that Fianna Fáil's profession of devout Catholicism was well grounded. A similar sort of response came from the Labour Party where a tradition of militant Catholicism had been growing in strength. In 1930, for example, its leader T.J. O'Connell supported the Mayo County Council in their refusal to employ a Protestant librarian.[80] As the Red Scare developed, the party moved to define itself more sharply in anti-communist terms. It refused to condemn the deportation of the Irish American socialist, Jim Gralton, from Leitrim and, at its 1934 conference, it passed a resolution deploring the communist menace and offered as an alternative a 'social order based on Christian teachings'.[81]

The Spanish Civil War which broke out in July 1936 brought the anti-communist campaign to a climax. The surge in support for Franco's regime was phenomenal in Ireland. The Irish Christian Front, which was formed by the Fine Gael TD Paddy Belton, conducted mass rallies in support of Franco with an estimated 120,000 people in attendance at the largest one in Dublin.[82] Partially because of the fact that the Irish supporters of Franco had their own fascist ambitions, Fianna Fáil adopted a neutral position on the issue. De Valera expressed concern at the rise of communism but also refused to recognise the military dictatorship of Franco. This stance brought considerable condemnation from sections of the Catholic Church and from Fine Gael. However, with neat political footwork de Valera defended himself on this score by pointing out that the Pope had not recognised the Franco regime either.[83]

The Spanish Civil War also presented an acute dilemma for the labour leaders. On the one hand, they saw fascism as a tangible threat to their very existence and had campaigned against the Blueshirts accordingly. On the other hand, support for movements which cloaked themselves in the banner of Catholicism ran very deep. Irish labour organisations solved this dilemma by adopting a neutralist position which paralleled that of Fianna Fáil. There was no condemnation of Franco despite his uncanny likeness to the Blueshirts, and the labour leaders declared themselves officially opposed to the twin evils of communism and fascism. In practice, however, they favoured accommodation with the anti-communist sentiment that was prevalent in the country.

The ITUC president's address to the 1936 congress provides a useful example of this scarcely veiled Catholic conservatism:

> neither communism nor fascism hold any solution for the social and economic evil of our country. Rather we must with confidence seek solutions on the lines adumbrated by Pope Leo XIII and by Pope Pius XI in the encyclicals dealing with the social question.[84]

At the Labour Party conference in 1937 the only reference to the war was a defence by the Labour TD Michael Keyes of his involvement with the Irish Christian Front.[85] The following year, when a speaker made a reference to 'fascist Spain' he was denounced by the Labour TD Gerard McGown, who claimed his faith had been insulted and that 'they were Catholics first and politicians afterwards'.[86] In line with the same philosophy, the Labour TD James Everett raised a question in the Dáil about the 'numerous Russian agents in various parts of the country who are suspected of having the intention of burning churches'.[87] Even the executive of the more openly left-wing union, the Workers Union of Ireland, banned its officials from speaking on anti-Franco platforms.[88]

Amongst some sections of rank-and-file workers, the anti-communist hysteria that arose during the Spanish Civil War reached unprecedented heights. In some cases, not only did union leaders go along with it, but they also sought to turn it to their advantage. In Galway, for example, a special meeting was called by 600 workers who belonged to the British-based Amalgamated Transport and General Workers Union to withdraw from membership because their executive committee had sent £1,000 to the 'Reds in Spain'. William O'Brien, the leading figure of the rival ITGWU, attended the meeting to accept the transfer of workers to his union. In a speech which studiously avoided any reference to the issue of Spain, he merely proclaimed that they were welcome into a union that was inspired by James Connolly![89]

The neutral stance of the official labour leaders had rather bizarre implications. A circular appealing for funds for victims of the war received only two replies from the unions – and both of them were British-based unions.[90] The issue of the Spanish Civil War also led Irish labour into greater isolation from its international counterparts. Fearful of being seen to offer any support to the republican side in the Civil War, William Norton gave assurances that the Labour Party had broken from the Second International – the international body which linked social democratic parties.[91]

The anti-communism which developed in the 1930s remained a strong factor in the Irish labour movement for decades afterwards.

As it easily translated into an attack on all left-wing thought, it helped many union leaders to define their goal in a similar fashion to Fianna Fáil's – namely, to build a society based on Catholic social teaching. Yet the shared ideological understanding between Fianna Fáil and the labour leaders was not in itself sufficient to establish an unofficial alliance. A key additional factor was the promotion of divisions inside the labour movement itself.

Divisions

This occurred in two particular areas: between male and female workers, and between members of Irish-based and British-based unions.

Catholic social teaching disapproved of the very notion of married women working and advocated a family wage for married men to whom preference should be given in employment. Yet the development of capitalism did not proceed according to rules laid down by the Vatican. Rather ironically, Fianna Fáil's industrialisation programme dramatically increased the number of women in paid employment. Table 2.6 shows that the female percentage of the labour force rose to virtually the same level as Britain's in this period. This occurred because while the number of jobs for both sexes increased, more women were recruited to the labour force than men. Thus between 1931 and 1936, male employment increased by 32 per cent while female employment grew by 67 per cent.

Table 2.6 Percentages of labour force by gender in Ireland and Britain, 1926–36

| | Ireland | | Britain | |
	Male	Female	Male	Female
1926	81.2	18.8	75.3	24.7
1936	75.3	24.7	73.5	26.5

Source: Department of Industry and Commerce, *Census of Production* (1936).

These changes became the focus of a backlash against women's rights as Fianna Fáil championed the rights of the married man. In 1935, the party introduced a clause into the Conditions of Employment Act which gave the Minister of Industry and Commerce power to exclude women from certain industries. The leaders of Irish labour, who by now shared the vision of the bishops and de Valera, also believed that women were more suited to the home. They had long rejected a syndicalist strategy of uniting workers in a militant fight against capitalism and so they concentrated on ways in which competition for male jobs could be removed. As a result, the ITGWU leaders were fulsome in their praise of the new restrictions on women. Senator Kennedy argued that it was 'the first measure to give male labour their rightful place in the new industries'.[92] William O'Brien even claimed that the particular section of the Conditions of Employment Act had been introduced at the request of the National Executive of the union.[93] This approach was by no means uncommon as was evident when a delegate from the Typographical Association told an ITUC conference that women 'were a menace to the industrial classes. Man was the breadwinner. He should earn enough to support women whose proper place was in the domestic sphere.'[94]

Not surprisingly, these attitudes were vigorously opposed by women workers, with the Irish Women Workers Union in particular mounting a strong campaign. A special leaflet it produced argued: 'Irish women do not go into factories as a form of diversion. They go because they are driven by necessity or by the honourable desire not to be an idle dependent upon a male relative.'[95] The Union warned male workers that they would not benefit as wages would still remain low, and it described the overall Conditions of Employment Act as the 'beginning of an industrial dictatorship' because it tried to tie the unions to the state.[96] Despite a magnificent campaign, the Irish Women Workers Union was defeated and the number of bans on women in paid employment multiplied.

The other issue which helped to pull labour more firmly into Fianna Fáil's camp was that of British-based unions. Fianna Fáil had long campaigned for a fully Irish labour movement, where British-based unions were discarded as national sentiment grew. It regarded these unions as suspect because they might not subordinate class interests to the goal of building up the Irish state and its industries. In reality, the party's demand for Irish-based unions also implied that labour needed to organise around the contours of the 26-county state. However, the idea of excluding British-based unions did not come from Fianna Fáil alone. In the early 1930s, thousands of craft workers left British-based unions to form Irish breakaways. The issue also exploded in a bitter dispute in the Dublin trams in January 1934 when 600 workers left the ATGWU to join the ITGWU. In accepting them as members, the ITGWU argued: 'It is inconceivable than an English organised and controlled union can continue to operate indefinitely in this country. Sooner or later this must be fought and the sooner the better for the working class of Ireland.'[97] The ITUC officially supported the ITGWU on this issue, claiming that the issue of Irish-based unions was a manifestation of self-determination.

Yet despite this campaign of hostility, many of the rank and file of British-based unions remained loyal to their organisations. In Cork, for example, the Amalgamated Society of Woodworkers unanimously passed a resolution condemning the ITUC for 'disorganising' Irish workers.[98] In the same town, the National Union of Railwaymen, also declared that nationalism and patriotism were irrelevant as regards union organisations, which stood for the 'emancipation of the working class'.[99] If the issue had been settled by voluntary debate and argument inside the ranks of labour itself, the damage might have been lessened. The very resilience of the British unions, however, led the ITGWU leaders to try to resolve the question by recourse to the law. They won a judgment from Justice Meredith that registration of ATGWU rules in Ireland was 'inoperative and of no legal effect'.[100] That judgment was largely symbolic, but a precedent had been set for the use of the state by one union against another. It also opened a path whereby the ITGWU moved closer to Fianna Fáil in order to reach their common objective of banning British unions.

The link between the ITGWU and Fianna Fáil on the issue became evident when the ITUC eventually established a special commission to try to resolve the question. This commission first met in 1937 and included the key figures of the Irish labour movement: William O'Brien from the ITGWU, Sam Kyle from the ATGWU, and the Labour Party leader William Norton in his capacity as leader of the Post Office Workers Union. O'Brien used James Connolly's idea of One Big Union to advocate the formation of a large Irish general union to replace the existing rivals. But where Connolly had seen the One Big Union emerging from workers' solidarity in struggle, it was clear that O'Brien saw unity coming from on high, with Fianna Fáil lending more than a helping hand. One of the commission members, Senator Farrell, claimed to have evidence that a 'prominent trade union' official had made representations to de Valera to include a clause in the new Free State constitution to ban British unions.[101] There seemed to be little doubt about whom the reference was made.

The full implications of these developments became clear when Fianna Fáil introduced its Trade Union Act in 1941, but a distinct trend had already emerged. In the increasingly nationalist atmosphere of Irish society, British unions were seen by the ITGWU and its allies as anathema that had to be dealt with by legislation. During the early 1920s when workers fought militant battles together, the issue had never been posed in these terms. Yet it now provided a new and vital point of contact between the ruling party of the 26 counties and its largest union.

Conclusion

If the period 1918 to 1932 is viewed as the playing out of the national revolutionary process in slow motion, then the latter date marks the point when the militant and intransigent wing of Irish republicanism finally came to power. The attacks on de Valera and Fianna Fáil from their opponents more than equalled similar denunciations of the Provisional or Official Sinn Féin in more recent decades. Fianna Fáil was supposed to be communist, or the harbinger of the communists, who would nationalise land and property, bringing disorder and bloodshed to the country. Yet the record of Fianna Fáil in government was one of studied moderation. All the early rhetoric about abolishing the army and supporting workers who took strike action was simply dropped. The one promise that Fianna Fáil remained faithful to was the creation of a framework whereby Irish capitalism could grow and prosper. To achieve this, it had to engage in conflict with the British Empire and with the large farmers in Ireland who favoured a continuation of the agro-export link with Britain.

That particular fight was of a limited duration and intensity. The large farmers in Ireland were far weaker than the latifundia owners in Latin America. The Land Wars of the previous century had broken the power of the older British landed aristocracy and the rising class of Irish large farmers never possessed the same form of patronage and local power as the landed elite in Brazil and Argentina. This meant that Fianna Fáil did not require the same scale of mobilisation as, for example, Peron, whose supporters openly won the leadership of trade unions and sometimes called workers out on demonstrations and strikes to promote his vision of national development. Although there were some violent clashes on the streets, the Blueshirt opponents of Fianna Fáil never mobilised a large section of the middle class or the rural poor. As a result, Fianna Fáil could mainly rely on the resources of the state to crush them and even had the luxury of also cracking down on its opponents on the left. By 1938, when it finally signed the coal and cattle agreement with Britain, Fianna Fáil had established some space for Irish capitalism to develop. Beyond that, it was more than willing to compromise with the world's imperial arrangements of the day.

Left-wingers in and around the Labour Party made the classic mistake of conflating Fianna Fáil's 'progressive role' in challenging the Empire with an image of a party that leaned to the left. It is from this period that a fundamentally mistaken view took hold on the Irish left: that Fianna Fáil had only a pragmatic relationship with capitalism and might even move to socialism if it was deemed popular enough. The fact that socialism was defined mainly in terms of nationalisation and the promotion of national development greatly added to this confusion. The most promising organisation of this period, the Republican Congress, began by identifying Fianna Fáil's commitment to Irish capitalism as the essential element which defined the party. But its own roots in the republican tradition and the influence of the small Communist Party in its ranks meant that it still sought to fight for a 'republic' that was ill-defined and hardly set apart from Fianna Fáil's actual capitalist republic. One of the undoubted costs was the loss of a small but significant section of Protestant socialists from Belfast who had gravitated to the socialist leanings of the Republican Congress but who had no interest in remaining tied to the umbilical cord of the greater republican family.

If the left had been clearer about the capitalist project of Fianna Fáil, they could have established a more solid current in the labour movement, but it is doubtful if they could have broken Fianna Fáil's hegemony over workers. The 1930s represented the most favourable decade for the establishment of Fianna Fáil influence. The weakening of the British Empire in international terms and the growing tendency to protectionism and autarky after the Wall Street crash helped to create a space for the expansion of Southern capitalism. Although the costs of Fianna Fáil's mini-industrial revolution were borne primarily by the workers, it also seemed that national development was really taking place. There were more jobs available, slum dwellings were cleared and replaced by new housing programmes, and minor improvements in social welfare were made – not much in terms of a transformation of working-class living conditions, but to a class who had suffered bitter defeats in the 1920s and remained demoralised by high levels of unemployment, these seemed to be small but tangible gains. In brief, the radical nationalism of Fianna Fáil could be associated with tangible economic advances.

And where those gains failed to satisfy, Fianna Fáil still retained significant ideological resources. Many of its leaders had risked their lives in an armed conflict with Britain just a decade previously. Their resilience in the face of Free State repression and blacklisting gave them an aura of austere, incorruptible figures who genuinely cared about eradicating poverty and Irish humiliations. More importantly, they made the successful transition from being excommunicated by the bishops to becoming their allies. In the process, the older goals of establishing a 32-county Ireland and continuing the fight against imperialism were transmuted into celebration of the Catholic identity of the 26-county state. De Valera was more than aware that the unity of spiritual and temporal forces was important as a source of discipline for a population which had become discontented when the earlier promises of radical nationalism were not met.

By the end of the 1930s, then, Fianna Fáil was already in transition. It had mobilised a populist alliance to weaken the grip of the older hangers-on of the Empire and had promised gains for workers in the process. It had carried this approach through into an informal alliance with a key section of Irish labour around the ITGWU leadership by being willing to exploit divisions over issues such as British-based unions and the employment of women. But these links with labour were never entirely contractual or based on the promise of material gains. There was always an ideological component which was articulated primarily through Catholic nationalism. The more the promise of material change receded, the more Fianna Fáil had to rely on this ethos.

CHAPTER 3

Tying the Knot: Fianna Fáil and Irish Labour, 1939–1945

The 'Emergency' of 1939–45 is often seen as a time when little of significance occurred in Southern Ireland. This has partially to do with the way in which the great events of history seemed to pass the country by. One historian has described it as the period when one part of Ireland experienced 'her almost total isolation from the rest of mankind'.[1] 'Stagnation', 'decay' and claustrophobia' are some of the common adjectives used to describe the country at this time.[2] Yet war conditions, even if they are experienced at one remove, produce tremendous strains on society, rupture old relationships and provide a stimulus for new forms of rule. Between 1939 and 1942, Fianna Fáil developed an elaborate structure of state intervention in the economy and, as part of this process, devoted considerable attention to the role of organised labour. In the process, intense conflicts developed, particularly as a result of the Wages Standstill Order and the Trade Union Bill of 1941. Nevertheless, these conflicts were blunted through the growth of a Catholic nationalism that was often associated with a defence of neutrality.

Irish neutralitry during the Second World War was so popular that even the more traditionally pro-British party, Fine Gael, supported it, with the sole exception of James Dillon who was forced to resign on the issue.[3] Enlistment in the defence forces reached extremely high proportions. In 1939, there there 12,000 men in the regular army. By 1945, this had reached a quarter of a million when the auxiliary forces are included.[4] When Sean Lemass proclaimed that 'the main task is to stay alive in a world where we have few friends',[5] the terms of the argument had shifted. The primary identity was the citizenry of the 26 counties. Ironically, while the policy of neutrality stemmed from a protest about the partition of Ireland, Terence Brown has pointed out that, 'neutrality and the experience of the war years mobilized Irish opinion for the first time to consider the 26 county state as the primary unit of national loyalty'.[6]

The cultural medium through which this sentiment expressed itself was overwhelmingly Catholic and conservative. Serious moves were afoot to debate the restructuring of Southern society along lines advocated by Catholic social teaching. The Commission on Vocational Organisation, which held its first meeting on March 1939, was hailed by *Irish Catholic* as a 'definite step to bringing the principle of the papal encyclicals to bear on Irish life'.[7] The paper recommended that the experience of Portugal and Italy be looked at. The rejection of most other strains of Irish life was overwhelming.

When James Joyce died in September 1941, the *Irish Independent* described him as one 'who reviled the religion in which he was brought up and fouled the nest which was his native city'.[8] Hatred and dislike of Protestants, Jews, and gypsies became officially quite acceptable. In 1943, for example, the Archbishop of Dublin, John Charles McQuaid, was appointed to chair a commission on youth employment despite the fact that he refused to sit with any official representative of the Protestant churches or even to take representations directly from Protestant associations.[9] A year later, Lenten regulations from the same archbishop barred entry for Catholic students to Trinity College lest they mix with Protestants. More sinister forms of anti-Semitism were also present. Ireland showed little sympathy with the plight of Jews who were persecuted by Nazi Germany and continued to maintain a strict anti-immigration policy. At a Fianna Fáil parliamentary meeting in 1944, the Minister for Lands could inform TDs that only 40 foreigners had purchased land in Ireland and of these 'only one was a Jew'.[10] Gypsies were regarded as akin to alien beings, with the Limerick County Council voting to have them interned while an outbreak of foot and mouth disease persisted![11]

Yet this very conservative Catholic society experienced a deepening class conflict. This is all the more surprising as it occurred at precisely the time when the nation was supposedly more united than ever before.

Warnings

The first signs of a clash came with a warning from the Fianna Fáil government in 1939 in which it promised to 'set its face against the effort of any class to obtain compensation for the rise in prices at the expense of the community'.[12] However, effective price controls never materialised and the remark seemed to be mainly directed at the unions. In May 1941, Lemass revealed that since the onset of the Emergency his department had investigated 426 cases of profiteering and found 72 companies guilty.[13] However, fines for overcharging were absurdly light and Lemass's figures were only the tip of iceberg since profiteering was rife. The social consequences of the widening gap between prices and wages were seen in disturbing levels of malnutritrion, infant mortality and tuberculosis.

The minister's call for an embargo on wage increases went unheeded by many groups of workers. At the end of 1939 and at the start of 1940 there was a wave of strikes for wage increases. The ITGWU had grown by 120 per cent between 1930 and 1938 and this all contributed to a new confidence among workers.[14] *The Torch*, the paper of the Dublin Constituency Council of the Labour Party, reported strikes of shop workers in Arnott's, pottery workers in Arklow, bakers in Drogheda, and railway workers on the Great Southern Railways.[15] At the end of November 1939, the powerful National Union of Railwaymen called a special delegate conference to coordinate action for a 10-shillings-a-week increase. In January 1940, 2,000 cinema workers struck for a 15-shillings increase. In February, the Dublin dockers came out on strike. Michael Colgan, a leading figure in the ITUC, later claimed that 'in 1939, there were strikes all over the place; there were pickets in every street in Dublin'.[16]

The new militancy provoked a strong reaction in Fianna Fáil circles. Speaking at the Cork Chamber of Commerce the Minister for Supplies, Sean Lemass, warned the unions that 'the uncontrolled actions by individual sections might produce consequences seriously detrimental to the interests of the working class'.[17] He added that,

> if democracy is to work, however, particularly in time of war, it can do so only by getting through voluntary co-operation with the central authority the same effective combination of all efforts to the same objective that in a totalitarian state is secured by regulation and control.[18]

Fianna Fáil anger was expressed even more bluntly by P.J. Fogarty, TD. Declaring that he 'had been a supporter of labour on all public bodies', he now believed that 'there is nothing in the country as bad as trade unionism'.[19] The most influential figure on the Fianna Fáil backbenches calling for an offensive against union militants was Erskine Childers. Childers was the general secretary of the Federation of Irish Manufacturers and acted as an unofficial lobbyist for its views within Fianna Fáil. The FIM had been founded in 1934 by those industrialists who had benefited from Fianna Fail's protectionist policies and by 1940 had come to represent 620 firms.[20] The organisation favoured restrictions on strikes in the public sector and an 'industrial court' to regulate worker–employer relations.[21]

Childers was a frequent contributor to Dáil debates on industrial relations. During one of his speeches he argued that 'we had better ask people to give up the extreme liberty they have in this country in industrial relations ... if they want their fundamental rights'.[22]

His appearance before the Commission on Vocational Organisation provided an occasion to articulate the feelings of the small Irish manufacturers and deserves quotation at some length as an example of the pressure this section of society placed on Fianna Fáil:

> *Question*: We take it that you believe that there is a lack of national and social discipline in this country?
>
> *Childers*: I should say that it was by far the greatest factor in our entire national situation. In actual fact what we should have said to our people was that we could not possibly have the party system which involved distributing benefits, for the country was morally diseased ... and that people should prepare for at least thirty years' hard work in which the benefits would come as the profits accrued and not be given in advance before profit accrued.
>
> *Question*: And how could this discipline be enforced?
>
> *Childers*: Looking back on it now and it is so easy to cry after the milk is spilt, it looks to me, as though we should have a sort of vocational organisation and a far more limited exercise of the franchise. I am speaking personally and not for the Federation.[23]

It was against this background that a number of crucial confrontations between Fianna Fáil and trade unionists developed.

Confrontations

The Unemployed

The first confrontation was on the issue of unemployment. Ever since 1938, de Valera had been exploring the idea of labour camps for the unemployed.[24] The Department of Industry and Commerce drew up a memo on labour camps where it took as its chief model the experience of the Construction Corps in America. The German experience was also considered, with the Department noting that among the claimed results were 'the disappearance of physical and moral slovenliness ... an appreciation of order, punctuality, cleanliness, self-control, obedience and a sense of duty and honour towards the nation'.[25] Matters were shelved until the outbreak of the Emergency, when the Office of Public Works (OPW) was charged with the organisation of a labour camp at the Clonast Bog in Portarlington 'as a practical experiment on a limited basis'.[26] In April 1940, 200 unemployed workers, mainly from Dublin, were selected to participate in the scheme. The minimum wage was set at four shillings a week after deductions for board. The workers could earn more with greater effort, although as the OPW memo put it, 'this is one of the matters the experiment is designed to test'.[27]

The response of the unemployed was one of uproar. A protest meeting was called on 27 April in Dublin but it was banned under the recently passed Offences Against the State Act. When the ban was defied, gardai broke up the procession and two officers of the Unemployed Workers Association were interned; the outcry from organised labour was so great, however, that they were released within a week.[28] Neverthless, the experiment went ahead, but with rather limited success. Of the 200 unemployed selected, only 57 reported to Clonast and, in the first week alone, 30 left, leaving eventually only 9 survivors.[29]

This did not diminish the enthusiasm of the FIM for the scheme, and Childers wrote to Dublin firms asking them to employ the handful who 'stuck it out'.[30] In the ranks of organised labour, there was, despite the first protests, a certain ambiguity towards the scheme from some quarters. At the ITUC Executive, the ITGWU members William O'Brien and Tom Kennedy urged support for the scheme, with Kennedy claiming that the problem of unemployment would have to be dealt with 'on the basis of camp life'.[31]

Despite the failure of Clonast, de Valera requested an informal meeting with William O'Brien as president of ITUC in October 1940 to discuss a new proposal for a Construction Corps.[32] The Construction Corps aimed at recruiting 2,500 unemployed, who would be technically classified as soldiers and would undergo military drill and gymnasium instruction. After receiving an assurance that the scheme would be voluntary and would not be in competition with civilian jobs, the ITUC Executive gave it a guarded welcome, noting 'the great interest, purpose and intention of the scheme'.[33]

The Labour Party, however, took a more hostile attitude to the scheme from the outset, arguing that it would not be voluntary and could be used to break strikes. Their fears seem to have been realised when it transpired that unemployment assistance was being denied to those who refused to enlist in the Construction Corps. Labour Party branches began organising protests against the scheme, but meetings were again banned under the Offences Against the State Act and five Labour Party members leafleting Labour exchanges in Dublin were arrested.[34] When the scheme was extended to Cork, violent protests ensued. Three hundred unemployed men who were called up for the scheme staged a demonstration that quickly turned into a riot.[35] This was only the most public sign of opposition amongst the unemployed. Of the 3,084 men offered places in the Construction Corps, just 680 accepted, and as a result, 2,395 were disqualified from receipt of unemployment assistance.[36] The Construction Corps was targeted mainly at the young urban unemployed – a group which, the OPW believed, represented 'a real danger of economic and social degeneration'.[37] Unfortunately for de Valera, this particular group did not share his image of a rural idyll based around hard physical work to produce 'social rehabilitation'.[38]

Union Militancy

Confrontation also occurred with the trade union movement. The strike wave at the outbreak of the Second World War culminated in a serious conflict in Dublin Corporation over a demand for an 8-shillings pay increase. The strikers' union, the Irish Municipal Employees Trade Union (IMETU), secured an agreement from the Dublin Council of Trades Unions for solidarity action. At a cabinet meeting held on 26 January 1940 it was decided that all assistance was to be given to the Corporation to resist the demand.[39] When both organisations met the Fianna Fáil minister, Sean McEntee, he informed them that if this action went ahead, the government would see itself as being 'forced into a position which would be nothing short of a revolutionary one'.[40] This threat and the intervention of a local bishop defused the situation, and workers returned without any substantial rise. Fianna Fáil had clearly won its first major confrontation of the Emergency. That at least is how the employers saw it. They sent their congratulations to the authorities for their 'refusal to submit to the Soviet from Winetavern St' – the headquarters of IMETU.[41]

The scene was now set for a wider offensive against the unions. During the course of the dispute, McEntee as Minister for Industry and Commerce had been instructed to draft anti-strike legislation along the lines of the British Emergency Powers Act 1920 and the Trade Disputes and Trade Unions Act 1927 which followed the defeat of the British General Strike the previous year.[42] The discussions at the Fianna Fáil cabinet and the memos circulated between ministers and civil servants during the preparation of this Bill revealed a strong anti-union bias in Fianna Fáil circles. McEntee, for example, showed a deep-seated loathing of trade unionists when he noted:

> The party in such disputes which is numerically the stronger is composed very largely of individuals whose every day occupation tend to make them more reliant upon physical strength than upon mental process for the solution of difficulty … it is from this fact that the danger to civil order and indeed the stability of the state, which is inherent in every major dispute, lies.[43]

Because trade unionists often relied on 'physical strength' rather than 'mental process', McEntee believed that police or army intervention might be dangerous. Instead, he proposed that economic sanctions be the principle weapon used against strikers and his notion became fundamental to the Department of Industry and Commerce's draft legislation.[44]

Part 1 of the proposed Bill was directed at strikes in essential services. The Bill granted the government power to declare a state of emergency if a strike might affect transport, fire, water or food on a local or national basis. Those who refused to return to work would be liable to imprisonment or a fine of £100 and loss of Unemployment Assistance. Part 2 of the draft Bill was directed at political strikes and made trade unions which supported such strikes liable to a fine of £1 a day for every one of their members on strike. Part 3 gave the minister power to set up Courts of Inquiry and an Arbitration Board in the event of strikes in the public sector. Part 4 required unions to register by placing a substantial deposit of money with the courts before obtaining the right to negotiate.[45]

These were extremely punitive measures and throughout all the discussions a degree of nervousness was in evidence, both from the civil servants who advised the minister and from Fianna Fáil cabinet members. One civil servant, for example, was particularly concerned with political strikes that might follow, noting that if these could 'be organised on a sufficiently wide front and maintained for a sufficiently long period it can be employed ... as the first step to revolution'.[46] Sean T. O'Kelly also drew attention to the 'dangers of large scale resistance [which] might lead to considerable disorder and commotion and damage to, or destruction of, property'.[47] Lemass, who is often presented as the most friendly figure to trade unionism in Fianna Fáil, had no problems with the notions of fines for strike activity but believed that the Bill should focus only on essential services.[48]

However, the biggest blow to McEntee's proposals came from outside the cabinet table. Clearly aware of the proposals being discussed, the ITGWU conference in June 1940 denounced the threat of 'reactionary legislation' being planned by Fianna Fáil and pledged the union to cooperate with the ITUC to 'take every effective step' to safeguard their rights.[49] The ITGWU threat confirmed the worst of O'Kelly's fears, namely, that the government was attracting hostility from the very union with which it had started to cultivate a strong relationship. Within a month of this development, McEntee's original proposals were simply withdrawn and Fianna Fáil decided to take a different route to curbing union power – one that involved collaboration rather than confrontation with the ITGWU. When Fianna Fáil's new Trade Union Bill emerged in 1941 it had a very different focus to the one originally envisaged by McEntee. So obvious was the scale of cooperation between Fianna Fáil and the ITGWU leaders in the drafting that the new Bill was colloquially known as 'O'Brien's Bill'.[50] How had this close relationship which was to be so decisive for the Irish labour movement for two decades become possible?

First, both Fianna Fáil and the ITGWU shared a passionate hostility to the existence of British-based unions in Ireland. After an ITUC conference in 1939 voted down the proposals that William O'Brien made to the Special Commission of Inquiry on reorganising the union movement, the ITGWU set up a Council of Irish Unions to promote its opposition to British-based unions. This included a number of right-wing nationalist union leaders such as Michael Colgan, who opposed 'offensive references' to the Portuguese dictatorship,[51] and Owen Hynes, who championed the work of the Commission on Vocational Organisation. This grouping moved increasingly to demand legislative action from Fianna Fáil to outlaw British-based unions. As well as banishing British-based unions, William O'Brien was obsessional in his hatred for Larkin's Workers Union of Ireland (WUI), which he saw as a red union. Generalising from his hostility to Larkinism, he even claimed that fascism in Italy 'grew out of an irresponsible, ill-controlled, foolish and wild trade union movement'.[52] The demand for more state control over unions, therefore, brought the ITGWU extremely close to Fianna Fáil.

Second, the Emergency itself introduced a new element into the Fianna Fáil–ITGWU relationship as the union became the most ardent champion of the 26-county state and the policy of neutrality. On the outbreak of war, the ITGWU president Tom Kennedy proclaimed that 'we in the union are in firm and determined agreement on this neutrality and we will do all in our power in maintaining it'.[53] Initially the ITGWU's position seemed to stem from a concern for independent working-class politics. Kennedy, for example, denounced the war as 'an imperialist blood lust',[54] while another ITGWU official, Cathal O'Shannon, then editor of *The Torch*, wrote:

> Let no man tell us after these last five shameful years that Chamberlain, Daladier and the capitalist and imperialist elements they serve are leading a crusade against Nazism and fascism and a holy war for democracy and liberty ... No, the issue now in 1939 is not so very different from that which it was in 1914–1918. It is a clash of competing imperialisms.[55]

The anti-war language was reminiscent of Connolly's anti-imperialism and O'Shannon was more than adept at writing in this semi-Marxist style as he had edited the *Voice of Labour*, the ITGWU paper, during the heady days of 1918–23. However, the language was entirely deceptive. The ITGWU's position on war had less to do with a general anti-imperialism than a concern for the integrity of the 26-county state. A debate at the Labour Party conference in 1941 more neatly illustrated the position of the ITGWU on neutrality. Paddy Trench, a Trotskyist member of the party, moved a resolution coupling support for neutrality with a more general championing of struggles against imperialism. He was denounced by P.J. O'Brien, a prominent member of the ITGWU in Cork, in terms which showed that there was little interest in events outside Ireland, and still less in any class approach to war. Trench's position, he claimed, would have meant:

> a full time job worrying about the position of oppressed people in India or China ... we were only a small island and should be better employed consolidating the labour movement. Surely we do not want a revival of the sufferings of 1916 and 1922, the days of the Fenian and the Penal Laws.[56]

O'Brien's plea to avoid a replay of the revolutionary period of 1916 to 1922 was particularly evocative. The ITGWU's concern was now with its own small state, and this was also reflected in the manner in which it related to the issue of partition.

While ITGWU leaders often used partition to expose the imperialist nature of British war aims, their interest in the matter rarely went beyond rhetorical statements. The purely symbolic nature of their concern about Northern events was illustrated in 1942, when six men were sentenced to death for the killing of Police Constable Patrick Murphy. Sean McBride headed a deputation to the National Executive of the ITUC on behalf of the Six County Reprieve Committee. He sought either support for strike action to save the prisoners or a day of mourning in the event of the executions being carried out, but the ITUC Executive refused to take any action.[57] Among the ITUC Executive, one who was most concerned to argue against any action was William O'Brien, the ITGWU general secretary, who was anxious to avoid any possible identification of the unions with the IRA.[58]

The Trade Union Bill 1941

The growing Fianna Fáil–ITGWU alliance was reflected in preparations for the new Trade Union Bill of 1941. Soon after McEntee's original plans for curbing union power were withdrawn, a series of private meetings took place between the ITGWU leaders and the Department of Industry and Commerce. In August 1940, a prominent civil servant suggested meetings with O'Brien and Kennedy, describing them as 'the better elements of the Irish Trade Union movement'.[59] When O'Brien and the Secretary of the Department of Industry and Commerce met on 23 September

1940, O'Brien insisted that there be no 'dictated record' of the conversation.[60] Despite this, it is clear that O'Brien suggested a tribunal system to decided which union could organise particular categories of workers.[61] This proposal would eventually form a central core of the new legislation. However, O'Brien by no means got his own way with Fianna Fáil. He argued against the proposal of McEntee for a system of desposits from unions before they could register for legal protection.[62] Fianna Fáil, however, decided to remain firm on this issue when it came to the final legislation. The outcome of the overall discussions was that McEntee's original project of direct confrontation with the union switched to a new objective of reorganising the trade union movement to benefit Fianna Fáil's nationalist allies.

When the Trade Union Bill finally emerged in May 1941, it contained two main proposasls. First, it required unions who wished to gain legal immunities under the Trade Disputes Act of 1906 to obtain a negotiating licence by depositing a fixed sum with the High Court. The aim of this section was claimed in an internal Department of Industry and Commerce circular to be 'the disappearance of small irresponsible unions'.[63] The WUI led by Jim Larkin was the prime target. Second, the Bill made provisions for the establishment of a tribunal which could bestow on a majority union in any particular industry the sole right to organise. British-based unions were excluded from the possibility of winning sole negotiating rights and thus faced eventual extinction. The tribunal was to be composed of two union representatives and an independent chairperson who were to be appointed by the Minister for Industry and Commerce. This gave the minister considerable scope, for example to appoint representatives who favoured the elemination of British-based unions.[64]

There was every indication that this was precisely how Fianna Fáil would proceed. Fianna Fáil speakers regularly poured vitriol on British-based unions and linked their removal to the eradication of strikes. McEntee charged that British-based unions 'regarded Ireland as very much in the position of a dog upon which to try a doubtful experiment'.[65] The Fianna Fáil backbencher Martin Corry claimed that 'it was in the interest of Britain to disorganise things and cause strikes or trouble here'.[66] The notion that British unions were engaged in a conspiracy with British capital to destroy Irish industry had considerable currency in nationalist circles, dating back to the great ideologue of the movement, Arthur Griffith.

From its discussion with O'Brien and others, the Department of Industry and Commerce were convinced that the Bill was 'not unacceptable to a number of responsible trade unions'.[67] This, however, was over optimistic as two issues were to cause concern even to right-wing nationalist union leaders. A number of unions in the Council of Irish Unions were small enough to have difficulty raising deposits in order to secure a negotiating licence. Fianna Fáil eventually side-stepped this issue by introducing a measure to waive a substantial part of the deposit for Irish unions. More seriously, in a major tactical error, the Trade Union Bill was coupled with the Wages Standstill Order which was promulgated on 7 May. The Department was by no means convinced that it could hold the line on the wage freeze. An internal memo stated it was 'a matter of opinion whether opposition by means of a partial [strike], or even an attempt at a general strike, would render it impossible to enforce order'.[68] Nevertheless, much to the irritation of the Council of Irish Unions supporters, Fianna Fáil pressed ahead with both measures simultaneously.

These factors forced O'Brien and the ITGWU leadership into a more public opposition to the Bill than their private discussions with the Department of Industry and Commerce would have suggested. O'Brien even called for 'protests in the strongest possible fashion', but by this he meant sending a delegation to Eamon de Valera.[69] If matters had been left in the hands of O'Brien and other union leaders it might have remained primarily at the level of token opposition. However, the Dublin Trades Council called a special meeting of delegates and agreed to set up a Council of Action to organise protests against the measures. It published its own paper, *Workers' Action*, to get around 'the official and unofficial censor'. Speeches by the Labour leader William Norton on the Trade Union Bill were in fact censored.[70] A small number of Trotskyists played an important role in the Council of Action although the Special Branch rather inflated their influence by claiming it was dominated by 'the Fourth International'.[71] On 28 June, the Council of Action organised a massive 10,000 strong demonstration against the Trade Union Bill and Wages Standstill Order, where James Larkin symbolically burned the Bill from the platform.

Inside the ITGWU, opposition to the leadership's collusion with Fianna Fáil developed when the Cork No. 1 Branch demanded that the union commit itself to not registering under the new Bill. The resolution was lost, however.[72] At the ITUC Annual Conference in 1941, O'Brien ensured that resolutions pledging not to cooperate with the Bill were removed from the agenda.[73] While protests mounted against the Trade Union Bill in September, the Council of Irish Unions held informal discussions with Lemass with the aim of pressing an amendment that the Labour Party refused to move in the Dáil.[74] Their suggestions for change were entirely insubstantial and, despite this attempt at compromise, 12,000 marched against Fianna Fáil's measures in October. However, at no stage was the campaign against the Trade Union Bill and the Wages Standstill

Order able to produce the type of action that the Department of Industry and Commerce feared most – industrial action.

The failure of the campaign against both the Trade Union Bill and the Wages Standstill Order brought a turning point in union relations with Fianna Fáil. By defeating opposition to both measures, Fianna Fáil ensured that the issue of Irish-based versus British-based unions remained at the top of the agenda for years afterwards. In effect, it also succeeded in making the language of class, which was expressed so eloquently by the representatives of the Dublin Trades Council, take second place to a concern for the 26-county state in its hour of emergency. A clear sign of the new discourse was in evidence from ITGWU speakers at an ITUC special conference in March 1942. One ITGWU delegate, Sean Byrne, asked the accusing question: 'In the last twenty years have we ever tried to assert our nationality in the Trade Union movement?'[75] The following year, the ITGWU president explained why militant action against the Wages Standstill Order was unacceptable when he said, 'they could not seperate themselves from the community. Would members of their own class who were in the Local Defence Force support the organised movement in action of the kind suggested?'[76] This notion of the country as a community that overrode the interests of any sectional group was at the heart of Fianna Fáil's project.

By convincing a large section of organised labour to think in these terms, the party had done much to consolidate its hegemony. Fianna Fáil had begun the Emergency facing an acute crisis in its relations with the unions, but had managed to overcome its difficulties by moving from the radical rhetoric of populism to promoting an identification with the 26-county state. A subsequent analysis of the period from William McMullen reflects the hegemony that this identification had achieved in the ranks of organised labour:

> The debt the Nation owes to the Trade Union movement during the period of the Emergency is incalculable. For had it not been for the sense of discipline and orderly method of reasoning inculcated into the minds of our members by the Trade Union movement over many decades, it is safe to say that as a result of repressive wage measures of the Government ... dislocation of industry would have been so widespread as to constitute a serious challenge to the economic policy of the government.[77]

The unconscious identification of the nation with the 26-county state was complete in McMullen's remarks. This is hardly surprising, however. The displacement of syndicalism with a more moderate social democratic outlook requires a decisive orientation on the state machinery to produce gradual reform. Winning the ear of government comes to substitute for a reliance on working-class struggle. In this sense every moderate social democrat develops a passionate loyalty to their own state and becomes a nationalist in the sense of promoting its interests.

The ITGWU leadership of the 1940s have often been presented as mean-minded empire builders determined to rid their country of British-based unions. Of their antipathy to British-based unions there is no doubt. But there was a broader dimension to their motives beyond mere empire building. For them, the nation was in jeopardy. The dangers of class conflict in the midst of the Emergency seemed awesome. Moreover, they had long decided that the success of orderly trade unionism depended on stable state structures. It was this which led them closer to Fianna Fáil. The full consequences of the new links would now become evident.

Resentments

In the short term Fianna Fáil's victory in 1941 encouraged the party to adopt an even more heavy-handed approach and, in the process, it managed to fuel considerable resentment from the working class. In 1942, it designed a pension scheme for the ESB and tried to make the scheme conditional on workers not taking 'wilful action' to interrupt supplies.[78] They also refused to negotiate an increase in bonus orders for the civil service and, according to the ITUC, 'virtually denied the right of Congress to intevene on wage issues between the state and its staff'.[79] However, the most dramatic clashes between Fianna Fáil and workers took place on the bogs.

The shortage of fuel supplies during the Emergency forced the government to look to turf as an alternative energy source. They were determined that wages paid to turf workers be kept as low as possible. Recruitment of workers for the bogs began in earnest in 1942 with the aim of cutting 100,000 tons of turf a week. An effective wage embargo of 32 shillings a week was set for the scheme, even though hours of work were lengthened from 48 hours to 54 hours. For those who had previously worked on the bogs this meant a considerable deterioration in pay and conditions. Discontent grew and an internal government memo admitted that vacancies could not be filled, 'due chiefly to dissatisfaction of workers with wages paid and conditions of employment'.[80] Stoppages began to develop in a number of areas in protest. In April, 1,000 workers assembled in Nenagh in a noisy demonstration and forced the reintroduction of a 48-hour week. Strikes and demonstrations also occurred in Westmeath, Meath, West Limerick and Tipperary.

In order to deal with this situation, Fianna Fáil turned to a policy of more stringent control over the supply of labour. Throughout the Emergency, emigration to Britian continued at high levels – there being, as T.D. Williams has pointed out, no embargo on enlistment in the British army from the republican government.[81] But in May 1942 an embargo was imposed on travel permits for those with experience in agricultural or turf production. In October, Fianna Fáil decided to establish a special register of agricultural and turf workers. If anyone on the register did not take up work on the bogs they were deprived of unemployment assistance for twelve months.[82]

Bitterness over the Wages Standstill Orders and the Trade Union Act, and Fianna Fáil's continuing attack on union conditions, led to increased anger from some of its former supporters. Although the leadership of the ITGWU were moving closer to Fianna Fáil, sections of its own rank and file both shared the rising sentiment of Catholic nationalism and began to express class grievances in political terms. One expression of this was the phenomenal growth of the Labour Party at this stage. In 1941, the Labour Party had 174 branches. By 1943, the number of branches had risen to 750.[83]

The rising discontent with Fianna Fáil must have been evident to de Valera, for he postponed the general election until the last possible moment. When it occurred in June 1943, the Fianna Fáil vote sank to its lowest percentage point since 1927. The party's vote dropped from 51.9 per cent to 41.9 per cent of the valid poll and its popular vote fell from 668,000 to 558,000. Labour, by contrast, seemed poised to make a breakthrough in Irish politics. Its share of the vote rose to 15.7 per cent – a full 10 per cent higher than its vote in 1933 when Fianna Fáil was on the crest of a wave. Having sensed the widespread worker opposition to Fianna Fáil, Labour ran 71 candidates – more than double the number for 1938 – and saw its popular vote rise from 129,000 to 209,000. In particular areas where workers had experienced a more intense period of class struggle, the Fianna Fáil vote showed an even more marked tendency to decline. In August 1942, just after the fight with the turf workers, the Fianna Fáil vote in Kildare in the county council elections fell by a full 75 per cent.[84]

Sections of Fianna Fáil were aware that one of their main targets in the election was Labour. An election leaflet in the Dublin Townships constituency, for example, stated that 'even in these most dangerous days when the nation should be firmly united, the Labour Party seeks to set class against class'.[85] Sean McEntee claimed that the Labour leader William Norton was the 'Kerensky of the Labour party' who was 'preparing the way for the red shirts'.[86] However, it is also interesting that these attacks caused nervousness inside Fianna Fáil. Many believed that it might alienate a working-class base that had been won by the populist politics of the 1920s and 1930s. A number of ministers – principally Lemass, Traynor and Ryan – claimed that McEntee's attacks were counter-productive. Lemass, for example, asked McEntee not to speak in Crumlin in Dublin, as 'it was a Labour stronghold' and his approach was alienating potential voters.[87]

In the aftermath of the election, a near crisis developed in the top echelons of Finna Fáil as McEntee tendered his resignation over the conduct of the campaign in Dublin.[88] He recognised that the main reason why the party had fared poorly was 'the dissatisfaction of public employees, in particular road workers and other county council employees with our wage policy'.[89] His resignation was not accepted. Instead, the party had to find a new strategy for maintaining its hegemony over the working class. It had won the sympathy of the union leaders in the ITGWU and many smaller Irish craft unions. Now it needed to translate that into a deeper sympathy from their rank and file.

Splits

Here the key lay in those elements of its ideology Fianna Fáil had begun to forge as a replacement for its populist rhetoric. As we saw, one of these elements was anti-communism which had emerged as a central theme in Irish labour in the 1930s, not because there was a massive 'communist threat', but rather as a touchstone for the full embracing of a Catholic social ethos. Fianna Fáil was more than in tune with this sentiment. It saw the campaign against communism as a code word for attacking any outlook that prioritised class over nation. Anti-communism and the vigour with which one pursued the tiny number of 'alien' supporters of Moscow was the litmus test for how far one had broken from all past radicalism and embraced the ethos of Catholic nationalism. The problem with McEntee's attempts in this matter was simply that they were premature and undertaken from outside the ranks of labour itself.

The immediate spark for a renewed anti-communist campaign lay in the candidacy of Jim Larkin for election on a Labour ticket in 1943. This set in train a series of labyrinthine moves in which the ITGWU leaders played an important role. Larkin and his son had applied for membership of the Labour Party in December 1941. The Communist Party of Ireland had, in fact, decided to dissolve itself into the Labour Party in July of the same year. Whether or not the Larkins entered the Labour Party on the Communist Party's advice is unknown, but it is probable that they simply had some loose sympathies with the party. When Larkin was nominated for a seat in Dublin North East, the ITGWU leaders used their positions on the Administrative Council to block the nomination. However, Labour Party branches in Dublin refused to comply with this, and so Larkin stood anyway and was elected with a high vote. After a failed attempt to expel Larkin, the ITGWU disaffiliated from the party on 7 January 1944 and five of the eight ITGWU-sponsored TDs broke away to establish the National Labour Party.

The creation of the National Labour Party has sometimes been presented as the result of an irrational feud between William O'Brien and Jim Larkin. This misses the political dimension to the split, which represented the most open move in the history of the 26 counties to align organised labour directly with the politics of Fianna Fáil. The abiding link between National Labour, Fianna Fáil and the bishops was a Red Scare, which one writer has described as 'the most effective in the state's history'.[90] The campaign had close parallels to the McCarthyite witch-hunt in the United States. Just as McCarthyism gave the funeral rites to the radical sentiment that began in US labour in the mid-1930s, so the Red Scare in Ireland buried for decades most traces of left-wing ideas that had been in existence during the revolutionary years from 1916 to 1923.

The first statement of the ITGWU on the split set the tone of what was to follow. The union claimed that the Labour Party 'has allowed the virus of communism too deeply into its system to permit any hope of the recovery of its independence'.[91] It was quite clear that the union was embarking on a joint course of action with others where information was being exchanged between papers like the *Catholic Standard* and Fianna Fáil. In March 1944, the *Catholic Standard* began a series of exposé articles on the activities of alleged communists in the Labour Party. It was unusually detailed and seemed to have its source in Special Branch files.[92] Even before the campaign began there is clear evidence of close links between the bishops and Fianna Fáil in tracking down individual communists. In 1942, for example, Bishop McRory wrote directly to de Valera to complain about the influence of the communist activist Verschoyle Gould who was detained in the Curragh Camps with republicans. Not only was McRory supplied with a detailed biography of Gould from Department of Justice files but it was also agreed to accede to his request to tranfer Gould to Mountjoy.[93]

The *Catholic Standard* articles and the ITGWU campaign neatly dovetailed with each other. The paper praised the ITGWU campaign as 'well founded'.[94] The National Party, in turn, reprinted a leading *Catholic Standard* article in its anti-communist campaign by Professor Alfred O'Rahilly.[95] J.P. Patterson, the chair of the NLP, noted that O'Rahilly's articles would help the NLP to stay 'clear and definite on fundamentals intertwined with Faith and Nationality'.[96] O'Rahilly also offered to help in drafting the NLP's programme, and one

ITGWU leader believed that this presented 'a golden opportunity for a party veering closer to nationalist issues'.[97]

Throughout these attacks the Labour Party was its own worst enemy. Instead of standing up for the mildest of left-wing principles, it attempted to compete with the NLP on its chosen ground of Catholic nationalism. It established its own Commission of Inquiry into communism in the Labour Party and expelled six members, including John de Courcy Ireland, a member of the party's Dublin executive.[98] During the 1944 election, Norton attempted to deflect the charge of communism by stating that 'the Labour Party proudly acknowledges the authority of the Catholic Church in all matters relating to public policy and public welfare'.[99] Denying the political rights of non-Catholics did little to help Labour's electoral fortunes. It managed to lose 70,000 votes and nine seats in the 1944 election. Fianna Fáil had clearly found an effective mechanism for maintaining its hegemony over workers.

Even greater long-term damage was to be done in the unions. Here the effectiveness of the ITGWU campaign to draw the labour movement closer to Fianna Fáil developed from the manner in which it articulated two other central concerns of the period: British-based unions and Irish neutrality. These were in turn, linked to the theme of anti-communism to produce a most potent brew. In February 1944, the key intellectual of the Irish right, Alfred O'Rahilly, advised the ITGWU to broaden out its campaign beyond pure anti-communism to embrace other issues. He suggested that it should connect the campaign to its previous attempts to outlaw British-based unions and eradicate 'the Belfast influence'.[100] When the report of the Commission on Vocational Organisation appeared in 1944 this provided a new opportunity to stoke up the fires of conflict over British-based unions. The Commission noted that there was a

> danger of this country being used [by British-based unions] as a field of experiment in regard to wage policies. These policies may result in strikes being called here irrespective of the feeling of the workers in this country or the likelihood of its success.[101]

How workers were to be coerced from Britain into taking such actions, seemingly against their will, was never fully explained. Not that explanations were really required. The campaign against the evils which British unions were importing into Ireland, however, really gained impetus when it was linked to a defence of Irish neutrality.

A loose left-wing axis had existed for some time in the Irish labour movement centred on the ATGWU, the Belfast Trades Council and the Workers Union of Ireland. It was influenced by the politics of both British labourism and, to some degree, the Communist Party.

Crucially, after Russia was invaded by Nazi Germany on 22 June 1941, both these tendencies saw the Second World War in anti-fascist terms. Both favoured the formation of a broad Popular Front against the war that might unite everyone from Churchill to the Communist Party. Both tended to deny that the war had anything to do with a redivision of the world between the foremost imperial powers. In practice, this led them to ignore or deny the national rights of the peoples of the British Empire to independence – at least, until after the war. While most socialists favoured a fight against Nazism no matter what country they came from, the particular strategy of seeking a popular front with Churchill proved an unmitigated disaster in Ireland, where memories of the Black and Tans were a mere 20 years old.

The left-wing challenge to the very concept of Irish neutrality first surfaced in 1941 when Sam Kyle of the ATGWU spoke against it at a Labour Party conference. He claimed that Ireland could not be, 'indifferent to the loss of national rights of France, Poland, Norway, Denmark, Belgium, Holland, Yugoslavia, Albania, Greece and Czechoslovakia'.[102] It was an interesting list as it excluded main centres of the world's population such as India where there had long been a demand for independence and national rights. The left's ambiguity on the role of British imperialism was adeptly exploited by O'Brien, who did not rely solely on clericalist fears to advance his cause. He denounced the left for the fact that the British Communist MP, Willie Gallacher, was 'prepared to shout and applaud Churchill in his way'.[103]

The issue exploded in 1944 when the newly formed World Federation of Trade Unions sent an invitation to the Irish labour movement to attend its conference. The meeting was to be attended by unions mainly from Allied powers. O'Brien charged that acceptance of the invitation would amount to a breach in the policy of Irish neutrality. When the ITUC Executive, which was now composed of more representatives of British-based unions, voted to accept, ten Irish unions walked out to establish a rival grouping, the Congress of Irish Unions (CIU). The split was to last a full 13 years.

By March 1945, when the CIU held its first conference, Fianna Fail's position had been immensely strengthened. There was a split in both the political and industrial wings of the labour movement, and the issues at stake – Irish neutrality, loyalty to the 26-county state and a virulent anti-communism – were a testament to the party's degree of influence in labour circles. The founding conference of the CIU confirmed the drift to Fianna Fail's positions. Delegates were informed that the CIU intended to take account of 'a national as well as a class point of view'.[104] One of its leaders, Michael Colgan, assured them that success would come their way just as surely as it fell to those 'who were most extreme in their nationality'.[105] W.J. Whelan probably summed up its mood best by stating that the CIU was 'equally oppposed to British imperialism as it was to the policy of dictatorship or the policy of communism'.[106] Opposition to imperialism was confined, however, to defending the sovereignity of the 26-county state and coincided with Fianna Fáil's approach to the matter.

Of the party's support for the split there can be little doubt and it is difficult to avoid the conclusion that considerable cooperation existed between the leaders of the ITGWU and Fianna Fáil to bring the situation about. A month before the founding conference of the CIU, Lemass assured a delegation that not only would they be recognised by the government, but also they would be regarded as the most representive body.[107] A later decision to appoint only CIU delegates to the International Labour Organisation seemed to confirm this. Privately, inside the machinery of the state, Fianna Fáil's support for the CIU was even more active. After the split, Lemass issued an instruction to all government departments to insist that the CIU be accorded 'at least equal status' to the ITUC. The document indicated a particular familiarity with key figures in the CIU when it advised that 'when informal opinion on trade union matters is sought', queries should be addressed to Cathal O'Shannon, the secretary of the CIU. Finally, it stated quite explicitly: 'It will be our policy to build up the Council of Irish Unions and to treat it as the most representative organ of Irish union opinion.'[108]

It was clear that the coincidence of interests between Fianna Fáil and a section of Irish labour which had begun to emerge in the 1930s had finally mushroomed to a full-scale alliance. Fianna Fáil had reached the high point of its hegemony over labour.

Conclusion

The Emergency marked the period when a more distinct and vigorous Catholic nationalism came to predominate over Fianna Fáil's earlier populist rhetoric. A defence of sovereignty and independence of the 26-county strategy finally replaced any real concern for partition. This did not mean that the issue of partition disappeared from the political agenda. It became, however, a symbol of a national wrong inflicted on Ireland by colonialism – an issue that could help bind the Southern community together by reinvigorating memories of past British oppression. It was not something which the politicians of Dáil Eireann aimed actively to overturn. Their primary interest lay in building their own state and nurturing their population with active support for it.

The political party that was most identified with the sovereignty of the 26 counties was Fianna Fáil. From 1939 onwards it made a transition to becoming a catch-all party. Its most significant achievement was to force Fine Gael to accept its political parameters. If 1932 represented the year when the Southern state was accepted by the republican minority, 1939 was the year when supporters of the neocolonial link with Britain had finally to accept Fianna Fáil's project.

The labour movement could hardly have remained immune from these developments. Populist organisations generally tend to move from a period of active mobilisation to one of binding their supporters to the state. In particular, the autonomy of the trade unions are often severely restricted. They are seen primarily as a vehicle for mobilising the masses to achieve the goals of the great leaders. For the reasons outlined previously, Fianna Fáil was never required to adopt these strong forms of populist mobilisation. Nevertheless, a related process is at work in this period as Fianna Fáil set out to restructure and impose a new loyalty on the labour movement. While it did not attempt to form direct institutional links between the state and the workers' movement, Fianna Fáil insisted that labour must mirror and develop an active loyalty to the structures of the 26-county state.

None of this emerged without considerable conflict. Indeed the years 1940–41 were remarkable for the degree of class struggle in Irish society. As on other similar occasions this found some expression in the growth of the Labour Party. But that party's traditional separation of economic struggles from political activity meant that it was in no position to press for the type of action which could have defeated Fianna Fáil's Trade Union Act. The growth in support for the Labour Party was very much a tenuous by-product of the short intense burst of conflict that was caused by Fianna Fáil's decision to freeze wages and interfere with the unions.

Fianna Fáil was able to turn back the rise of the Labour Party by a vigorous anti-communist campaign which demanded that workers' organisations openly accept Catholic social teaching. The scale of the frenzy over communism was remarkable if we measure it against the tiny size of the Communist Party. But this is to misunderstand the nature of the particular campaign. On the one hand, it represented a pride in the Catholic ethos of the 26 counties and a desire to reject all 'alien' influences that detracted from an enthusiastic loyalty to the Southern state. Thus anti-communism was a means by which former radicals like O'Brien and McMullen cleansed themselves of their own history and ensured that the politics of Connolly and Larkin was finally put to rest. On the other hand, it allowed for a more active espousal of class harmony against 'alien influences'. The more the 26 counties faced an external threat, the greater the scope for ITGWU leaders to join with Fianna Fáil to play down class conflict.

The left found itself dramatically exposed in this process. A right-wing nationalist current around O'Brien was able to reclaim the traditional memories of anti-colonialism in the South to promote a new loyalty to the Southern state. The left, by contrast, put itself in a position where it seemed to be profoundly ambiguous about this tradition. It backed the British Empire as a progressive force in the Second World War, seeing it as a bulwark in the fight against fascism. It often ignored the fact that for all his rhetoric about freedom of small nations Churchill was more than willing to deny very basic rights to such large nations as India and to continue to interfere in Ireland.

The process by which the left was marginalised is similar to the way Islamic fundamentalists replaced the Arab left when it sought an accommodation with large colonial powers. In Palestine, for example, many look to organisations like Hamas precisely because the Palestinian Liberation Organisation became so anxious to reach a settlement with both Israel and their superpower sponsor, the United States. The comparison, while not exact, serves to make the point that the isolation of the left in this period was not simply an inevitability, but owed something to its own outlook. The tragedy for many Irish socialists is that they have often vacillated between seeing Irish republicanism as nearly an anti-capitalist movement and, at other times, completely ignoring any fight against the influence of British imperialism.

CHAPTER 4

Fianna Fáil's Failure, 1945–1958

After the Emergency Fianna Fáil hoped to capitalise on its new relationship with a section of the labour movement and move to greater state control over the unions. Its aim was to promote a sense of class harmony, but it soon became clear that the party faced substantial difficulties. Its populist appeal of the 1930s had rested on the promise of real material improvements for workers. The Emergency had allowed it to shift its emphasis to promoting a more generalised sense of loyalty to the 26-county state, but once the external threat was removed the emperor was revealed as having very few clothes. Ireland of the late 1940s and 1950s became a byword for poverty and emigration, and this threatened to eat away at Fianna Fáil's dominance over Irish labour.

As soon as the war ended the Fianna Fáil cabinet was gripped by what might be called 'the great fear'. During the Emergency, an estimated 100,000 Irish people had emigrated to Britain and their return after the war was seen as a distinct threat to stability. According to F.H. Boland, Assistant Secretary of External Affairs:

> Whatever the danger of social revolution in this country may be, it is certain to be at its maximum during the last year of the war and during the next year or two after it ... immediately the 'ceasefire' order is given, the whole aim and purpose of the British authorities will be to rush all these workers back to the country as quickly as they can.[1]

Some unusual schemes were proposed by Fianna Fáil ministers to deal with returned emigrants. Frank Aiken, for example, suggested concreting all the roads of the country. He estimated that the job would take between 10 and 20 years; that those employed could be paid 25 per cent less than the normal rates; and that as work was available in each district, Fianna Fáil could 'legitimately shut down the Unemployment Assistance part of the Labour Exchanges'.[2]

Lemass was also keenly aware of the postwar problems. As early as June 1942, he sent a memo to de Valera on labour policy in which he pointed to the danger of disputes if wage controls were lifted. He proposed the establishment of a Ministry of Labour and argued that:

[the] general scheme of control of labour, introduced to cope
with the circumstances of the Emergency should be retained
after the Emergency has passed and become a permanent
feature of the state's labour organisation.[3]

State regulation of the labour market had obvious implications for
the unions and Lemass believed that this degree of state intervention
would either 'necessitate active co-operation with the unions' or
alternatively 'a prohibition of trade union interference with it'.[4] What
was certainly not desirable was any form of militant or independent
labour movement. Lemass also argued inside the cabinet for
expansionist, full employment policies to meet the new dangers but
again he believed that this had to be accompanied by a strategy for
both involving and reshaping Irish labour. According to Lemass:

a full employment policy is incompatible with the old practice
of settling wages rates by due negotiation between employers
and trade unions or by strikes and lock-outs ... in return for the
removal of the fear of unemployment the workers must be
willing to accept supervision of wages rates by a public authority
charged with policing the real value of all wages.[5]

As free negotiation on wages was to be circumscribed by greater
state control, Lemass argued that the unions should be encouraged
to participate in industrial management. He believed that such
participation was a 'necessary preliminary to the acceptance by them
of responsibilities in relation to the maintenance of discipline'.[6] This,
then, was an ambitious project for remodelling the unions and
subjecting them to greater state discipline. Shorn of their political
ties, and facing a diminished scope for free collective bargaining,
they were to enter a relationship with the state where the key word
was 'responsibility'. In return for imposing greater discipline on their
members, they were to gain a voice in production.

There were many attractions in this scheme for the union leaders.
During the Emergency, limited wage increases were granted through
a Wages Advisory Tribunal, while strike action was prohibited. The
result was that by 1944, the ITGWU, for example, was spending
a mere 0.6 per cent of its income on industrial action.[7] Moreover,
as the system of wage control only allowed licensed unions to
apply for a wage increase, there was a strong incentive for workers
to join unions. Between 1941 and 1945 membership of trade
unions grew by 50,000, or by 29 per cent on the 1941 figure.[8] The
more favourable attitude by the union leaders to the wartime
system for regulating wages was expressed by William McMullen
when he noted that 'a more comprehensive and objective view reveals
it brought in its train advantages to the workers which might
otherwise not have accrued'.[9]

The immediate result of this shared desire for a different model of union organisation was that discussions began on a new Industrial Relations Act. At first, the Department of Industry and Commerce sought to restrict strikes in essential industries. They also wanted a system whereby agreements between union and employers were registered and made legally binding, thus effectively outlawing unofficial strikes.[10] The two union federations gave two quite different responses to these proposals. The ITUC made it clear that it would oppose any limitation on the right to strike, while the CIU was far more welcoming. The CIU wanted a National Labour Board to adjudicate on issues, with a ban on strikes and lockouts for 14 days after the Board had given its decision. However, it drew a distinction between recording agreements with the court and registering them. Only the latter would be legally binding and the union and employers could therefore retain the option on how much state regulation they wanted in particular cases.

When Lemass brought the outcome of these discussions back to cabinet, it was clear that he had placed special emphasis on winning union cooperation. There was no reference in his draft Industrial Relations Bill to the original proposal for banning strikes in essential services even though he was criticised inside the Fianna Fáil cabinet for appeasing the unions.[11] Instead, the Industrial Relations Act, which became the cornerstone of the whole structure of industrial relations for decades to come, contained a number of elements. First, the act provided for the principle of voluntary mediation and arbitration under a Labour Court system. In deference to union wishes, Labour Court recommendations were normally not binding but relied on moral authority. Second, the old Trade Boards which set minimum rates of pay were renamed Joint Labour Committees and were given more powers to regulate conditions of employment as well. The Labour Court could establish these JLCs, and when it confirmed their orders these became legally binding. Third, it provided for the voluntary registration of agreements between unions and employers. Once registered, these also became legally binding – all employers in a particular industry had to comply and no union could disperse strike funds in contravention of these agreements.

Lemass saw the Industrial Relations Act as only the first step towards greater regulation. After the Supreme Court ruled that a section of the Trade Union Act of 1941 was unconstitutional as it impeded the right to free association, Lemass wrote to the union leaders suggesting a new system of certification. He urged that all unions would have to be certified before an independent authority and pay a deposit. Significantly, he also wanted to include provisions whereby some unions could be decertified. He informed one delegation that, if there were complaints about disruptive tactics … then in his opinion, it would be desirable at some stage for a competent authority to step in and say that due to financial mismanagement or disruptive activities, the union concerned should cease to exist.[12]

However, while Lemass was working on proposals that could see some unions banned, his strategy was blown off course by a growing revolt from below.

The Revolt from Below

The revolt began at the end of 1945 with a strike of the Irish Women Workers Union in the laundries. The point at issue was a demand for a fortnight's holiday, and Fianna Fáil were intent on backing the employers in resisting it. Lemass spoke out against the strike, and his department went as far as refusing permits for striking laundresses to go to Britain to work during the stoppage. Yet the strikers were able to call on considerable solidarity from the rest of the labour movement, and after a long strike the employers were forced to concede the fortnight's holiday. Fianna Fáil hoped that the strike would not set a precedent, but the claims for extra holidays and shorter hours were to feature in many of the postwar disputes.

Soon after the laundry strike ended, 1,000 farm labourers who were members of the Workers Union of Ireland came out on strike for the 48-hour week, a week's holiday and a 14-shillings increase. They called on workers in the city for help in stopping farmers selling their produce in the markets, and on busy market days lorryloads of vegetables heading for the markets were often overturned. In some areas, broken glass and barbed wire were spread on the road to puncture the tyres. Through these, often violent, tactics, vegetable supplies to the Dublin market were halved and the big farmers were forced to meet with the WUI. New wages rates were eventually agreed and the farmers accepted in principle the claim of a 48-hour week and a week's holiday. Such was the success of the strike that plans to establish a new organisation for rural workers were brought rapidly to fruition. In May 1946, the Federation of Rural Workers (FRW) was launched by the ITUC with the help of loans from other unions.

The next big group to strike were teachers who began their action on 30 March 1946 over a claim for a new salary scale. A special subcommittee was formed within the Fianna Fáil cabinet to resist the strike, composed of de Valera, Gerry Boland and Tom Derrig, the Minister for Education, who explained the general Fianna Fáil philosophy on strikes in the public sector when he stated:

An effort has been made to secure the sympathy of the public by suggesting that the strike was on a parallel with trade union action. There was a very important difference. In this case in his opinion, there was a definite challenge to the authority of the state if the teachers or any other body of public servants should adopt strike action.[13]

Derrig ruled out any mediation because he argued that the dispute was 'between the community as a whole and several sections which have demands to make on the public purse',[14] while Gerry Boland justified this stance by pointing to the fact that the British Labour government also took a strong line against strikes. The teachers' strike was one of the few struggles to provoke significant dissension within Fianna Fáil. In more rural societies teachers are often accorded a higher social status and influence than in more developed industrial societies. They sometimes function as an intellectual stratum that articulates the ideology of the ruling elite to the population of the wider countryside. Irish teachers certainly played an important role in inculcating the main elements of Catholic 26-county nationalism in both their educational and non-educational activities. Many were drawn into the fold of Fianna Fáil and ensured that its ethos permeated such organisations as the Gaelic Athletic Association (GAA), where they played an active role.

Not surprisingly, therefore, some Fianna Fáil TDs objected that a strong stand against the teachers was having an adverse effect on the party. At the Fianna Fáil Ard Fheis in October, there were no less than 14 branch and district resolutions seeking arbitration to end the dispute. Despite this support, the teachers were defeated after the cabinet's stance wore them down and they returned to work with no gains won after a plea from Archbishop McQuaid. Even after this defeat the Fianna Fáil government rubbed salt in their wounds by making a point of paying a special bonus to 40 strikebreakers. It was an insult that was not forgotten easily.

In August 1946, the focus shifted once again back to the farm labourers when 600 workers in Clane, Maynooth and Celbridge came out on strike to demand that the recent Dublin agreement be applied to them. A Kildare Farmers Association had been formed some months beforehand with the explicit purpose of preventing just this development. As a result, the strike quickly escalated into what one newspaper called an 'agricultural civil war' as farmers sent in 'flying columns' from neighbouring counties to break the pickets and save the harvest.[15] Large numbers of gardai were billeted in the towns to protect the strikebreakers and workers complained of so much harassment that 'it was worse than the "Tan times"'.[16] The *Catholic Standard* added its voice to the fray by launching a ferocious witch-hunt, claiming that 'the Red element

[were] endeavouring to foment class war in the countryside'. It claimed in somewhat colourful imagery that 'no normal decent farm labourer' would want anything as 'ridiculous and unnatural holiday as a half day' because,

> in the natural traditional way of farm life – at least since the bad old days have ended – real half holidays and whole holidays were not those ones which are counted on the clock but real holidays such as ... a wet day on a loft where the conversation was often weird, wonderful and romantic.[17]

The labourers chose, however, to pursue the more modern form of holidays, as the strike lasted until the end of September. After it finished inconclusively it became the focus for a huge organising drive among rural workers, with membership of the FRW growing to 17,000 just one year after its launch.

These strikes served as a prelude to what was to come in 1947. The root cause of the unrest was a surge in inflation, with the Consumer Price Index rising by 31 per cent between August 1946 and August 1947. Fianna Fáil fuelled resentment by introducing a special budget in May which raised consumer taxes while removing the excess surtax on profits. The ITGWU's report for that year claimed that 'not since 1923 had there been so many strikes' and indeed 89 per cent of the union's income for that year was spent on strikes.[18] Throughout the strike wave, Fianna Fáil attempted to keep doors open to union leaders to encourage their sense of 'responsibility', but even the CIU leaders were forced to respond to the anger from within their ranks. In the process, Fianna Fáil found the existence of two competing union federations could militate against their interests.

The escalating strike wave took on very serious proportions when workers in the flour mills rejected a Labour Court recommendation on a pay rise and served notice to take strike action from 28 May. De Valera immediately informed the mill workers' union, the ITGWU, that the strike 'would be considered a National Emergency and that the Government would take steps to declare such a strike illegal'.[19] The warning was no idle threat as the Fianna Fáil cabinet instructed Lemass to draft immediately an amendment to the Protection of the Community (Special Powers) Act 1926. When the proposals came back to the cabinet three days later, they gave the government powers to prohibit 'the organisation, declaration or maintenance of, or participation in, any specified strike or lock-out'.[20] The far-reaching powers to ban strikes reflected both the scale of the crisis and Fianna Fáil's deep-seated aversion to union action. Punishments for breach of this order included fines for every day the strike went ahead, or imprisonment for up to six months with hard labour. Upon discussion at the cabinet table it was decided that union funds should be the principle target of fines.

Fianna Fáil were fully intent on invoking the measure if the flour mill strike went ahead. De Valera, however, held a last-minute meeting with the CIU leaders where he told them of the threat of anti-strike laws, claiming they were necessary because of 'the high degree of organisation now existing between workers of all classes [sic]'.[21] This was enough to intimidate the union leaders into backing down – although higher awards for the flour workers were later established.

Disputes spread to the countryside as road and turf workers took strike action against a long-standing attempt by Fianna Fáil to peg their wages to the rates laid down by the Agricultural Wages Board for farm labourers. Sean McEntee explained the rationale for this policy when he argued that 'the farmers should get the best men who are needed on the land'.[22] Wages for other rural workers could therefore not exceed those paid by the farmers. Fianna Fáil's policy was designed to ensure that the local authority workers lived 'in admittedly frugal conditions in a cottage provided by the local authority ... with all the produce he might be expected to produce for himself by the thrifty use of the plot that surrounded his cottage'.[23] It was clear that the party's rural ideal was somewhat harsher than de Valera's vision of comely maidens dancing at the crossroads.

On 9 May, this policy was challenged when the recently formed FRW began a strike of road and bog workers over demands for increased wages and a fortnight's holiday. The turf workers in Offaly had a high degree of organisation, with Labour Court rec-ommendations being referred to a 'camp council' composed of delegates from different bogs. Strike action was also undertaken against the advice of union officials when hundreds of workers began a 'stay-in strike' at Bord na Mona establishments. They eventually won a substantial pay increase and their union was also recognised by the company.

The strike wave throughout the country was by now at a very high level. Between May and July several groups of workers engaged in industrial action. Unskilled ESB labourers in Boyle, road workers in Co. Dublin, insurance staff in Irish Life, and employees in the Dublin Wholesale Drug trade were some of the varied groups of workers who struck. The strike wave rankled with the union officials and, according to one, the demands 'were out of all proportion to the increased cost of living and left union officials ... in a very invidious position'.[24] In September, 2,500 bus workers came out on strike to demand a 30-shillings wage increase and a 40-hour week. Despite their intention of building a close relationship with Fianna Fáil, the ITGWU leaders were forced to make the strike official.

Any failure to do so would have led to mass defections to the rival ATGWU. The strikers eventually won a 5-shillings increase above a Labour Court recommendation.

The strike of bus workers set the pace for a new round of industrial struggles. The day after the bus strike ended, the traditionally moderate Irish Railwaymen's Union proposed that 'the whole movement, Irish and foreign, consider declaring a two day general strike against government policies'.[25] Shop stewards at the ESB also called for joint action from the two congresses but other elements in the CIU were determined to pull back from confrontation. The Cork Council of Irish Unions, for example, warned of the danger of 'undesirable elements' and argued that since Irish-based unions were 'an integral part of the state they ought to work for stability'.[26]

The sense of crisis in 1947 was palpable. The *Irish Times* declared that 'our society is drifting towards anarchy'.[27] At a public meeting in Letterkenny, Lemass articulated the deep worries in Fianna Fáil when he warned that the 'wrecking of the Labour Court cannot be allowed'.[28] He also attempted to put the strikes in a wider context by arguing that the situation in Europe generally was very favourable to the activities of communist organisations 'whose aim is the destruction of civilisation as we know it and whose instrument is social unrest arising from economic difficulties'.[29] The Federated Union of Employers also denounced 'the fanning of the flames of class war' and saw the main culprits as being 'Moscow, the World Federation of Free Trade Unions, the United Nations and the International Labour Organisation'.[30]

In October 1947, Fianna Fáil faced two by-elections in Waterford and Dublin in which the newly formed Clann na Poblachta offered a radical populist challenge to its rule. The party had been formed the year previously by the ex-Chief of Staff of the IRA, Sean McBride. He combined together in the new republican party those who campaigned to win freedom for the republican internee, Sean McCaughey, who died after only 31 days on a hunger strike. Clann na Poblachta was a replica of the early Fianna Fáil, with a resonant radical republican message but seeking also to address immediate economic issues. Fianna Fáil attempted to use the by-elections to stoke up anger against the union militants. When de Valera spoke at a by-election in Waterford, the *Irish Press* ran the banner headline, 'The Class Conflict cannot continue, says the Taoiseach'.[31] Typically, McEntee engaged in unashamed Red baiting and claimed that the Labour Party leader Norton had supported a call for a general strike, 'the weapon most commonly used by the communists in their march to power'.[32] Notwithstanding all this, the by-elections represented a considerable setback for Fianna Fáil. The Dublin seat was won by Clann na Poblachta, and in Waterford, Labour and Clann na Poblachta took 30 per cent of the vote.

The escalating revolt from below ensured that Fianna Fáil's plans for state regulation of industrial relations became a distant dream as the strikes pushed any thought of banning disruptive unions off the agenda. The section of the Industrial Relations Act which sought to register agreements so that they took on the force of a legal contract also looked very flimsy when the Labour Court itself was not even accepted as a fully legitimate institution. Instead of a grand strategy, Fianna Fáil was forced to resort to a carrot-and-stick approach to defuse the crisis.

The carrot came in the form of the Industrial Efficiency and Prices Bill. It proposed to establish 'development councils' in industry whereby the unions got a direct voice in the promotion of measures to raise efficiency. The employers saw the Bill as a major concession to the unions and the Federation of Irish Manufacturers denounced it as 'the negation of private enterprise' because it brought about 'an unprecedented degree of state management'.[33] This opposition only confirmed the enthusiasm of the union leaders, both right and left, for the measure. The general secretary of the CIU claimed that if the Bill was fully implemented 'the whole field of production, management, overheads will be in the hands of the trade union movement'.[34] Jim Larkin Junior, a key left-winger once associated with the Communist Party, was a keen advocate of the measure. Yet the aim of Lemass was hardly a dramatic transfer of industrial power to workers. He sought instead to co-opt the unions to follow the dictates of market competition.

If the Industrial Efficiency Bill served as the carrot for the union leaders, the stick came in the form of new measures to contain rank-and-file militancy. The Fianna Fáil cabinet gave permission to the banks to lock out their staff if they pressed for a wage rise. In October, de Valera announced that he wanted a voluntary agreement with the unions to limit wage rises, but if this were not forthcoming he would introduce a legal wage freeze. In fact, even as Lemass was inviting union leaders to talks on the issue, his own department was drawing up an Industrial Emergency Bill which would have given him power to order a pay freeze throughout industry and impose severe penalties on those who defied it.[35]

The union leaders found themselves confronted with a relatively straightforward choice. They could either support the growing rank-and-file revolt, or they could work more closely with the government and form partnership arrangements at industry level. Their whole history predisposed them to the latter option and, before long, both union federations agreed to enter talks with de Valera on pay restraint. However, the very government which was offering the partnership arrangements had also become politically discredited.

It faced new challenges from Labour and, more significantly, Clann na Poblachta, which appeared like a ghost to haunt it with its own populist politics from the 1930s. The intense feeling of national unity around the Emergency had faded in the realities of postwar class conflict.

By 1948, when de Valera decided to call a general election to nip the Clann na Poblachta challenge in the bud, the tide was already running out. One of the measures which fell as a result of the election was the Industrial Efficiency Bill, on which the union leaders had pinned much of their hopes. It was to become a benchmark to which future union leaders would aspire.

The 1948 Election and the Inter-Party Government

Despite the upsurge in union militancy in 1947, the leaders of the ITGWU remained extremely close to Fianna Fáil. That party had, after all, actively promoted the ethos of the 26-county state and was the most militant opponent of British-based unions in Ireland. The ITGWU hoped to develop their alliance with Fianna Fáil on to a more political level, and their main vehicle for achieving this was the National Labour Party. It pressurised the rest of the CIU to endorse the party as its main political representative. Once it won this backing, the National Labour Party ran an election campaign which simply dovetailed with Fianna Fáil. Both parties used the anti-communist theme extensively, despite the fact that the official Communist Party had almost disintegrated at this time. Once again, anti-communism was a cover for attacking all left-wing ideas and demanding full loyalty to the Catholic nationalist ethos of the 26 counties. In the course of the campaign the CIU issued a powerful statement on the reformation of the Comintern, claiming that 'alien notions of politics and trade unionism must be recognised and defeated'.[36] It argued that only Fianna Fáil and National Labour stood for a restructuring of the trade union movement on a 'self-contained and national basis'.[37]

When the results of the election were returned, the full extent of the close ties between ITGWU leaders and Fianna Fáil were revealed. The ITGWU Executive quite simply ordered the National Labour Party to support Fianna Fáil in forming a government. It drew up a programme for the small party which was mainly designed to add extra welfare measures on to Fianna Fáil's own platform. It included, for example, demands for a national scheme for social security and an end to the policy of low pay for rural workers.

Unfortunately for the ITGWU, its own creation rebelled and the National Labour leader, James Everett, informed the union that under no circumstances could they vote for Fianna Fáil. Most of his deputies had won their seats on the basis of a labour sentiment and, while many of their electors went along with the anti-communist arguments, they also wanted some changes which benefited workers. The postwar experience had led to intense hostility to Fianna Fáil and the National Labour TDs felt it would be electoral suicide to support that party for office. Instead, they joined with the rest of the Dáil to form the bizarre Inter-Party government which united the Fine Gael with the radical republicans of Clann na Poblachta and the National Labour Party with their supposed communist friends in the Labour Party!

The rare opportunity to achieve the much vaunted aspiration of a Fianna Fáil–Labour government, so desired of the ITGWU leaders, was missed. The project of the ITGWU leaders of adding a welfarist ethos to the Catholic nationalism of Fianna Fáil would never again have the same potency. For Fianna Fáil, the failure to capitalise on gains it had made during the Emergency meant its relationship with organised labour became more precarious after this point. Nevertheless, they still held on to one important trump card: there was strong support for a radical alternative to Fianna Fáil at the end of the 1940s but it was an ambiguous radicalism. It sought to express itself within the culture and climate of a 26-county state that had been so starkly reshaped by Fianna Fáil and the Catholic Church. This meant that the limitations of the new radicalism were all too quickly exposed.

Expectations of change were certainly high with the Inter-Party government. When the Irish Labour Party leader William Norton took up the post of Minister for Social Welfare there were high hopes that he might lay the basis of a comprehensive social security system which offered protection for workers in sickness, old age, and in unemployment. Moreover, Fianna Fáil were particularly vulnerable on this issue. The radical rhetoric of the early 1930s was now almost a mirage as McEntee argued against a family allowance system as an unnecessary financial burden on the state. McEntee even claimed that such allowances would 'induce the less fitted to marry at the expense of everyone else in the community'.[38] McEntee's approach to social welfare met with considerable opposition, even inside Fianna Fáil. At the 1945 Ard Fheis of the party, no less than 20 resolutions were tabled which called for increased pensions and the abolition of the humiliating means test. Norton had only to carry through on the mildest of measures to gain some real credibility for himself and his party.

After he took office, Norton certainly set out on this road. Throughout the 1950s there were reports that he was working on a social security bill which would eliminate the means test from many areas. Yet accounts at union conferences also indicated that the Bill was 'being delayed for some reason not apparent to the public'.[39] Later, the Labour Party would be more precise and claim that the measure was attacked by a 'privileged elite'.[40] In fact, the attack had begun in the cabinet itself. Noel Browne, the radical Minister of Health from Clann na Poblachta, has described how 'queries, counterqueries, objections, tendering of memoranda on ideological grounds accumulated around Norton's proposals with each successive Cabinet'.[41] The more right-wing ministers objected to the mildest of reforms that might extend welfare benefits.

There was also a deeper ideological assault from the Catholic Church on the issue. Norton was unlucky to find himself in office when the bishops' opposition to the welfare state was at an all-time high. Later, they would soften their position to accept a modified welfare state that did not conflict with the Catholic principle of 'subsidiarity', whereby individual families, and not the state, were responsible for their own economic plight. During Norton's stewardship, however, *Christus Rex*, the magazine of the intellectual militants of the Church, proclaimed that 'comprehensive state welfare schemes are opposed to the moral, legal, social and economic principles and are utterly discredited by experience and history'.[42] Norton had no stomach for challenging the bishops on their use of theology to stop reforms. As a member of a government whose members included some who were more than anxious to look after the interests of the 'privileged elite', he was even less likely to pursue the matter. In the end, Norton's Social Security Bill faded away.

A more dramatic case of the failure of the Labour Party and the unions to pursue mild reforms was the Mother and Child Scheme. The Clann na Poblachta Health Minister, Noel Browne, had proposed to give free medical care to mothers and children up to the age of 16. It called forth outrage from the medical establishment and the bishops, who saw it as the foundation stone of a British-style National Health Service. Bishop Browne of Galway used his opening speech to the CIU Congress of 1951 to launch a tirade against the 'totalitarian outlook' and 'slave plantation theory' which underlay the proposals.[43]

Nevertheless, the Mother and Child Scheme appealed to working-class people who, no matter what their wider political persuasion, could either not afford to pay for doctors or had to endure the degrading means-test ritual. Indeed, despite the strictures of Bishop Browne, Frank Purcell of the ITGWU called for the speedy introduction of the measures to ensure that 'restricted means shall not be a barrier to any mother and child being enabled to avail of the best possible medical service'.[44] Later he relented somewhat and accepted an amendment from a Limerick Trades Council delegation which demanded that the scheme be in accordance with 'Catholic social and moral teaching'.[45] This equivocation showed that there was a desire in the more nationalist section of the labour movement for a welfare scheme which put them significantly at odds with the bishops.

This presented a great opportunity for the social democratic wing to begin to restore its hegemony, and at first it seemed that the ITUC might indeed champion Noel Browne's proposals. Its Executive endorsed the Mother and Child Scheme and called for its early implementation. Its President, Helen Chenevix, went to Noel Browne to urge him to stand firm on the proposals and not to resign.[46] However, once the bishops issued their formal pronouncement denouncing the Mother and Child Scheme, ITUC retreated from any public support for the scheme. The same Helen Chenevix who visited Browne to express support told the ITUC conference that the unions, 'being concerned with the industrial side, rather than the political side of the workers movement, are not called upon to comment on all aspects of these happenings'.[47]

If the ITUC lacked courage in the matter, the same could not be said of the Labour Party – they simply joined the bishops in opposing a free medical service for mothers and children! The party's report for 1951 condemned Noel Browne for not appreciating the 'seriousness of the bishops' ruling', and behind the scenes they worked even more assiduously to defeat him.[48] Noel Browne has revealed that one of his most vigorous opponents in the cabinet was the Labour Party leader, William Norton.[49] Labour's failure to stand up for this important reforming measure was disconcerting enough to its own supporters, but to a wider audience who were influenced by the political culture of Catholicism it only seemed to confirm that there was no alternative. The strains that arose between the bishops and their followers could not be exploited and the ultimate beneficiary of Labour's failure was to be Fianna Fáil.

As if all this was not difficult enough for the social democratic wing, the period of the Inter-Party government also saw dramatic developments over the issue of partition. In September 1948, the government declared the 26-county state to be a republic. It was motivated partially by a desire to appease the radical claims of Clann na Poblachta, but also to signal that Fine Gael had re-entered the field of constitutional nationalism. The move set in motion a new train of events as the Unionist Party in Northern Ireland used it as an opportunity to call a general election on the constitutional issue, claiming that the declaration of the republic represented a dire threat to the Protestant people. In the heightened sectarian atmosphere that arose during the 'crisis', the Northern Ireland Labour Party behaved little differently from their Southern counterparts: they bowed to the prevailing ethos and voted to change their position to endorse unequivocally the constitutional position of Northern Ireland. After an overwhelming victory in the polls, the Unionist government demanded more measures from the British Labour government to strengthen the link between the United Kingdom and Northern Ireland. The result was the Republic of Ireland Act, which effectively consolidated partition.

Throughout the 26 counties there was a wave of outrage, and thousands went on demonstrations and marches against the Act. The anger was also reflected inside the ranks of the unions, as it was, after all, a British Labour Party which had acted to strengthen partition. If anything was designed to add to the stature of Fianna Fáil and its Catholic nationalist allies this was it, and the CIU was not slow to respond. One of its leaders summed up their mood when he said:

> So far as partition is concerned we are a class. We are 100 per cent Irish and we are against partition. I do not believe that there should be no aggression. Nothing worth having was ever got by trade unionists without a fight.[50]

The ITGWU immediately affiliated to the newly formed Anti-Partition League and distributed its literature through its branches. But the CIU leaders also sought to turn the anti-partition mood on to British-based unions in Ireland who had links with the British Labour Party. They pointed out that many of these unions paid a political levy to that party and argued that British-based unions had been revealed as 'enemies of democracy and of a free united Ireland'.[51]

Undoubtedly, the attacks had a powerful impact, and the ITUC found itself in a most embarrassing position because it had publicly called on Irish emigrants in Britain to vote for the British Labour Party.[52] Its appeals to the British TUC to make some protest against the Republic of Ireland Act were also brushed aside. Inside its own ranks it tried, by means of some extraordinary contortions, to balance between Irish nationalist sentiment in the South and the demands of its Unionist supporters in the North. On one occasion, the Executive of the ITUC issued a protest against the Republic of Ireland Act – and then concealed this stance from delegates to their conference in Belfast by not including the item in their annual report.[53]

These developments brought the ITUC to the brink of a split. At one congress there was a crisis over a resolution to expel a delegate from the Northern Ireland Labour Party (NILP) and in December 1950, it was reported that a number of Irish-based unions were about to leave to join the CIU.[54] Although unity was preserved by a series of intense manoeuvres, the overall decline of the ITUC compared with their nationalist rivals in the CIU could not be disguised. The outrage over the Republic of Ireland Act coincided with an outstanding period of recruitment for the unions and the CIU won the lion's share of the new members. Between 1945 and 1953, the CIU grew more rapidly than their rivals in the ITUC. The decline in the relative position of British-based unions was even more dramatic. In 1945, British-based unions represented 22.9 per cent of the overall trade union movement, but by 1955 this had declined to only 13.6 per cent.[55]

The difficulties which the ITUC faced related in no small way to the manner in which social democracy was powerless to challenge Catholic nationalism. As we have seen, the Fianna Fáil–CIU axis faced considerable problems during the upsurge of militancy in 1947–48, but the ITUC and the Labour Party could not take advantage of the difficulties of their rivals. When Labour joined the Inter-Party government it proved unable to promote reforms which Fianna Fáil would later take up. Its behaviour during the Mother and Child Scheme showed that it was as deferential to the bishops as any other party, and this allowed them to eventually re-unite with the National Labour Party. To add to its misery, its fraternal allies in the British Labour Party and the NILP showed that they were willing to respond to British nationalism to the same degree as the Irish Labour Party (ILP) was unable to resist the pressures of Catholic nationalism. All of this meant that the social democratic challenge to Fianna Fáil's hegemony dissipated as quietly as the melting of snow.

The Bleak 1950s

By the early 1950s, then, the Irish labour movement was dominated by a right-wing nationalist politics. It wanted some element of reform for workers but it subordinated this desire to the dictates of the bishops. Sometimes it is the minutiae of events that reveal the political sway of Catholic nationalism. One such was the national pilgrimage of union leaders to meet the Pope in 1950 which was led by the ubiquitous John Charles McQuaid. There was not the slightest embarrassment about a supposedly non-sectarian labour movement going on a journey to pledge its loyalty to the head of the Catholic Church. If anything, the union leaders were more concerned about the details of who would be seen with the pontiff. A particular worry, for example, was whether all union leaders could be photographed beside vestments that were to be presented to the Pope. The minutes book of the CIU Executive conveys in its dry and precise language how the particular dilemma was solved:

> Dr O'Connell [the secretary to Dr McQuaid] had arranged for a special audience with His Holiness and also suggested that

the form of presentation be a set of white vestments ... After a long discussion it was agreed that the vestments be photographed ... that after the delegation had returned from Rome all visiting trade union representatives of this Congress who are visiting Rome later should be photographed ... that the photograph of the vestments should be superimposed on the other photographs.[56]

In this way every trade union leader had a chance to have their picture taken with a set of vestments which would eventually reach the hands of the Pope! This approach was perfectly congruous with the general ethos of the CIU. The following year, for example, the CIU sent a telegram to Rome in which they claimed that their organisation was 'humbly prostrate at the feet of his Holiness' and expressed 'their dutiful congratulations on the 12th anniversary of his coronation'.[57] The small number of non-Catholics who were trade union members simply did not count. It was almost as if they did not exist.

A variety of institutional arrangements underpinned the virulent anti-communism which acted as a cover for naked Catholic domination. One was the Catholic Education Programme for Trade Unionists which was designed to strengthen the grip of Catholic social teaching on an important leadership cadre of the movement. Dr Alfred O'Rahilly was the main inspiration for the programme and he claimed to have copied the method of the communists of seeking to 'work from inside through a vigorous minority with a clear objective'.[58] Another principal institutional support was the link with the US embassy in Dublin. It was common for a representative of the US embassy to update CIU conferences on the progress of the battle against communism during the Cold War. Trips were also organised to the United States for both the CIU and ITUC leaders by the anti-communist Mutual Security Alliance and were sometimes subsidised by the Irish government.

Yet even in these bleak conditions there were forces at work undermining the old certainties. A key argument throughout this book is that nationalism should not be viewed as a semi-mystical ideology that resolves all contradictions in society. People may share a nationalist sentiment for long periods of time, but they only tend to sustain active mobilisations for a nationalist cause when it is associated with material improvements. Such was the power of Fianna Fáil's appeal in the 1930s, when their populist politics promised and – within key limits – delivered some gains for workers. The challenge that nationalism offered to the neocolonial status of Ireland resulted in some direct improvements that could sustain a mobilisation around these sentiments. When these improvements began to run out, Fianna Fáil could still, for a period, rely on a growing identification with sovereignty for the 26 counties during the Emergency. Nevertheless, by the 1950s it was absolutely clear that a sovereign independent Ireland was reaching its own cul-de-sac and this meant that new contradictions were bound to emerge.

One of the key factors which undermined the ethos of traditional Catholic nationalism was that the Southern Irish economy was quite simply in an appalling state. A growing balance of payments problem arose as Irish industry came up against the limits of its protectionist strategy. Industry still needed to import raw materials and other inputs, but its own inefficiency, which had been fostered by protectionism, meant that it could barely pay for them. Total industrial employment actually began to fall throughout the 1950s and emigration regularly exceeded 40,000 a year. Jokes about the last person to leave the country having to turn off the lights were commonplace. All of this was bad enough, but this depression coincided with the great postwar boom that was occurring in the rest of Europe. Between 1949 and 1956, the volume of gross national product (GNP) in Ireland grew by only 8 per cent compared with an average of 42 per cent for the countries in the Organisation for European Economic Co-operation.[59]

This was the situation which Fianna Fáil faced when they returned to power in 1951. Political desolation sometimes produces bizarre political developments. None more so than the fact that Fianna Fáil was dependent for office on the support of two of the most left-wing TDs in the Dáil, Peadar Cowan and Noel Browne. Cowan had set up a tiny party known as the Vanguard Party whose declared aim was to 'end capitalism in Ireland, establish a socialist republic for all Ireland and undo the British conquest in all its phases, political, cultural and economic'.[60] He claimed that he supported a Fianna Fáil government 'as a follower of James Connolly' in order that the Labour Party be released from 'the tentacles of reaction'.[61] This was a reference to the party's previous coalition with Fine Gael. Cowan argued that there was a fundamental difference between Fianna Fáil and Fine Gael because 'one is more socialist than the other'. Browne apparently agreed with this view, for he took it one step further by actually joining Fianna Fáil in 1953.

This extraordinary decision can only be explained by reference to the dominant outlook of left-wingers at the time. In the heyday of the Cold War and Stalinism, many socialists comforted themselves with the fact that while conditions in their own countries were difficult, there was a 'socialist homeland' which cared for a large proportion of humanity. Often their main objective was simply to support the most 'progressive' party in their own country, and sometimes the choices were quite unexpected. If Irish socialists favoured Fianna Fáil, Cuban communists at one stage even more implausibly looked to the dictator Batista who was eventually overthrown by Castro. Irish left-wingers also had an understandable but nevertheless deeply pessimistic view of the political consciousness of their own working class whom they regarded as immutably dominated by clerical reaction. They believed that the only way of relating to workers was through the filter of the dominant republican ethos. Connolly's argument that capitalism was introduced to Ireland by Britain was magnified out of all proportion to claim that republican sentiment contained within it a potential to move further left. The republican ethos of Fianna Fáil was therefore seen as a natural respository for 'progressive' politics. The more depressing the actual conditions for socialists became, the more this illusion grew for individuals. Browne and Cowan quite simply exaggerated the difference between Fianna Fáil and Fine Gael to claim that the former was qualitatively better, and so justified their own, somewhat desperate, support for it.

In reality, Fianna Fáil was engaged in a major offensive against the workers just as Noel Browne was applying to join. As an avowedly pro-capitalist party, Fianna Fáil had little option in terms of economic policy, as the depression of the 1950s forced it on to ever greater attacks on its own supporters. The strains opened up dramatically with Sean McEntee's budget in 1952. McEntee wanted a severe deflationary budget to reduce the balance of payments deficit, and so income tax was raised by one shilling in the pound and subsidies on staple household items were removed. The result was that the price of bread rose by a staggering 38 per cent, sugar rose by 63 per cent and the price of butter doubled.[62] The budget signalled a new and more explicit right-wing drift in Fianna Fáil politics, with Erskine Childers denouncing all social spending as 'slush'.[63]

The budget had a major impact on Fianna Fáil's supporters in the unions. Even William McMullin of the ITGWU, who had become an active Fianna Fáil supporter, described it as 'stunning blow'.[64] But worse was to follow. In March 1952, McEntee's Department of Finance removed recognition from a civil service union after it decided to impose an overtime ban in the Department of Post and Telegraphs. Efforts by the ITUC to discuss the matter with de Valera were rejected on the grounds that civil service matters were not appropriate subjects for a union federation. Fianna Fáil also suspended payments of an arbitration award for civil servants granted under the new Conciliation and Arbitration Scheme. This measure again provoked an outcry and a large demonstration of civil servants was held on May Day, 1953.

Attitudes inside Fianna Fáil were clearly hardening on a variety of issues. When the Labour TD, Sean Dunne, tried to bring in a Bill in the Dáil to increase the wages of agricultural workers he was denounced by one Fianna Fáil TD for bringing 'trade union rancour and conflict' to the countryside.[65] Fianna Fáil TDs also adamantly opposed demands for equal pay. When William Norton introduced a Bill on the subject, Lemass claimed that it would only encourage married women to seek paid employment, something which was 'contrary to our way of life'.[66] Another Fianna Fáil TD claimed it would lead to a 'baby sitters union and other undesirable developments'.[67] Fianna Fáil also found themselves in conflict with the newly formed Dublin Unemployed Association which was backed by both union federations. Confrontations between the gardai and the unemployed developed after a sit-down on O'Connell bridge.

A disillusionment with Fianna Fáil became evident in many quarters. Sean Moore, for example, a prominent union leader who supported the party, was particularly incensed with their treatment of civil servants. He claimed that when Fianna Fáil gave jobs to their followers it was as 'messenger boys' on starvation wages. Renouncing his support, he declared:

> God forgive me. I was loyal follower for a long time myself but it is hard to think of what the Fianna Fáil government has done for the men and women who brought about the establishment of the Republic in this country.[68]

A number of voices were also raised inside the ITGWU calling for reaffiliation to the Labour Party. At its 1952 conference the issue almost came to a vote but was deferred after a heated and protracted debate.

These growing strains with organised labour brought a change of direction from Lemass. As the most far-sighted strategist within the party, he saw that a simple appeal to the Catholic nationalist ethos was losing its potency and so he quietly dropped his plans to bring in a new Trade Union Act and to take up the battle once again with British-based unions. Instead, he focused on the competitive pressures for militancy that arose from two rival union federations. He had come to favour one strong centralised centre in the unions that might become a partner in social partnership-type arrangements that would involve the unions in reinvigorating Irish capitalism. He therefore made two major speeches on the need for trade union unity in 1953 and linked it with the concept of development councils which would help to imbue the unions 'with the idea of giving a service to the community'.[69]

Lemass's calls and the growing strains of the 1950s all had their impact. Negotiations soon began on a united union federation on the basis of 'the Irish trade union movement being wholly Irish based and Irish controlled'.[70] Increasingly, the negotiations took on a momentum of their own, so that by 1955 when they were completed there was not a single dissenting voice inside the ITGWU when it was agreed to form the interim Provisional United Trade Union Organisation.

Conclusion

In Latin America some labour movements were tied very closely to populist currents and their autonomy from the state was severely curtailed. In Ireland, as we have seen, this did not occur because Fianna Fáil did not require the same scale of active mobilisation from their supporters to hold office. Nevertheless, as we saw in the previous chapter, an analogous process was at work whereby Fianna Fáil sought to restructure the labour movement around a loyalty to the 26-county state. When the party tried to take a further step and create more open links with a section of the Irish labour movement, it failed.

That failure did not occur for want of a desire amongst the leaders of the ITGWU to forge just such an alliance. The programme that the ITGWU leaders presented to the National Labour Party as the basis for a coalition with Fianna Fáil after the 1948 election probably represented the pinnacle of their ambitions. It was designed to add mild welfare reforms to Fianna Fáil's traditional championship of 26-county Catholic nationalism. The failure of Fianna Fáil's populist project stemmed from an altogether different source: after the Second World War the party was powerless to grant the type of material improvements to workers that it had done in the 1930s. The protectionist strategy had run aground and by the 1950s the Irish economy was in a parlous state. The failure of Fianna Fáil was made all the more acute by the fact that in Britain, workers made significant gains with the formation of the National Health Service and a comprehensive welfare system.

Ireland at this time shows that there are significant limits to the appeals of populism and nationalism. These ideologies do not simply grip people's hearts and transfix them for all time. The political culture in any social formation has certainly a degree of autonomy from its economic base, but that autonomy is very much circumscribed. The failure of Fianna Fáil to deliver reforms to its supporters led to a period of debilitating stagnation for the party and between 1948 and 1957 its hold on office was severely weakened. When it did briefly form a government its core supporters in the CIU became seriously disillusioned as the party tried to manage a declining economy. By the end of the 1950s, the party's populist project had reached a dead end and its hegemony over labour was only rescued by a radical shift in economic strategy after 1958.

Irish social democracy has sometimes been viewed as a victim of the political culture of nationalism. In fact, its marginalisation by Fianna Fáil was by no means an inevitable process – the Labour Party contributed significantly to its own failures. The failure of either the union leaders or the Labour Party to champion a welfare programme during the Mother and Child Scheme debacle seemed to confirm that there was no real alternative to Catholic nationalism. On the one comparatively rare occasion when the status of Northern Ireland directly impacted on Southern politics, the social democratic tradition also lost out. The fact that it was a British Labour government who introduced the Republic of Ireland Act and that British-based unions gave the impression of supporting it, again contributed to the hold of Catholic nationalism.

Irish society in the 1950s had all the signs of stagnancy and demoralisation. In the main, this stemmed from near economic collapse and the successive waves of emigration that robbed the country of its youth and vitality. On a political level, however, there was also another dynamic at work. The failure of Fianna Fáil in this period was more than matched by the weakness of Irish social democracy.

CHAPTER 5

State Intervention, Social Partnership, and Rank-and-File Militancy, 1958–1965

On 16 December 1957, the Fianna Fáil Minister for Finance received a note from his top civil servant, T.K. Whitaker. It drew attention to the all too obvious 'mood of despondency about the country's future' and called for a decisive change in direction.[1] Within a week, Whitaker was given permission to draw up a document which later became known as *Economic Development*. It advocated the abandonment of the protectionist programme which Fianna Fáil had pioneered since the 1930s. In its place Whitaker called for a strategy of inviting in multinationals and opening up the country to free trade.[2] At first he argued that this needed to be accompanied by a sharp attack on public spending and a pay freeze, but later this was not regarded as the essential element of the switch. The change in economic direction, conventionally known as the '1958 turn', was to have unforeseen and dramatic consequences for Irish society. Yet the motivations for the change have often been misunderstood.

Some analysts believe that civil servants like Whitaker managed to impose their own views on Fianna Fáil and see this as confirmation of the theory that the state is genuinely independent of all classes. This argument is given some support by Bew and Patterson, despite the fact that they once claimed to write from a Marxist perspective. In their classic biography of Sean Lemass they argue that the autonomy of the state enabled it to impose its strategy on a reluctant bourgeoisie.[3] They stress that key sections of this class were fearful of foreign competition and that the state bureaucracy had to break with them, at least temporarily, in order to bring about the new turn. In this analysis, the mystery players after 1958 become the native capitalists who are not regarded as the primary beneficiaries. Thus the authors of *Understanding Contemporary Ireland* claim that the large farmers and overseas investors were the direct and immediate beneficiaries of the turn, and neglect even to mention the native capitalist class.[4]

For those influenced by a republican perspective, the 1958 turn represented the point at which Fianna Fáil most clearly abandoned its original ideals. Here the party is seen as abandoning both its

106

opposition to neocolonialism and its attempt to forge an 'independent economy', and the shift in strategy is regarded as 'selling out' Irish industry to foreign interests.[5] Key economists of the time such as Patrick Lynch also saw the turn as 'an attempt to fuse the two economies' of Britain and Ireland'.[6] The view that Ireland was once again becoming a neocolony was by no means confined to republicans. When Fianna Fáil rescinded the Control of Manufacturers Act, which stipulated that Irish shareholders own a majority stake in companies, the veteran left-winger Noel Browne simply read out Lemass's speech supporting the original Act in the 1930s to add to the charge of a sell-out.[7]

There are, however, a number of fundamental problems with these perspectives which lead to a misreading of the nature of the changes in Irish society. In the first place, the 1958 turn was not dictated exclusively by the interests of the state bureaucracy. As Eoin O'Malley has pointed out, the new economic orientation was the culmination of a series of policy changes that had begun in the 1950s.[8] The establishment of the Industrial Development Authority in 1949 and the introduction of an Export Profits Tax Relief in 1956, for example, had the support of most of the political and business establishment, even though these measures helped to open the way to greater foreign investment and a shift to an export-orientated industrialisation programme.

Second, neither Whitaker nor the state bureaucracy generated their policies in isolation – they were operating within a framework of political decisions to reintegrate Ireland into the world economy under the aegis of US-dominated institutions. In 1955, for example, the Irish government signed an agreement with the United States giving guarantees against the expropriation of the investments of US citizens or any ban on the reconversion of their earnings into dollars. It was another important step towards preparing the way for US multinationals to begin investing in Ireland. Whitaker's own report was drawn up after unofficial discussions with the World Bank, and this body was also shown the report prior to its publication. In addition, there is evidence that the World Bank was giving 'an unusual extent of attention' to Ireland at this point.[9]

Third, it is quite simply historically wrong to ignore how the new economic strategy was formulated with the direct and immediate interests of the native capitalist class in mind. Lemass made it clear from the outset that this class was not being abandoned:

> We must guarantee the firms which were established here on the assurance of the Control of Manufacturers Act that powerful external organisations would not be permitted to open branch plants to supply the home market and thus bring about in time the very position which these Acts were designed to prevent.[10]

By and large this promise was fulfilled. The grants and subsidies that were directed to foreign firms after 1958 went to those which were geared almost exclusively to export markets. In other words, they went to companies which posed little threat to the domination of native capitalists over the home market. Moreover, the state subsidies to industry were not directed exclusively at foreign firms but were also given to native companies as well. Indeed, as the Telesis Report later pointed out, Irish industrialists received a higher grant per job created than their counterparts in foreign firms.[11]

In reality, the 1958 turn should not be seen as an abandonment by Fianna Fáil of its original ideal, but rather as a continuation of its central project of promoting native capitalism. The party sought to revive the Irish business class by connecting it to an expanding world economy and by using the multinationals to inject a new dynamism into the Irish economy. Protectionism was simply one strategy that had become outmoded, and the evidence suggests that Fianna Fáil were correct in their assessment that the new economic turn would benefit native capitalism. O'Malley has estimated that even if foreign multinationals are left aside, the rest of industry in Ireland grew at the rate of 3.6 per cent per year throughout the 1960s.[12] Compared to the stagnation of the previous decade this was an achievement. Small business mushroomed after 1958 as new opportunities were created in the home market. By the end of the 1980s they were employing one-fifth of the manufacturing workforce. At the other end of the scale, a small number of the firms which were established in the era of protectionism managed to outgrow the Irish markets.[13]

The New Economic Nationalism

The 1958 economic turn was crucial in allowing Fianna Fáil to revive its hegemony over the leaders of organised labour. The connecting link between the party and many labour leaders was a concern about the development of the 26-county economy and its state. The continuity with its own past allowed the party to argue that the 26-county Catholic nationalism had to be translated into a concern to win the battle for production. In one sense this theme was always present, and Lemass's argument at the 1959 Ard Fheis that 'patriotism was the motive force necessary to build up a progressive nation with a viable economy' could have been made at any time since the party's formation.[14] But after the demoralisation of the 1950s, there was also a new emphasis in Fianna Fáil policies that contrasted sharply with de Valera's stress on the virtue of frugality. At the following year's conference, Lemass told delegates: 'We used to say that we would prefer freedom in the hair shirt to the fleshpots of serfdom but that is not a choice we have to make. We believe in the beneficial force of disciplined nationalism.'[15] It was Fianna Fáil's ability to replace the hairshirt with fleshpots that would give it a continuing influence on the workers' movement.

From the outset the omens were good for the party. Despite minor reservations the shift to free trade and an export-orientated development programme was accepted by the union leaders. Prominent ITGWU leaders praised the party for 'its imagination, initiative, enthusiasm and tendency to long-term planning which had attracted many new industries to the country', while the union's newspaper, *Liberty*, called for all possible assistance to be given to Irish industries which were geared to exports.[16] The newly formed Irish Congress of Trade Unions also accepted that 'further expansion will depend on our ability to develop our exports of manufactured goods'.[17] The union leaders had already begun to see themselves as team players who were entering a world league. This form of nationalism went beyond rhetoric. The ICTU became an enthusiastic supporter of the Irish National Productivity Council, which brought together union leaders and employers to find ways of raising productivity. The ITGWU president John Conroy claimed that when workers were being more productive they were showing a 'true and practical form of nationalism and patriotism'.[18]

The union leaders were only slightly more ambiguous about the influx of foreign capital. There remained lingering demands for more control but, rather ironically, these were directed more at foreign workers than foreign capital. The ICTU regularly called for restrictions on immigrants entering Ireland, claiming that they would cost Irish workers their jobs.[19] In general, the welcome for the multinationals was overwhelming and any action against them was viewed as akin to national sabotage. When electricians took strike action at the newly opened Whitegate Oil Refinery, their union leaders called on them not to be 'misled into action which is against their national interest'.[20] Typical of the new enthusiasm was a feature in *Liberty* about the Shannon Industrial Estate, which attracted many of the first multinational firms to arrive in Ireland. The paper was delighted that the new employers were 'very pleased with the adaptability of Irish labour' and, in particular, 'their keenness of eye and deftness of hand'. Its only regret was that they had taken on so many women, who made up 40 per cent of the workers in Shannon![21]

Fianna Fáil and the union leaders were more easily able to arrive at a shared perspective because the newly united Irish Congress of Trade Unions, which was formed in February 1959, refused to affiliate to the Labour Party. Before the split in 1944 every large union had a political link with the Labour Party, yet the only political reference in the founding statement of the ICTU was a pledge to uphold the democratic system of government. Moves by the Labour Party to offer the ICTU representative places on its leading bodies were rejected and when it requested an invitation to the ICTU conference in 1960, it was told that the 'time was not opportune for the exchange of fraternal delegates'.[22] Even if it had not been able to sustain its right-wing Catholic nationalist alliance with a section of labour, Fianna Fáil had at least achieved its ideal of a labour movement shorn of all political links.

The lack of formal political affiliation did not stop some union leaders having strong views that were almost identical to those of Fianna Fáil. This emerged clearly when Ireland applied to join the Common Market in July 1961. The older right-wing nationalist axis in the ITGWU saw it as an important step that was necessary for 'European civilisation to be saved',[23] and believed that it represented a bulwark against communism. There were some suggestions that entry to the Common Market might be tied to Ireland's willingness to join the North Atlantic Treaty Organisation. The Fianna Fáil attitude to Irish neutrality was like its policy on protectionism – highly pragmatic and ready for discarding when necessary. Lemass argued that the size of Ireland's army meant that it could make little contribution, but that 'if it was considered that by joining NATO we could make a contribution to Western defence – which is our defence also – then we might have to think again'.[24] One of his ministers, Michael Moran, claimed that neutrality was not a policy to which Ireland wished to remain committed, and, in an interview in the *New York Times*, Lemass also reiterated that Ireland had no qualms about taking on defence commitments.[25] These comments provoked some interesting responses from the ITGWU. Its newspaper, *Liberty*, defended Lemass wholeheartedly and even argued that joining the Common Market might mean 'building up a much larger armed force with a substantial increase in arms expenditure'. It also defended Moran by claiming that neutrality was useless in a period of atomic warfare.[26]

In general, then, the ideologies of the past were in transition. Fianna Fáil was shifting towards a new form of economic nationalism that promised real improvements for workers. They managed to retain the emphasis on 'developing Ireland' while still giving the multinationals a chief role in the process. The labour leaders, who had once dreamt of greater 'planning' in a protected Irish economy, also made the transition fairly easily. The change did little to shake Fianna Fáil's or the union leaders' faith in the battle against communism. Indeed, it added a more modernised appeal to an old message which was in keeping with developments in the United States itself where the more suave Cold Warmonger John F. Kennedy had taken the reins of power.

Rumblings

Between 1959 and 1963, the Whitaker revolution was implemented through the First Programme for Economic Recovery, and as the Irish economy opened up, impressive growth rates were recorded, with an annual average increase in GNP of 4.5 per cent. The signs of the new wealth were visible everywhere: a major building boom was underway in Dublin, for example, while in Shannon there was 'a stay at home in Ireland' campaign to assist in the building of a new town.[27] It seemed that the spectre of mass unemployment and emigration was lifting.

One of the side effects of the new boom was a growth in trade union militancy, as grievances that had been bottled up in the depressed years of the 1950s began to be unleashed. For many workers the boom was an opportunity to catch up with some of the gains their counterparts had made in Britain. An early sign of the shift was a resolution passed at the ICTU conference in 1959 seeking a 40-hour week throughout industry. A new term, 'leapfrogging', entered the vocabulary of industrial relations as workers began to press for higher increases than those negotiated in the wage rounds. The seventh wage round, for example, was agreed in 1959, but a year later various clerical grades pressed for and won higher increases than the going rate. The financial statements of the ITGWU (see Table 5.1) bear out the fact that the early 1960s saw a sharp rise in militancy.

Table 5.1 Strike pay as a percentage of ITGWU expenditure, 1958–64

Year	Percentage
1958	3.1
1959	3.2
1960	2.7
1961	24.8
1962	4.4
1963	26.1
1964	11.6
1965	26.2

Source: ITGWU, *Annual Reports*, relevant years.

The strikes introduced a new element which had rarely been seen before: they embodied a revolt not only against the employers, but also against the very union leaders who had so enthusiastically embraced Fianna Fáil's new turn. The first beginnings of rank-and-file organisation became evident as workers found a confidence to defy their own union leaders. For Fianna Fáil, however, these problems were summed up under the general rubric of 'union indiscipline'.

One of the first strikes to bring this new issue to the fore occurred in the ESB in August 1961. The strike began after electricians decided to reject a Labour Court recommendation on their claim for higher wages and reduced hours of work. The Irish Congress of Trade Unions totally opposed the action and called on workers who were not directly affected to pass the pickets. The directive was almost universally disregarded by manual grades in what the *Irish Press* described as a 'complete flouting of Congress authority'.[28] When a new offer was made which exceeded the Labour Court recommendation, pickets were lifted briefly, but the strike itself continued. One ITGWU official summed up the exasperation of the union bureaucracy: 'We advised everybody to return to work but ... they are just taking the law into their own hands.'[29] Manual workers who supported the electricians' pickets now set up their own committee that was independent of the official union structures. The statement of this rank-and-file organisation expressed a new mood which was to become very common in the 1960s:

> We are determined we will not pass any picket. We are determined to uphold the principles of trade unionism to the letter. We resent the pressure put on us by the unions through the medium of the press and radio to 'scab' and act as 'blacklegs' in this dispute.[30]

The tension between the rank and file and the officials was so high that the venue for negotiations between the official unions and the ESB had to be kept secret because they feared a demonstration from the unofficial strike committee. When these talks finally produced settlement terms the recommendation for acceptance was overturned by a strike committee composed of rank-and-file workers.

Fianna Fáil saw these events as a significant humiliation for the union leaders, and their first response was quite traditional – they reached for new legislation to control the militants. In September, Lemass recalled the Dáil to deal with the growing emergency and submitted an Electricity (Temporary Provisions) Bill. This proposed to establish a tribunal in the ESB that would set rates of pay which would be legally binding for six months. In effect, it made strike action in the ESB illegal for this period. Lemass justified the measure by arguing that they were 'facing a crisis for trade unionism as well as for the country'.[31] The Labour Party opposed the Bill, though on the most moderate of grounds, claiming that it 'invaded rights recognised by the Constitution and the Papal Encyclicals'.[32] Fianna Fáil saw the measure more as a threat and promised that it would not be used if the strike was settled by other means. In the end, this tactic worked, as agreement was soon reached between workers and the ESB.

The rank-and-file revolt, however, was by no means over. Shortly after the ESB strike ended, the ITGWU leaders found themselves in serious difficulties with bus workers in Dublin. A strike began after 1,500 workers met to protest at a proposal to introduce one-man-operated buses, and very quickly a big gap again opened up between officialdom and the rank and file. The union leaders pleaded for a deferment of the strike until seven days' notice was given and ordered their own members to 'resume work forthwith'.[33] When the strikers heard this they marched on Liberty Hall, the headquarters of the ITGWU, in protest. There they were told that the union leader, Fintan Kennedy, would not discuss the matter with them as he 'could not deal with a mob'.[34] This so incensed workers that ITGWU officials were shouted down, jeered and slow handclapped at a meeting of 3,000 bus workers the following day. Control of the strike was taken away from the officials and a rank-and-file committee began to direct activities. The matter was only resolved after mediation between the union leaders and the unofficial strike committee was organised by two Dublin priests.

These two strikes illustrate how the labour movement was being pulled in two contradictory directions by the industrialisation programme. The removal of the fear of unemployment led to a new confidence among rank-and-file trade unionists who were determined to push for higher wages and shorter hours. Paradoxically, the same process of industrialisation was also pulling their leaders into a closer relationship with Fianna Fáil to help win the battle for more exports. This contradiction played an important role in Fianna Fáil's strategy of developing a form of social partnership to cope with the revolt from below.

Social Partnership

Social partnership, or corporatism as it is referred to in academic circles, is a particular style of organising the relationship between organised labour, employers and the state that emerged in a number of countries in the 1960s. Panitch has provided a succinct definition of the concept when he claimed that it was

> a political structure within advanced capitalism which integrates organised socio-economic producer groups through a system of representation and co-operative mutual interaction at leadership level and mobilisation and social control at mass level.[35]

This definition is useful, provided we understand it in a number of quite specific ways. 'Mutual interaction', for example, should not be taken to imply any degree of equality between capital and labour. One can mutually interact and still be subject to the dominant power of the other party. Nor should it be taken to imply that the substance of decision making between the economic interests is anything but quite limited.

On the other hand, it is important to recognise that the unions do not become integrated into the state in the way in which some vocationalist organisations strove for in the 1930s. Integration simply means that they work closely with, and develop a deeper loyalty to, state institutions – often against the interests of their own members. None of this, however, stops the union leaders being subjected to extremely contradictory pressures. They may seek a closer relationship with the state, but the basis on which they are recognised stems from the claim that they represent their members. The contradictory pressures to which the union leaders are subject is often ignored by academic writers who believe that corporatism provides a structure which effectively replaces class conflict. As the term 'corporatism' has come to have this particular connotation, we normally use the more common phrase by which the process has become known in Ireland – social partnership.

Some writers, such as Joseph Lee, have argued that Fianna Fáil's strategy of social partnership was part of its dynamic drive to rid Ireland of traditional stagnation. In his highly eulogistic account of Lemass, Lee sees workers' organisations as 'conservative' and unable to realise 'the enormous long-term gains from a more dynamic society'.[36] According to this view, Lemass had to establish social partnership structures to drag the unions towards a more positive and modern attitude to the national economy. This is clearly an ideological account which operates from a shared perspective with Fianna Fáil, because it divorces the notion of a dynamic economy from any consideration of class relationships and assumes that there are equal benefits to be had by all.

Bew and Patterson were pioneers in challenging this approach and insisted that Lemass's new strategy had to be analysed in the context of 'the irrepressible reality of class conflict generated by the capitalist structure of the Irish economy'.[37] They argue that it arose as part of an attempt by Fianna Fáil to rebuild its hegemony over a relatively strong industrial labour movement. The precondition for social partnership was an expansionary state budget that promised increased gains for workers, and this was only achieved, according to Bew and Patterson, when Lemass fought a vital battle both within his own party and against the state bureaucracy to increase the public spending programme. His principal opponent was the architect of the 1958 turn, T.K. Whitaker who favoured large cutbacks in 'unproductive' spending during the First

Programme for Economic Expansion. The considerable overshoot on the figures for public spending first envisaged in 1958,

> represented the triumph of the Lemass line, concerned as it was with the reconstruction of Fianna Fáil's hegemony over the masses, as against the Whitaker line which reflected not expertise but the interests of particular sections of the dominant class.[38]

There are a number of problems with this account which tends to add credence to the image of Lemass as more favourable to the interests of workers than other Fianna Fáil leaders. For one thing, too much is made of the overshoot in spending targets in Whitaker's programme. Gareth Fitzgerald has pointed out that the methodology of the First Programme was particularly weak in formulating targets[39] and, therefore, to infer a major conflict between two factions of the political establishment from the overshoot may be a little grandiose. It is also one-sided, and indeed conspiratorial, to analyse the rise in public spending in Ireland solely in terms of an attempt to maintain hegemony over the working class. In the 1960s many of the advanced industrial economies experienced a dramatic rise in public spending as a proportion of GNP. As O'Connor has pointed out, the increased role of the state in providing 'social capital' – that is, expenditure that facilitated profitable private accumulation – stemmed for the need of business itself to have a more educated and better-cared-for workforce in a period of boom in capitalism.[40]

The social partnership structures that grew up in the 1960s arose from two main sources. First, there was the 'external threat' to the Irish economy when it began to integrate into the world system. Fianna Fáil was able to call on older forms of nationalism that had been built up since the 1930s to argue for cooperation to meet this challenge. The union leaders had to be closely involved in the detailed restructuring of older industries if workers were to support changes geared to raising productivity. Second, there was the 'internal threat' that grew with rank-and-file militancy. Fianna Fáil saw a formal structure of social partnership as a device for drawing the union leaders closer to the state, flattering them with notions that they were engaged in planning, and so pressurising them to discipline their own members. These structures offered a substitute for the decomposition of the older populist rhetoric which had come adrift in the 1950s.

The first formal institution which set the new trend was the Commission on Industrial Organisation (CIO), which arose directly out of Ireland's application to join the Common Market. Originally, this body grew out of a series of meetings between the Department of Industry and Commerce and the employers' organisation, the Federation of Irish Industry. The ICTU, however, made strenuous

efforts to be included and, according to one union leader, forced
its way on to the Commission, as they believed that it contained
the embryonic seeds of planning.[41] In fact, there was not much force
needed since Lemass quickly saw the opportunities presented by
the request of the union leaders. CIO survey teams were established
for each industry and Lemass suggested that they consult the
relevant unions about retraining and redeployment of workers. By
1962 an elaborate structure was established whereby employers in
particular industries met in Adaptation Councils to promote rationalisation of their firms, while workers were represented in parallel
Trade Union Advisory Boards which were supposed to be consulted
on the details of change. Government grants were made available
for the running costs of the Trade Union Advisory Boards. The
CIO carried a certain leverage because it could make recommendations on the payment of grants and it used this to press for
partnership arrangements at industry level.

For the labour leaders participation in the CIO was akin to
having a say in planning the economy and they were fulsome in
their praise for the new structures. Jim Larkin Jr, who had moved
steadily away from the left-wing views of his youth, even claimed
that the CIO was 'a tribute and, in a limited way, a culmination
of the policies pursued by the labour movement'.[42] In fact, even
within their own terms, they grossly exaggerated what was happening.
The Trade Union Advisory Boards and the Adaptation Councils
rarely met to discuss how industry was to be restructured, for there
was a distinct lack of enthusiasm among employers about this
degree of worker involvement.

The other important institution which was established at this time,
the Employer–Labour Conference, became a hallmark for future
developments. It was formed in November 1961 after the ESB strike
and its principle aim was to stop the practice of 'leapfrogging' in
wage rounds. Its exclusive focus on the pay levels of workers reveals
the real core of 'planning' in this period. The Employer–Labour
Conference was supposed to take expert advice on the movement
of pay and prices so that it could issue general guidelines for wage
negotiations. Yet the only element which could be controlled was
pay as no mechanism has been found in a capitalist economy to
regulate the pricing policy of individual firms. The unions insisted
that the whole process be subject to voluntary agreement, but they
accepted that there were certain objective pay norms which might
be good for the national economy. Ideologically, the
Employer–Labour Conference was an attempt to remove the issue
of pay bargaining from the realm of distribution of resources to one
which centred on 'the national interest'.

The End of the Class War?

The transition to the new arrangements was by no means smooth for Fianna Fáil and sometimes they made serious misjudgements about the degree to which the union leaders were willing to move in order to discipline their own members. One such occasion arose in 1963 when, in response to a slowdown in the economy, a government White Paper, 'Closing the Gap', called for a public sector pay freeze and low increases in the private sector. Lemass tried to push the Employer–Labour Conference to produce wage guidelines which would be binding on the unions, but he was trying to gain advantage from the new arrangements too quickly. The outrage of the union leaders was demonstrated when they withdrew from the Employer–Labour Conference and also threatened to resign from other institutions such as the CIO.

Lemass had to work hard to restore the new arrangements. He eventually conceded that wage increases could be negotiated voluntarily, but insisted that they be related to the growth in national production. He also made a major speech in the Dáil that became famous for the single ambiguous line which advocated that 'the time has come when national policy has to shift left'.[43] 'Shifting left', however, had little to do with a move towards socialism but rather implied a need for greater state intervention in the economy. Lemass argued that the possibilities offered by the growth in the world economy would only be seized provided the state played a more active role in guiding investment in the economy. Lemass was under no doubt that 'private enterprise would continue to be the main spring of our progress',[44] but he was also acutely aware that the degree of restructuring of the Irish economy was bound to require greater state management. In particular, the formal institution that linked the unions and the employers, and which had been established a few years previously, needed to be fully restored.

These overtures were enough to restore the confidence of the union leaders, and as a sign of their enthusiasm, Sean Lemass was invited to address the ITGWU conference for the first time in June 1963. In a rather presumptious fashion he claimed that James Connolly would have been a happy man if he had foreseen the day 'when the head of the Irish government would come to a conference like this to argue for a national plan'.[45] The plan included little more than the measures outlined in his 'shift left' speech, but crucially Lemass also argued for a reshaping of the trade union movement itself:

> In any free democratic society, a strong well organised and competently administered trade union movement is essential for economic and political progress. The more highly developed

a national economy, the more obvious does this become. All of us who are concerned with the preservation of our free democracy as well as our country's economic progress have therefore a vested interest in the development, the efficiency and the effectiveness of our trade union movement. It cannot be a concern of its members alone – it is far too important for that.[46]

Here then was the essence of Fianna Fáil's strategy. The trade unions were organisations that were too important to be left to their members alone. In other words, they could not simply be representative bodies, but had also to become vehicles for mobilising their members for the good of the 'economy's progress'. The assumption that 'progress' would benefit all equally did not have to be justified – the audience he was addressing had long been used to a rhetoric of pulling together to develop the nation.

After his historic address to the ITGWU conference, Lemass took another important step in developing the social partnership framework when he established the National Industrial and Economic Council. This was composed of ten representatives of the employers, ten union leaders, and nominees of the government. Under its first chairman, T.K. Whitaker, it was charged with drawing up periodic reports on the national economy that were to provide the background from which the Employer–Labour Conference would issue 'objective' advice on wages. It also played a pivotal role in formulating the Second Programme for Economic Expansion and so gave the union leaders the impression that they had achieved their historic goal of winning a say in 'planning'. What the plans were for or who they were designed to benefit had long taken second place to a veneration for the abstract concept of 'planning' itself.

In reality, the main success of the new institutions was to intensify the rhetoric about a team approach rather than a class-based approach to the economy, and here, one of the new leaders of the ITGWU, John Carroll, played a prominent part. Carroll did not belong to the old guard who had directly aligned themselves with Fianna Fáil in their advocacy of a Catholic nationalist Ireland, and he sought instead to present a more modernised version of the union. At one seminar for union officials, where he shared a platform with the employers' leader, Dan McAuley, Carroll reiterated the team message:

If we are steadfast in our demand for a greater share of the national income, then we must play our part to the full in making the national cake bigger. No excuses, no protests, no opposition can justify this holding back of our efficiency or our productivity.[47]

The idea that 'productivity' was simply a technical matter that would benefit everyone disguised the more concrete reality of redundancies, rationalisations and speed-ups. Even to put more detailed names on the process is to point to the divergent class interests. Yet the new institutions of social partnership had already strengthened the economic nationalist instinct of the union leaders, and soon, tangible benefits began to flow for the Fianna Fáil government. On New Year's Day 1964 a national pay deal was concluded between the unions and the employers whereby wage increases amounting to 12 per cent over two years were agreed under the prodding of Lemass. At the same time, discussions were underway with the Minister for Industry and Commerce, Jack Lynch, on changes in trade union law. Initially, these discussions began after a case involving the Educational Company of Ireland raised a question mark over the right of unions to place pickets on workplaces where they were seeking to form a closed shop. Lynch used the occasion, however, to press for far wider changes which involved the registration of unions. Although these discussions did not go as smoothly as Fianna Fáil expected, Lemass had every confidence in the effects of the new arrangements. In January 1964 he claimed that the new agreement on pay signalled the end of the old idea of class war.[48]

This claim was a little premature, however, to say the least. While the union leaders were fêting Lemass at the ITGWU conference, their own rank and file had become increasingly restive. In April 1963, bus workers once again came out on strike over the issue of one-man buses, and the industrial correspondent of the *Irish Times* wrote that he detected a 'bitterness abroad such as Dublin has not seen for fifty years'.[49] The leaders of the ITGWU were torn between a new generation of militants and a Fianna Fáil government that was offering them a new collaborative relationship. The language of national responsibility was now demonstrated more concretely by John Conroy, the main ITGWU official involved in the dispute. He said that 'no group of busworkers will be allowed to use the union for any wrongful or unjust purpose such as challenging a management decision in what is clearly a management function and responsibility'.[50]

The gap, which had already opened between the union leaders and the rank and file, had reached breaking point. Rather typically, the ITGWU tried to blame 'a small number of Reds among the busworkers' for fomenting the divisions.[51] This Red baiting did not stop the majority of its Dublin membership resigning to form a breakaway union, the National Busworkers Union. This set a pattern whereby 'breakaways' became an attractive, if flawed, route for rank-and-file revolts throughout the 1960s.

This revolt, however, did not deter the union leaders from trying to reshape their own movement. At the ICTU conference in 1964 the Executive tabled resolutions demanding that no strike should start until 28 days had elapsed after a Labour Court recommendation and that pickets should only be placed a week after strikes began. This latter bizarre proposition was designed to give workers the opportunity to 'assess intelligently and in a voluntary manner their attitude to the trade dispute'.[52] Their proposals were, however, denounced as a 'blacklegs' charter' by rank-and-file delegates at the conference and were decisively thrown out.

Then, in mid-August, one of the great landmark battles of the 1960s occurred when building workers struck to demand a reduction of their working week from $42\frac{1}{2}$ hours to 40 hours. Nearly 20,000 workers were involved in a strike which involved extensive use of mass pickets, with hundreds picketing at any one moment at the sites in Dublin. Lemass tried, at first, to stiffen the resolve of the employers, but when the strike dragged on to September, matters became very serious. A special conference of the ITGWU was called and it agreed to 'respond loyally and in strength to any call to action' which might be organised in support of the building workers.[53] Soon afterwards the building bosses began to crumble, and the Minister of Industry and Commerce intervened and allowed workers to secure the 40-hour week. It established the headline on the working week for decades to come.

The collapse of Lemass's prediction that the class war would end had dramatic consequences inside the Fianna Fáil cabinet when one of its key ministers, Paddy Smith, who sat on its economic committee, resigned his office. It was the first resignation that Fianna Fáil had suffered over an openly political division of opinion in its whole history and it reflected the strains within the party as it attempted to re-establish its hegemony over a more militant labour movement. Smith's resignation letter expressed an extraordinary bitterness about the very union leaders with whom Lemass was endeavouring to work closely. He wrote that the union leaders

> can be quite glib on the rising cost of living, profits and price control and at the same time, with their tongue in their cheek and being really led from the rear, make demands that they know, when conceded, can only have one result – rising costs and so on.[54]

Even if it was written from an anti-union stance, the letter certainly reflected the contradictory pressures the union leaders were under, as the reference to leadership from the rear indicates. Smith advocated a break from the strategy of collaborating with the union leaders and called for a fight against the 'plague' of militant trade unionism. Lemass's acceptance of his resignation implied that Fianna Fáil was afraid to take up this particular battle.

Conclusion

Fianna Fáil's switch from protectionism to an export-orientated programme after 1958 has sometimes been regarded as an abandonment of its traditional aims. This simply begs the question of what these aims were. Officially it sought to end partition and restore the Irish language, but these were always the ideological gloss for a more practical project: the expansion of native capitalism and the defence of the Southern state.

Far from abandoning these goals, Fianna Fáil found a different and more effective way of achieving them after 1958. The multinational firms which entered the Irish economy did not compete with native capitalism but rather created new opportunities for its expansion. In the longer term, they also helped to realign the Southern economy away from a dependence on Britain and towards a greater integration into the world economy. Far from Fianna Fáil promoting a new form of neocolonialism, it could reasonably argue that its primary motivation was always a form of economic nationalism. The notion, therefore, that the 1958 turn either represented a break with Fianna Fáil's tradition or indeed that it had to be forced on the party by a state bureaucracy is misplaced.

The post-1958 shift, however, had important consequences for the way the party related to the labour movement. Henceforth it could no longer rely solely on the close ideological affinity that arose from the shared perspective of Catholic nationalism. Ireland's re-entry into the world economy brought about a certain modernisation and rendered obsolete the previous discourse of standing up to the old enemy, Britain. Moreover, a variety of practical measures were also required both to raise productivity and to rationalise Irish industry if the Irish economy was to survive in free-trade conditions. In brief, Fianna Fáil established a number of institutions which sought to organise the unions, employers and the government around social partnership arrangements. This strategy aimed at further reform of the unions to ensure that they established discipline over their own members, and was part of a push towards greater productivity and flexibility.

The union leaders were not free agents, however, and were not always able to deliver on promises they made. Paddy Smith's resignation and his complaint about the 'glibness' of the union leaders pointed to a deeper problem. The condition for acceptance of the ICTU as having a voice in national decision making was that it claimed to represent the workers. By themselves, prominent ICTU officials such as Ruaidhri Roberts or Donal Nevin were simply talented individuals with whom the government had little incentive to engage. It was their representative capacity which counted, and this, in turn, meant that they were subject to pressures. They often swung between the demands made on them as social partners of the government and a desire to stay in touch with their own members. As the 1960s progressed, these conflicting pressures were stretched to breaking point.

CHAPTER 6

The Fire Last Time, 1965–1973

In the mid-1960s, as Fianna Fáil sought ways of bringing industrial peace, a wave of political radicalisation had begun to sweep the world. The war in Vietnam and the struggle for black civil rights in America itself led many to question the old ideas of the Cold War. Initially the centres for radical ideas were often the colleges, but soon many young workers were also attracted to a desire for fundamental political change.

Ireland was by no means immune to these developments. Just as workers set out to enjoy the first fruits of the economic boom, the general instability throughout the world system began to make itself felt. The black movement in America provided a direct inspiration for the nationalist minority in Northern Ireland and soon their grievances exploded into mass demonstrations on the streets. Simultaneously in the South, there was a mood of political restlessness as the labour movement pressed for new gains. The combination of worker militancy with a movement which questioned the very arrangements of partition brought Ireland closer to a destabilising social upheaval than at any time since the early 1920s.

Yet the potential threat that existed to capitalist rule has been ignored by many writers. Even those who express some sympathy with the left have tended to portray Irish workers as victims of history rather than as possible agents of their own liberation. Some have pointed to the degree of multinational involvement in the economy to claim that there was a form of economic dependence which militated against the full development of a labour movement. According to this view, foreign-led development produced a 'disorganised' working class which was incapable of political advance.[1] Others have argued that the industrialisation programme only increased the opportunities for clientelist practices which were supposed to atomise and divide workers, making it easier for right-wing parties to dominate.[2] What is missing from these accounts is any notion of the contradictory effect of the Irish industrialisation programme. It suggests that the Irish elite was in full control of the process, able to manipulate a passive working class, and in a position to suppress all the tensions that were thrown at it. This was patently not the case.

The Effects of Industrialisation

The industrial programme that began with the 1958 turn transformed the social structure of the Republic of Ireland. At the heart of the changes was a dynamic economy whose growth rate matched the rest of Europe for the first time. The boom, for example, accelerated the flight from the land, changing forever the image of Ireland as a rural society. In 1951, 40 per cent of those gainfully employed earned their income from agriculture, but 20 years later only a quarter did so. Similarly, the boom brought marked changes in the family and in the role of women in society. The new electronics factories, for example, concentrated on employing women on the assembly lines and this contributed to a major exodus from the home. In 1961, for example, only 5 per cent of married women were in paid employment, whereas 20 years later the figure had risen to one-fifth. It was still small by international standards, but the changes set in train tensions which eventually helped to undermine the dominance of the Catholic Church.

The multinationals came to Ireland for a variety of reasons. By moving across the Irish Sea, a company could enjoy the fact that 60 per cent of Irish industrial workers earned under £10 a week in 1960, whereas only 10 per cent earned a similar figure in Britain.[3] Another reason was the high level of state grants, which rose dramatically with the entry of foreign companies. In 1958, the Irish state paid out only £398,000 in capital grants to industry, but 15 years later this had risen to an astounding £20 million.[4] These new subsidies were not accompanied by any rise in taxes on capital as the increase in state revenue was born primarily from the expansion of the PAYE tax sector, which grew from 180,000 in 1960 to 605,000 a decade later.[5] Table 6.1 shows the divergent trends as regards tax on labour and capital.

Table 6.1 Percentage of tax receipts of central government derived from income and capital, 1958–73

Year	Tax on income (%)	Tax on capital (%)
1958	18.0	1.8
1962	18.3	1.5
1966	21.4	1.4
1970	21.6	1.0
1973	21.2	1.2

Source: Central Statistics Office, *National Income and Expenditure Report*, various years.

Although workers bore most of the costs of the industrialisation programme, they did not feel this so sharply as long as living standards seemed to be improving. Moreover, the growth in the economy was also accompanied by a big expansion in social spending. In 1967, Fianna Fáil introduced free secondary education and the following year instituted a limited programme of grants for third-level education. It also passed a series of laws that laid the basis for a rudimentary welfare state, and which included an occupational injuries scheme, provision for redundancy payments, a choice-of-doctor scheme, and pay-related benefit as a cushion against the immediate hardship of unemployment.

These measures certainly benefited workers, but they were not introduced for altruistic reasons. The dramatic expansion in the Irish economy meant that a more educated and secure workforce was required. Moreover, the degree of militancy that grew in the 1960s meant that it was in the employers' own interest to reduce pressure points in industrial relations. The introduction of redundancy payments and pay-related benefit, for example, lessened the danger of worker occupations of factories and helped to ease in rationalisation programmes. While there was a minor 'trickle down' effect from rising profit levels, the new measures were largely funded by increased state deductions from workers' incomes. Between 1953 and 1974, for example, social insurance contributions for workers grew by 376 per cent whereas benefits such as unemployment benefit for a single man only increased by 126 per cent.[6]

Nevertheless it would be wrong to see the industrialisation programme as simply another strategy to 'rip off' workers. It also brought a number of unintentional changes which led to a restructuring of Irish labour and so facilitated its growing militancy. For one thing, there was a major expansion of union membership as 90,000 new workers joined the unions between 1965 and 1973.[7] This overall growth in the unions was accompanied by changes in the relative weight of different types of union in the ICTU. Table 6.2 illustrates this.

Table 6.2 Percentage of members in different types of unions in the Republic of Ireland, 1965–75

Year	Type of union			
	General	White-collar	Craft	Other manual
1965	55.8	22.0	13.6	8.6
1970	52.9	24.9	13.7	8.5
1975	48.6	31.3	11.5	8.6

Source: W.K. Roche and J. Larragy, 'The trend of unionisation in the Republic of Ireland' in *Industrial Relations in Ireland*, Department of Industrial Relations, UCD (eds), (Dublin: UCD, 1987) p. 25.

The main growth was in white-collar unions which grew from one-fifth to nearly one-third of the ICTU membership in this period. While many white-collar workers may not have shared in the traditional ethos of manual working-class solidarity, neither did they share in the defeats of the 1950s. Their very isolation from the labour movement served as a form of insulation from the effects of demoralisation. As a result, groups like the ESB clerical workers, who were often concentrated in large offices, became key wage leaders who set targets for other workers to aim at. White-collar unions were often to the fore in raising claims for relativity increases, fringe benefits and service pay, and their demands were taken up in turn by other groups. A related factor which helped to strengthen militancy was the growth in public sector employment. Kelly and Brannick have claimed, after a detailed analysis of strike figures in this period, that public sector employees were much more prone to engage in strike activity than their private sector counterparts.[8] High rates of unionisation and a certain security in employment certainly added to union confidence. However, Kelly and Brannick tend to exaggerate the point, as there was also a growth in strike activity in the private sector when older industries based on clothing and textiles began to decline and were replaced by metals and engineering.

Fianna Fáil were mindful that the industrialisation programme brought with it the danger of a stronger working class and tried to disperse factories to rural areas. The industrial estates, for example, were pioneered in towns like Shannon, Galway and Waterford, and higher grants were offered to multinationals who located in less developed areas. However, all the factors I have mentioned above meant that Fianna Fáil could not control the very process it had helped to initiate. Wickham's argument that industrialisation weakened the working class because it took place outside areas where the unions were traditionally strong is misplaced. As Lindsey German points out, this type of claim rests on an assumption that there are set 'vanguard' groups within the working class who preserve and maintain patterns of labour militancy.[9] It fails to recognise that the working class undergoes a constant process of recomposition and that it is often the less experienced sections who play an important role in taking the movement as a whole foward. Ginsborg has demonstrated in the case of Italy that rural workers who have fewer union traditions, can also be less hidebound by some of the more conservative habits that grow up with more bureaucratised structures.[10] The Irish experience also confirms the fact that industrialisation opened a Pandora's box of militancy and political radicalisation beyond Fianna Fáil's worst fears.

The First Shots

At first, the growth in the Irish economy seemed to confirm Fianna Fáil's message that national development was in the best interest of workers. Lemass's phrase that 'a rising tide lifts all boats' became a familiar one in this era and he remained supremely confident that economic nationalism would continue to dominate the workers' movement. Describing this period later, he notes: 'The trade unions were completely on our side. I suppose this was true even in the political sense, apart from support for the policies we were pursuing.'[11] The modernisation of the country also allowed Fianna Fáil to argue that strikes and class conflict were outdated forms of behaviour which belonged to the anglicised culture of the Victorian period. In the new era, it was claimed that strikes were directed at 'the community' itself rather than at the individual capitalist, who had now receded into the background. Indeed, industrial conflict only occurred as a result of either misunderstandings or the activities of hotheads or agitators. It could be avoided if professional managers and professional union leaders understood the sophisticated practices of industrial relations. Here is how Lemass emphasised the new ethic:

> The professional trade union negotiator like the professional personnel manager of a well organised business concern understands what is practicable at any particular time and that, within the limits of practicality, his job is to negotiate and compromise, not the organisation of strife.[12]

However, this rather comforting ideology was abruptly punctured by a record-breaking strike wave in 1965 and 1966. The Labour Court noted that pay claims for the latter year were 'fought with a tenacity seldom previously experienced'.[13] As militancy escalated, Fianna Fáil was forced to look to more repressive measures for dealing with the unions.

The trouble began in October 1965, when the Irish Telephonists Association, a militant breakaway union, began picketing telephone exchanges to demand recognition. The Minister for Posts and Telegraphs responded by taking out a legal injunction against the pickets, and when this was breached, three strikers were jailed. If this was designed to intimidate the union activists it failed miserably. Within hours, ITA members began picketing the Dáil itself and this time Fianna Fáil responded by using the Offences against the State Act. This law was normally designed for use against the more 'subversive' tradition of republicanism, but Lemass saw no reason why it should not be extended to trade unionists because, as he put it, 'if they want to involve themselves in anti-state activities, they cannot expect to be treated differently to anyone else'.[14]

Support for the jailed telephonists began to grow, however, when the National Busworkers Union pledged its support. Dublin dockers and workers at Gouldings Fertilisers walked off their jobs and marched to the headquarters of the ITGWU where they shouted abuse at their leaders for not supporting the strikers. Meanwhile the jailed telephonists began a hunger strike in protest at Fianna Fáil's actions and 1,500 people marched through Dublin in a demonstration called by the National Council of Civil Liberties to demand their release. The Fianna Fáil minister Brian Lenehan was not impressed, though, and denounced the NCCL as a 'front for anti-state, communist and physical force elements'.[15] The situation was only defused when an agreement was reached between the Attorney General and the hunger strikers whereby they were released in return for a promise not to picket the Dáil.

Anger with Fianna Fáil in this instance was confined to a relatively small number of militants, but the escalating series of wage demands, coupled with a government demand for restraint, set the scene for wider confrontation. In January 1966, in an effort to moderate wage rises the ICTU advised its members to accept a £1 a week rise as the maximum target they could demand. In reality, it became the minimum that growing numbers would accept. Groups like the dockers, confectionery workers, and engineering craftsmen in CIE went on strike or threatened to do so. In the last-named case, the agitation was led by a rank-and-file group and their statement expressed both a self-confidence and a resentment with their official leaders which was typical of this period: 'We are not plebians and have no intention of being treated as such. Accordingly as people who are paying you and keeping you in office we demand that you arrange for the officialising [sic] of this stoppage.'[16]

These pressures considerably dented the 'professional' role which Fianna Fáil wished to assign to the union leaders, who were forced to adopt a more radical rhetoric and even to start attacking 'the establishment' in order to keep in touch with their membership. John Conroy of the ITGWU, for example, used the commemoration of the 1916 rising to argue that Connolly had died fighting 'the establishment and organised employers for political freedom and social justice'. He added that in 'this commemoration year the enemy is not foreign employers and not the agents of a foreign government. No, this time the employers and government agents are home based.'[17]

Conroy and the ITGWU leaders had little intention of acting according to this new class-based rhetoric, but they were no longer masters of events. When the Fianna Fáil government announced that it was unilaterally fixing a 3 per cent ceiling on wage increases, there was further outrage among the rank and file of the unions. From this point onwards, the number of strikes quite simply escalated, and within a short space of time Fianna Fáil were left reeling, looking for an escape from the very wage norm they had imposed weeks before. Eventually, the Labour Court was called in to find a way out and it was forced to recommend that the ICTU demand of a £1 increase be accepted throughout industry. At the time the advice was issued, 5,000 workers in the confectionery trade, 3,000 in the clothing industry, 3,500 in bacon curing and 1,700 in Dublin dairies were on strike for precisely this demand. The union victory was simply a taste of the militancy that was to come.

Unionising the Multinationals

Another issue which became a prominent source of confrontation was that of union rights within the multinational firms. Fianna Fáil was initially well disposed towards the unions recruiting in these plants, since it saw them as playing a positive role in encouraging greater productivity. In the Shannon Industrial Estate, for example, meetings were often arranged between foreign business interests and union leaders prior to the opening of a plant. The multinationals were given a package which included not only grants and tax breaks, but also a recognised union which was established even before the first worker was recruited. The ITGWU was more than willing to take part in these 'sweetheart' arrangements, claiming that it would behave in 'such a constructive and responsible way that employers would be as anxious to have their workforce unionised as the unions would be'.[18] Despite this studied moderation, however, there was no question of compelling foreign firms to recognise unions, as this would have militated against the vigorous free enterprise climate that Fianna Fáil espoused.

The issue of union rights at the multinationals came to a head in Shannon at EI, a subsidiary of the giant US firm General Electric, which had a long record of opposing unions. The ITGWU had begun organising at the plant in 1966 but management refused to negotiate with them, and in March 1968, 380 union members from the 600-strong workforce went on strike to win recognition. From the outset the strike was fought with an extraordinary intensity, with strong pickets from the mainly female workforce blockading entrances to the plant. The placards the strikers carried included slogans such as 'Yankee, Yankee, you can't dictate'.[19] Flying pickets were placed on the petrol stations that supplied the cars of the strikebreakers and the CIE bus which brought them to work was withdrawn after union pressure. Aer Lingus workers in the nearby airport also refused to move goods from the strike-bound premises. When the company won an injunction at the High Court to prevent picketing, workers simply defied the order until the Supreme Court reversed that decision.

The company fought back by trying to raise fears about the Irish programme of industrial development. They issued a statement claiming that 'they refused to believe that Ireland can become an industrial nation if industry must constantly pay the price of obtaining a union official's permission to remain in business'.[20] EI placed advertisements in the press for new employees and hired 150 applicants. As the strike dragged on, buses that took non-union employees to work were burnt by the IRA and death notices for these strikebreakers also appeared in the press. A very heavy police presence was established in the town, with union members complaining that they were billeted in houses of strikebreakers.

At the start of the strike, Fianna Fáil took a neutral stance, with Paddy Hillery condemning the 'rigid attitude of both sides'.[21] It soon became clear, however, that Fianna Fáil effectively supported the company's freedom of action because it refused to bring in any measures to compel EI to recognise the union. Sean McEntee even claimed that the real issue was one of workers being 'coerced into making union contributions'.[22] Another minister, George Colley, agreed with EI's position that the strike endangered the industrialisation programme. He argued that the Irish government could not tell 'foreign industrialists grudgingly that they may come in, but that we are going to ensure that they behave themselves'.[23]

The issue came to a head when the Executive of the ITGWU finally decided to call a national stoppage of its entire membership if the matter was not resolved. The threat was taken very seriously and the Department of Industry and Commerce called a hurried meeting between the EI management and the union. EI were eventually prevailed upon to take the strikers back and, although a closed shop was not established, the ITGWU won some degree of recognition from the company. The scale and militancy of the EI workers set a precedent which ensured that multinationals were more willing to recognise unions in future. Fianna Fáil had to reverse its policy of awarding grants to any multinational, regardless of whether it was willing to concede union recognition or not. In 1971, the then Minister for Labour, Joseph Brennan, confirmed this shift when he told the Dáil:

> The current policy of the Industrial Development Authority is to approve [grant] applications only where there is an understanding that management, if approached by trade union members employed in the factory, will negotiate with the union in relation to pay and working conditions of such members.[24]

The EI strike was fought by a new workforce who were not steeped in the older traditions of union solidarity. If Fianna Fáil's policy had been to relocate industry outside Dublin to ensure a less union-conscious workforce, then the EI dispute showed that it was a policy that was destined to fail.

Anti-union Laws

The strike wave of 1965–66 exposed the limits of institutionalised collaboration by showing that the union leaders were not entirely free agents. They had tried to keep up with their rank and file by attacking 'the establishment', but this in turn only stimulated further militancy. When it became clear that the union leaders were too weak to control their members, Fianna Fáil changed tack and looked to anti-union laws to curb the growing militancy. In the process, they exposed an authoritarian streak that was never far below the surface when it came to dealing with those who interfered with the drive for profit.

The first area where the unions came under legislative attack was in the ESB. After a brief strike by ESB fitters in June 1966, the Minister for Labour, Paddy Hillery, introduced the Electricity (Special Provisions) Bill which gave legal effect to the rates of pay and conditions and outlawed any strike against them. It imposed a fine of £5,000 on unions who supported strike action, with an additional £100 fine for every day the strike went on. Individual strikers were also subject to a fine of £25 a day – a measure that was an exact replica of Sean McEntee's proposals for dealing with ESB workers back in 1940. Fianna Fáil tried to justify the new measure with alarmist propaganda. Hillery argued that giving workers the right to strike in the ESB was like 'putting a nuclear warhead on a conventional weapon'.[25] One of his backbenchers, Martin Corry, claimed that the Bill was only opposed by 'an alliance made here in the Pale between the Freemason element and the Communist element'.[26]

Although the ICTU condemned the Act, they quickly took up Fianna Fáil's invitation to discuss a voluntary no-strike agreement in the ESB in return for repeal of the legislation. As the talks dragged on, another strike developed in March 1968, this time led by the Dayworkers Association – a rank-and-file group which had been formed amongst unskilled ESB staff to press for higher pay rises. Hillery immediately invoked the Electricity (Special Provisions) Act against them, and nine strikers were summoned to appear before the courts. The 40-strong National Committee of the Dayworkers Association assembled to pledge itself to all-out strike action across the country if any of its members were jailed. Jailing of the strikers started, in fact, at the end of March when over 50 workers were sent to prison. A mood of alarm seized the ICTU and one of their number later wrote that they feared 'there might be a general movement of workers springing from this, a general revolt, a contestation such as was experienced in France some months later'.[27] As nothing seemed to terrify them more than this degree of class solidarity, the ICTU promptly advised that no action be taken. The strikers, however, continued to escalate their strike, and the ESB was threatened with a complete close-down of the national grid as other workers respected the unofficial pickets of the Dayworkers Association. Faced with this degree of militancy, the Fianna Fáil government simply capitulated. It entered prolonged discussions with the union leaders to see how the release of the strikers 'could be done within the due process of the law'.[28]

The solution they eventually found was for the ESB management to pay the fines of the strikers. To add to their humiliating climb-down, managers had also to send a fleet of taxis to Mountjoy Jail to take the strikers directly home to their families. The Electricity (Special Provisions) Act had been defeated by the militancy of one of the unofficial rank-and-file groups which Fianna Fáil loathed. The Act was quietly repealed, but the defeat had far wider implications because it introduced a nervousness in government circles about other frontal assaults on union power. This became evident in the way in which plans for other legal changes were eventually jettisoned.

Before the defeat of the ESB (Special Provisions) Act, proposals had already been well advanced to curtail the right to strike. In April 1966, union leaders were presented with a memorandum of 49 points which was designed to lay the basis for two new bills, the Industrial Relations Bill and the Trade Union Bill.[29] The main provision of the former was to outlaw strikes for three months after the Labour Court issued a recommendation. This provision was deemed necessary because growing militancy had meant that Labour Court recommendations were increasingly discarded by workers, as Table 6.3 indicates.

Table 6.3 Percentage of Labour Court recommendations accepted by workers (various years)

Year	Percentage
1957	95
1958	98
1960	77
1961	80
1965	53
1966	49

Source: Labour Court, *Annual Reports* (various years).

The Trade Union Bill promised to be even more comprehensive in scope. It sought to define the concept of unofficial strikes and render them illegal. It proposed that only those strikes which won the support of 51 per cent of all those eligible to vote be permitted. Every abstention was to be counted as a vote against striking, thus raising the hurdle for a pro-strike ballot very high. The Minister for Labour was also to be given powers to revoke the licences of individual unions and to force them into group negotiating schemes whereby they would be bound by the decisions of other unions.

Hillery claimed that the purpose of both these measures was to help 'the top men [sic] of the union [to] ensure that necessary and unpalatable economic truths are communicated down the line as they should be'.[30] The ICTU raised some objections to the proposals, but not being totally averse to all the measures, they entered into a working party with the Fianna Fáil government to discuss them. They came to an agreement to ban unofficial picketing and to make secret ballots compulsory before strikes could take place. In return Fianna Fáil agreed, among other things, to make grants available for union amalgamations and to repeal those sections of the Offences Against the State Act which applied to strikes.[31]

However, once again the ICTU leaders discovered that they could not act like independent 'professionals' in imposing discipline on their members. In an atmosphere of increasing militancy, delegates to the ICTU annual conference ordered their leaders to leave the working party and to withdraw cooperation from Fianna Fáil scheme's for controlling strikes. This was a bitter blow to Fianna Fáil's strategy, and when Hillery decided to press ahead on his own he could only introduce an Industrial Relations and Trade Union Bill that was extremely bland . He claimed that he had to drop some of the stricter provisions because 'whatever about the merits of those particular proposals, it would have been futile to go ahead with them in the light of trade union reaction'.[32] By that time, he had learnt how devastating the power of groups like the ESB workers could be. It was an eloquent testimony to the strength of rank-and-file trade unionists in this period.

Politicisation

The process by which industrial militancy produces a wider politicisation in the working class has often been a source of controversy for Marxists. One writer, John Kelly, has used detailed empirical data to show that a political class consciousness can often develop in conjunction with major strike waves, such as those which occurred in Britain between 1915–22 and 1968–74. Building on earlier arguments of the German Marxist, Rosa

Luxemburg, he claims that when strikes face state intervention, they tend to produce a political radicalisation. The extent of the radicalisation is dependent on a variety of factors: the scale of strike action; the degree of participation by strikers in running the action; the context of economic and political crisis; the strategies of the employers; and the nature of the ideological leadership of the strikers.[33]

Kelly's framework helps to make sense of a considerable part of the Irish experience of the late 1960s. While the level of strikes was particularly high, the degree of resistance by the state and the employers was not particularly strong. Fianna Fáil's retreat on wage norms and its general tendency to resort to borrowing to overcome economic difficulties helped to lower the intensity of struggle. By the late 1960s the party had also become more aware of the dangerous politicising effects of government intervention in industrial disputes. Paddy Hillery noted in 1968 that

> official restraints on employee income were an important factor in recent disturbances in France. The British and French experiences illustrate the drawbacks of government intervention in pay matters and would not encourage a government to meddle without the strongest compulsion.[34]

The spectacular growth of the Irish economy gave Fianna Fáil room to manoeuvre and retreat in order to build bridges again with the union leadership. They were also helped by the fact that left-wing ideas were also extremely weak in a country that was just beginning to question the ideological dominance of the bishops and traditional nationalism.

Nevertheless, as we have repeatedly stressed, Fianna Fáil were not masters of events. Despite the fact that socialist ideas were in a minority, the fact remains that the degree of industrial struggle was exceptionally intense in the Republic. Moreover, it took place against a background of growing radicalisation throughout Europe and an uprising in Northern Ireland. All of this contributed to the creation of a link between industrial militancy and the growth of political ideas. The focus of this politicisation was not the revolutionary left, which was too tiny, but rather a Labour Party which was using a radical left-wing rhetoric that had not been heard since the 1920s. For workers who started to become politically aware through their own experience of struggle, Labour was the first port of call.

A number of indicators bear this out. First, there was a considerable growth in Labour Party membership, which expanded by 68 per cent in the space of three years, as illustrated in Table 6.4.

The late 1960s has been justifiably called the party's 'brief golden age' by one historian.[35] Until this point, the Labour Party was primarily a collection of rural personalities, but afterwards it came to resemble a political machine built around a more distinct ideology.

Table 6.4 Labour Party growth, 1966–69

Year	Members	Branches
1966	9,100	372
1967	11,200	440
1968	13,700	540
1969	15,300	606

Source: M.A. Busteed and H. Mason, 'Irish Labour in the 1969 election', *Political Studies*, Vol. 18 (1970).

Second, in urban areas the Labour Party made considerable electoral gains. In the 1965 general election, the Labour Party vote grew by 4 per cent, but in Dublin city its percentage vote doubled to 19.5 per cent, the highest level ever achieved. In the local elections of 1967, the Labour vote quadrupled in Dublin and it came within two seats of overtaking Fianna Fáil. In the 1969 general election, the Labour vote again increased and reached 24 per cent in Dublin. In effect, a contradictory pattern had emerged: in rural areas, the radical image of the Labour Party lost votes, but in the urban areas it brought gains.

Third, a series of unions affiliated to the party in this period, often after important debates at rank-and-file level. The WUI began the process in 1965 when they formally affiliated, but the crucial shift came with the opening of a debate inside the ITGWU. The issues had been discussed since the early 1960s but the leadership postponed making a decision on the matter. Then, in 1966, the Drogheda branch used the commemoration of Connolly's death to argue for a political link, and after a year-long discussion in the branches, the union voted overwhelmingly to affiliate. Other unions such as the ATGWU, the third largest union, and DATA, the draughtsmen's union, also affiliated. The one partial exception was the ICTU itself. It established a joint council with the parliamentary Labour Party but kept its distance by forbidding its officers to hold Labour Party office.

Fourth, within this growing Labour Party there was also a decisive shift to the left. After 1966, leading figures of the party began to call themselves socialist and its general secretary, Brendan Halligan, noted that 'it is almost respectable now to be a socialist'.[36] A consultative conference in 1968 committed the party to 'a radical socialist philosophy', and the following year its policy document proclaimed that 'Labour's objective is a fundamental change in society, not a mere reforming programme'. Items such as workers' participation in management that have become standard Labour policy in subsequent years were denounced as 'a device to ensure co-operation with management for the purpose ... of exploiting for private profit'.[37] If this was the language of the official documents, then at rank-and-file level the radicalisation was even more uncompromising. Delegates rejected the very possibility of coalition with right-wing parties, backed strikes and were more than willing to cooperate with left-moving republicans as well.

Thus the Republic of Ireland shared in the 1968 international experience but it did so under its own particular conditions. Unlike the more industrialised countries of Europe, it had never experienced a Labour government which had ruled on its own. Instead of a significant number of former social democratic supporters moving to the far left as was the case in France and Italy, the pattern in Ireland was for former Fianna Fáil supporters to move to a more radical-sounding Labour Party. There were also small signs of a more revolutionary left emerging, with groups like the Young Socialists numbering their membership in hundreds, but their links with labour politics were never fully broken. As a result, when a deep political crisis engulfed Ireland from 1969, social democracy was the main banner under which the left responded.

Fianna Fáil's Response

The growth in support for the Labour Party forced Fianna Fáil to adopt a mixed response. On the one hand, the old anti-communist rhetoric made a vigorous reappearance, reaching a crescendo during the 1969 general election when the party's new leader, Jack Lynch, did a tour of the convents to warn against Labour's Cuban-style socialism. Not to be outdone, Sean McEntee claimed that the Labour Party stood for Stalin and 'the red flames of burning homesteads in Meath'.[38] As usual, there was also an appeal to the great national tradition to ward off the foreign communist menace. Here, for example, is Lynch's warning about a Labour Party document on Workers Democracy:

> I ask Irish workers, the descendants of those who fifty years ago, so bravely and so unselfishly helped to free our country from one invader, to think hard and long about the kind of utopia which is now offered and I ask them not to make the mistake of facilitating or inviting, however unwittingly, an insidious tyranny, to conquer the same land whose freedom was so dearly bought.[39]

However, alongside the traditional response there was also an attempt to relate to the growth of left-wing ideas. The 1967 Ard Fheis of the party was organised under the theme of 'Cherish all the children of the nation equally', and afterwards, the *Irish Press* ran a banner headline proclaiming Fianna Fáil to be 'The Social Welfare Party' because of the number of welfare measures it had introduced.[40] The party also set up a Trade Union Affairs group which advised the unions to move beyond 'economistic' ideas to, for example, sending around trade union inspectors to visit the houses of sick members! It sought to draw a contrast between the harsh industrial militants and the caring policy of Fianna Fáil which looked after the poor and the 'social welfare classes'. The Fianna Fáil Trade Union Affairs Group opposed the Electricity (Special Provisions) Act but coyly pointed out that socialist ministers in England were also adopting measures to restrict the right to strike.[41]

Fianna Fáil's attempt to present itself as a caring social welfare party was weakened by some of its own policies and tactics. Despite the party's supposed concern for the low paid, it remained adamantly opposed to equal pay for women until entry to the European Economic Community demanded it as a requirement. In 1968, for example, Paddy Hillery told the Dáil that,

> I recently said at a meeting of women who are very interested in this [equal pay] that I did not think the community was yet ready for this equal pay for equal work. I got out of it alive but not much along with it.[42]

The caring image was also damaged by a growing advocacy within the party of repressive measures. In 1967, it introduced a Criminal Justice Bill which demanded that 24 hours' notice be given to the police for outdoor meetings and also prohibited meetings taking place within a half-mile of the Dáil. The Fianna Fáil TD Lionel Booth argued that the measure was necessary because student radicalism was spreading throughout Europe and that if the government did not act its successors would be forced to 'take the most brutal measures which will kill freedom for many years'.[43] The Bill was regarded as so draconian that it was condemned by the grass-roots of Fianna Fáil at their 1968 Ard Fheis.

In addition to these policies, Fianna Fáil's approach to fund-raising left a deeper question over its concern for the underprivileged. In February 1967 a secret meeting of wealthy backers of the party was held in Dublin to form TACA, a financial support group. The 200 prominent businessmen who enrolled in the organisation were given access to government ministers on numerous social occasions. The suspicion that membership of TACA brought special favours was by no means allayed when the Education Minister, Donagh O' Malley, in answering the charge of patronage, simply replied that 'of course, we look after our own'.[44] The Minister for Local Government, Kevin Boland, who was responsible for Fianna Fáil's house-building programme, later explained how a TACA function worked:

> We [the cabinet] were all organised by Haughey and sent to different tables around the room. The extraordinary thing about my table was that everybody at it was in some way or other connected with the construction industry.[45]

As the 1960s grew to a close, Fianna Fáil's image as a 'workers' party' was fading fast. The new confidence of its business backers meant that they no longer tried to hide their wealth or access to power. The wider unease in Irish society pushed the party towards a more authoritarian outlook where it sought to restrict or even crush street demonstrations against its policies. On the other hand, a layer of union activists were becoming more politicised as a result of their experience of widespread struggle. The Labour Party was presented with a notable opportunity to make a quantum leap, but it had to do so under conditions of even deeper industrial and political crisis. Its failure to develop an adequate response, however, dramatically exposed its own weakness.

Labour and the Crisis of 1969–72

Between 1969 and 1972 when the Stormont parliament was abolished, the previously stable foundations of Irish society were rocked to their very foundations. The most visible signs of turmoil were evident on the streets of Northern Ireland, but these events had a more profound influence on the South than at any other time in its history. Many began to question the failure of the Southern state to match its anti-partition rhetoric with any concrete actions. Some wondered if the Southern establishment had developed a vested interest in perpetuating a border that seemed a guarantee of the dominance of right-wing policies throughout the island. This questioning coincided with the re-emergence of strike action in the South among groups like the maintenance workers and cement workers which once again demonstrated the power of the picket line. If Labour had been able to build on this new tide of political and industrial militancy, it might have severely weakened Fianna Fáil's influence. Yet the whole tradition of social democracy, with its respect for the rule of law and its focus on parliamentary elections, placed such a shift in role well beyond the realms of possibility.

The Northern Crisis

Catholic grievances against discrimination led to the formation of the Northern Ireland Civil Rights Association (NICRA) in February

1967. NICRA demanded a number of measures: the abolition of multiple voting for rate payers and the establishment of the principle of one person, one vote; an end to the gerrymandering of constituency boundaries to ensure Unionist majorities; and a points system in the allocation of housing to remove discrimination. These very moderate demands were to provoke both a huge revolt and a fierce reaction in Northern Ireland. Starting with a civil rights march in Derry in October 1968, the movement escalated to a point where the very existence of the state came under question. The background and development of these politically charged events is told elsewhere, and the primary concern here is with the manner in which the Southern labour movement responded.[46]

At first, the Irish Labour Party was most sympathetic to the demands of the civil rights movement. In 1969, it sent a high-profile delegation consisting of leading figures such as Frank Cluskey, Michael O'Leary, Noel Browne and Conor Cruise O'Brien to Derry and Armagh to investigate the events for themselves. They gave their full support to civil rights groups which were confronting the RUC and the notorious B Specials, and considered the representatives of the Derry Citizen's Defence Committee whom they met as the 'de facto government of the Bogside'. They praised the 'courage, determination and tactical skill of the Bogsiders [who] without outside aid, had undermined Stormont's constitutional position in its entirety'.[47]

This type of response began to change after the Labour government in Britain sent in the army. Initially, the troops were seen as coming to the relief of Catholic areas who were under attack from loyalist mobs and elements of the RUC. Very quickly, however, they found themselves in conflict with those same Catholics when they attempted to shore up the institutions of the Northern state. The British strategy was to first establish stability and afterwards to pressurise the Unionist government in Stormont to introduce some measure of reform. In practice, this often meant harsh repression of Catholic rioters and the imposition of a curfew in the Falls Road in July 1970 which resulted in the death of five people.

As these events unfolded, the Labour Party adopted a new rhetoric about the need to 'normalise' the situation and warned against the arousal of republican passions in the South. It went out on a limb to support the role of the British army in Northern Ireland. When Fianna Fáil called for a United Nations peacekeeping force to be sent in, the Labour leader Brendan Corish insisted that the British army 'instead of being an occupation force, could be turned into a peacekeeping force'.[48] He pressed for the 'normalisation of politics in the six counties' by implementing a reform package and allowing it to 'operate for a few years'.[49] Party spokespersons argued firmly against raising the question of partition in the short term, and Barry Desmond claimed that 'one must be content to see the unity question evolve over a number of decades'.[50]

The main danger in the North was no longer sectarian structures of the state, but the 'extremism' that might emerge on the Catholic side. Desmond opposed any tendency for the South to become involved in destabilising partition, arguing that 'under no circumstances should state aid – to use a polite term – be subvented from the Republic into Civil Rights organisations in Northern Ireland lest we provide succour to any Unionist reaction on this basis'.[51]

As the IRA emerged to challenge the very basis of partition, the Labour Party became even more adamant that gradual reform of the Northern state was the only feasible option. In practice this meant looking to the British army as the vehicle by which the IRA could be suppressed and law and order restored. This view was enunciated most dramatically by the party's Northern Ireland spokesperson, Conor Cruise O'Brien, when he outlined the three main principles of the party's philosophy in 1970. These were, first, 'to leave law and order to the British and admit that is what we are doing'; second, to 'remain in touch openly and not clandestinely' with the British; and third, to support 'working with the British, really working with them in conditions of trust, not at the same time going around blackguarding them or nagging at them'.[52] In line with these principles, the party opposed calls to abolish Stormont and called instead for new structures whereby the opposition could play a constructive role in the government of Northern Ireland. It not only envisaged that the Northern state could be reformed, but indeed also claimed that socialism itself could be established within the framework of partition. The party's policy statement in 1971 stated:

> The attainment of socialism in the 26 counties would be a step of vast importance towards the goal of an all Ireland socialist republic. Similarly, the attainment of socialism in the Six Counties would be a long step towards a socialist united Ireland.[53]

The position of the trade union leaders was virtually identical with that of the Labour Party, and, if anything, was even more concerned with 'normalising' the situation. When internment was introduced in 1971, for example, the Northern Ireland Committee of the ICTU issued a most ambiguous statement claiming that 'a democratic state requires such powers as are necessary to protect it'. There was no condemnation of internment and no support for the civil disobedience campaign that grew in its wake.[54]

These political positions of both the political and industrial leaders of the labour movement became a particular source of disillusion for their supporters on both sides of the border. As the situation in the North escalated up to the abolition of Stormont in March 1972, many moved from a demand for reform to outright opposition to partition. It was noticeable that the very people who supported the Labour Party in the South because of its new-found radicalism were precisely those who wanted stronger action to end the border. An Irish Marketing Survey of 1971, for example, found that Labour Party supporters were the most militant on the national question, with 30 per cent demanding an immediate British withdrawal and 16 per cent even supporting the supply of arms to the North.[55] At the ITGWU conference that year, the rank and file rejected their leaders' advice and called for the immediate release of prisoners held in England and Northern Ireland. This resentment found expression among Labour TDs when a more republican wing began to crystallise around Sean Tracey, David Thornley and Stephen Coughlan. Tracey, for example, claimed that while he did not advocate force, he did 'advocate defence, united defence against the designs of Stormont and Westminister'.[56] This group, however, were more closely aligned to the more traditional nationalism of Fianna Fáil than to any coherent socialist response to imperialism.

Whereas Labour up to 1969 was able to project a distinct class identity against Fianna Fáil on a range of questions, it failed to do just that when it came to the Northern crisis. After initially supporting the demands of civil rights, the party shifted to backing the status quo, claiming that extremism was the main problem. In practice, it positioned itself as a supporter of the British army, albeit claiming that the troops had to stabilise the situation in order to bring reform. The Labour Party's concentration on the problem of 'extremism' also led it increasingly to believe that the Southern state itself was under threat from republican supporters. This view was to play a predominant role in its decision to quench the radical rhetoric of the 1960s. It also left the door open to others, often on the right, to give expression to the frustration felt against the Northern state.

Coalition

In 1967, the Labour Party voted with only 20 dissenters to oppose entry into a coalition government. Two years later, the party leader Brendan Corish reaffirmed this strategy by stating that if the party ever changed its mind, 'my continued fight for socialism will be from the backbenches'.[57] The electoral results in 1969 began to shake this position as the rural branches suffered from Fianna Fáil's Red Scare and the loss of transfer votes from Fine Gael. In general, however, the rhetoric about 'the 1970s will be socialist' continued.

What changed all this was the social explosion in Northern Ireland. The party's desire to normalise the Northern situation undermined its own left-wing rhetoric. The immediate catalyst for the about-turn came in May 1970 when two ministers of the Fianna Fáil government, Charles Haughey and Niall Blaney, were sacked and later tried for importing arms to the North, although they were later found innocent. Haughey had shown little sympathy with militant republicanism and as Minister for Justice in 1961 had reactivated the Special Criminal Courts to crush the IRA. Nevertheless the scale of the crisis in Northern Ireland led both Haughey and Blaney to press for a more interventionist line. They believed that it was necessary for Fianna Fáil to seize the leadership of a powerful movement which was directed at partition – lest that movement took a direction which opposed the Southern state as well. They were particularly concerned by the left-wing rhetoric of sections of the IRA and wanted to encourage more right-wing elements to come to the fore.

The Labour Party saw the whole arms trial as confirmation of its worst fear that instability was spreading to the South. It claimed that these events were the beginning of a 'hot emergency' where the institutions of the Southern state were threatened by an element in Fianna Fáil intent on using force to end partition.[58] In the aftermath of these events, Conor Cruise O'Brien signalled a new closeness with Fine Gael when he praised the role of its leader, Liam Cosgrave, during the arms crisis. Increasingly, the Labour leadership argued that it was necessary to abandon the anti-coalition stance in order to protect democracy from the wilder fringes of Fianna Fáil. A special conference was called on December 1970 where it was argued that only the Labour Party could supply to a government the 'policies necessary in certain circumstances for the defence of democracy', and in this atmosphere of panic the leadership were given a free hand to make arrangements for coalition.[59]

From this point on, the Labour leaders placed even more stress on the dangers to state institutions and the need for cross-party support for these institutions. In doing so, they revealed that a core value of social democracy was defence of their own state. After Bloody Sunday in 1972, when the British army shot dead 13 civilians in Derry, Michael O'Leary claimed that

> one consequence of this continual confrontation between the streets and the British army must be a growing movement away from Parliament and free institutions in this part of the country. In such a situation we will have to consider something like a national government.[60]

The call for a national government, however, was short-lived as Fianna Fáil continued to be seen as the chief cause of instability.

At one point in its history, Labour had toyed with the idea that Fianna Fáil was more 'progressive' than Fine Gael because of its role in promoting industrial development. Now it came to the conclusion that the party which had forged the identity of the Southern state was flirting with its very destruction and so was worse – far, far worse – than Fine Gael.

The Maintenance Dispute

If the political arm of social democracy was thrown into crisis by the events in Northern Ireland, then the industrial wing experienced a similar crisis with the maintenance strike of 1969. During this strike, the power of the picket line was demonstrated as never before and, in the process, the issue of who controlled its use came to the fore. Was it to be the ICTU leaders, or the strike committees thrown up by the rank and file?

The maintenance strike began on 24 January 1969 in pursuit of a claim for higher wages. The ICTU Executive had pleaded for it to be deferred but this was ignored by the craft workers. After the strike began, negotiations between the unions and employers started immediately and pickets were lifted for a time to allow them to progress. However, a settlement that was reached between the union leaders and the employers was eventually turned down by the rank and file of two small craft unions. Pickets were placed again on 5 February, and, from then onwards, control of the strike fell into the hands of a committee thrown up by rank-and-file strikers. An ICTU report later claimed that 'its authority was unique' as every recommendation from the official leaders was rejected simply on the word of this committee.[61] Extensive picketing took place which involved tens of thousands in the dispute. In desperation, right-wing union leaders from the Marine Port and General Workers Union placed curious 'retaliatory pickets' to protest at the effectiveness of the maintenance workers' strike. By March, the employers were in headlong retreat and eventually voted to concede the full claim – a 20 per cent pay rise, and one of the biggest increases granted throughout Irish industry.

Fianna Fáil reacted to the strike with intense anger. Hillery denounced the strike as a threat to democracy and called for a fostering of 'pride in race, pride of kinsfolk, pride of family' to resist the 'rotten strikes' that were spreading like a 'killer disease'.[62] He also pointed to the role of union leaders as a factor that could be positive or negative for stability. He argued that their attacks on the establishment had caused serious damage to the government and, ironically, to their own institutional structures. For their part, the union leaders were equally shocked by the effects of the strike. Almost echoing Hillery's argument, the ICTU president Jimmy

Dunne denounced the 'do-it-yourself brand of trade unionism which treats with contempt all the institutions, practices and procedures that our trade union movement has created in this country over the last sixty years'.[63]

Stability and Renewed Social Partnership

If the Northern crisis led the Labour Party to drop its radical rhetoric in favour of coalition with Fine Gael, the maintenance strike led the union leaders to seek a new accommodation with the Fianna Fáil government. Social democracy abhors a crisis almost as much as nature does a vacuum. The condition for its very existence is the resolution of grievances within the structure of capitalism. Once that structure comes under strain the reflex of both union and political leaders is to restabilise it before pressing further with any demands for reform. Instead of building on the new expression of radicalisation, labour leaders far preferred to accept, if needs be, a relatively minor role within Irish politics, rather than to risk upsetting the very system that caused the turbulence.

Soon after the maintenance strike, the ICTU moved quickly to impose discipline in its own ranks. Playing on certain divisions between craft and general workers, it pushed through a new concept of picketing at its conference in 1970. Henceforth, decisions on the use of the picket were deemed to be too important to be left to those at workplace level. Instead a new 'all-out strike' placard was invented which had to be introduced in strikes involving more than one union. These pickets could only be sanctioned by the ICTU after some weeks of deliberation. In the meantime, those not directly involved were encouraged, even instructed, to pass the pickets. Despite being labelled a 'scabs' charter' by Jim Kemmy, a future Labour Party chairperson, these proposals were passed by a conference largely dominated by full-time officials.[64]

The next move towards a restabilisation came from the Fianna Fáil government. At the end of 1970 they introduced a Prices and Incomes Bill to limit wage increases to 6 per cent at a time when inflation was running far higher than this. The ICTU went through the motions of protest, establishing a political action committee to rescind this decision. It refused, however, to call any stoppages against the measure, and it quickly became clear that the ICTU was looking for an accommodation with Fianna Fáil. The Prices and Incomes Bill was mainly a device by the Fianna Fáil government to pressurise the union leaders into standing up against their own militants. Under the threat of a legal wage freeze, the ICTU leaders entered negotiations with the government and the employers on a new structure for handling wage claims. When a National Wage

Agreement finally emerged from these discussions, Fianna Fáil duly withdrew their Bill to freeze wages and prices.

Despite its title, the National Wage Agreement was not simply about pay increases, but rather involved a fundamental restructuring of industrial relations. Alongside the dropping of Labour's radical rhetoric, the agreement became an important factor in the resta-bilisation of the South. In effect, it restored the social partnership model that Fianna Fáil had championed in the early 1960s, though at a much stronger and deeper level. It established the Employer–Labour Conference once again, which met monthly to monitor and control wage demands. It set up subcommittees to enforce a new respect for procedure in the conduct of grievances. Alongside the changes in picketing policy, these moves all served to confer a new authority on the ICTU. Fianna Fáil also followed up by introducing another Trade Union Bill in 1971, the aim of which was to help shore up the authority of the ICTU leaders by making it more difficult to establish 'breakaway unions'.

The ICTU faced some opposition over the re-emergence of centralised bargaining, and had to expel one union and suspend another over their failure to comply with the National Wage Agreement. For a brief period a Dublin Shop Stewards Committee, which linked together hundreds of rank-and-file representatives, managed to slow down the drift to social partnership. Yet in the main, the ICTU was successful in curbing militancy. By 1972, for example, it was able officially to call on ESB workers not only to pass the pickets of the ESB Shiftworkers Association, but even to take over their jobs in order to break the strike.

The militancy of the late 1960s was predominantly sectional, and where political generalisation occurred, it was mainly around the ambit of social democratic politics. For a period, the limits of this tradition were stretched to allow for a radical rhetoric that seemed to challenge the structures of capitalism. But as the crisis in Irish society deepened, the inherent conservatism of social democracy was exposed. In many instances, social democracy placed itself to the right of Fianna Fáil, particularly in its support for the British army in Northern Ireland. Labour's traditional separation of industrial and political activity meant that it often saw strikes as a form of disruption, rather than as a training ground through which workers come to see their strength and begin to question received ideas. For a generation of new militants who had become radicalised by the 1960s, it provided no basis on which they might respond from a class point of view to the crisis. Some drifted into an apolitical form of syndicalism, others looked briefly to republican politics, many simply became disillusioned. Orderly industrial relations were re-established mainly because there was no political alternative available to bring together the experience of workers' self-activity and the resistance of an oppressed group in Northern Ireland.

By the early 1970s, the elements of political stability were already in place. The Labour Party was once again on the path to a coalition that would further disillusion its own supporters, and the union leaders were renewing their corporatist arrangements with Fianna Fáil. That party had also begun to overcome its splits over the arms trial by subordinating its concern about the Northern situation to an internal anti-subversive campaign. The party introduced the Prohibition on Forcible Entry Act in 1971 to deal with factory occupations and squatting, or what one TD called 'organised mob law or organised hi-jacking'.[65] Fianna Fáil followed it in quick succession with measures which allowed for military detention of republican prisoners in the Curragh, censorship of television through the infamous Section 31 of the Broadcasting Act, and the establishment of non-jury Special Courts. None of these measures saved the party from electoral defeat in 1973, but it did succeed in reuniting the party around its primary objective: the defence of the Southern state.

As social democracy proved unable to make political gains from the crisis of Irish society, some of the older and more ambiguous traditions of the labour movement also began to reappear. This was best expressed by a small incident in October 1970. Almost immediately after he was acquitted of charges of conspiring to import arms, Charles J. Haughey was invited to the ITGWU headquarters in Liberty Hall as a special guest of the National Executive Committee. In reply to a welcoming address, Haughey remarked: 'For my part, I shall always be proud to be associated in every way possible with the ITGWU in helping to make Ireland a better place to work in, and above all, live in.'[66] A new leader and a new alliance were waiting in the wings.

Conclusion

According to Hazelhorn, 'nationalism combined with traditional clientelism over decades' to become the most effective way in which Fianna Fáil maintained the status quo in Ireland.[67] Nationalism helped to transcend class conflict, while clientelism encouraged workers to think of themselves as individuals rather than as part of a collectivity. An alternative analysis of the late 1960s however, seriously questions this approach.

As argued above, Fianna Fáil's nationalism was never entirely an ephemeral ideology but tended to be linked to the promise of material gains. In the 1960s, this promise seemed to be more credible as rising living standards became the norm and a limited welfare state came into existence. The majority of workers did not experience these gains through an extensive patronage system, but rather as the fruits of an expanding economy. Sometimes workers fought hard through their unions to make gains. On other occasions, there was enough fat on the bone for improvements to be ceded more voluntarily. The 1958 economic turn therefore laid the material base for continued Fianna Fáil dominance by allowing it to claim the mantle of an 'expansionist' party that could promise gains for all classes in Irish society.

However, by the late 1960s, substantial contradictions emerged within Irish society which created other openings. Writers who have adopted the model of dependent development from Latin American sociologists have often overlooked these contradictions. They have exaggerated the practice of clientelism and have seen it as the principal device through which Fianna Fáil hegemony was established. Implicitly, they assumed that foreign-led development was unnatural and tended to produce distortions in society which would not exist if a healthy form of indigenous capitalism was dominant. The result has been to view the Irish working class as a victim of neocolonial development – a disorganised, cap-in-hand, immature class that could never reach the level of political consciousness until there was a fully independent economy and a genuine national development.

The arrival of the multinationals in Ireland, however, produced far more complex consequences. The economic boom which followed certainly brought a new confidence to the 'mohair suited' brash businessmen who began to occupy cadre positions in Fianna Fáil. Yet it also had the effect of helping to recompose the labour movement so that the memories and experience of defeats were overcome. Indeed, the bitterness that often lay below the surface in Irish society was given new forms of expression when workers felt themselves needed by the thriving industries. The result was an explosion of industrial militancy that laid the basis for rank-and-file forms of organisation ranging from 'breakaway unions' to unofficial shop stewards' committees.

This degree of industrial militancy and ensuing confidence had a politicising effect, at least on a minority of workers. Even though Fianna Fáil often sought to retreat from outright confrontation and even though left-wing ideas were relatively weak, the fact remains that the scale of the struggles which took place against a background of an uprising in Northern Ireland meant that a radicalisation was bound to happen. The real question, therefore, is not why Irish workers were 'disorganised', but rather how the strong desire for fundamental political change was quenched.

Here it is necessary to move beyond the determinism of the dependency school, which reads off political developments from

the supposed neocolonial structure, and to look at particular
ideologies. The boom uprooted thousands of former supporters of
Fianna Fáil from the countryside and brought them to the cities,
where they experienced class conflict as workers. Having never
previously encountered a Labour government, many looked to the
radical rhetoric of that party as the focus for their hopes of change.
The political response of social democracy to the crisis which
engulfed Ireland after 1968 is therefore an important key to
understanding the situation.

In reality, the Irish Labour Party and the union leaders could
only react to the uprising in Northern Ireland and the growth of
militancy in the South with an increasingly shrill plea for
'normalisation'. This is no surprise as the core value of social
democracy lies in protecting the supposedly democratic institutions
of the state. In practice, this resulted in the Labour Party leaders
giving implicit support to the British army as a stabilising force. It
also took them on the road to coalition with Fine Gael when the
Southern state seemed to be threatened after the arms trial of
1970. And while this process was unfolding at a political level, a
similar and related process was occurring at an industrial level. The
union leaders saw the rising tide of industrial militancy as a threat
to their relatively privileged social position, and this time, the
desire for normalisation led to a renewed search for an agreement
with the Fianna Fáil government.

All of this created considerable disillusionment and eventual
cynicism amongst labour supporters. As always, the Labour Party
proved that its own conservatism was the best ally Fianna Fáil had.

CHAPTER 7

The Rise and Fall of Charles J. Haughey, 1973–1990

In 1979, two unique events occurred in the Republic of Ireland within months of each other. One was the first big tax march of PAYE workers, and the other was a papal mass in Phoenix Park. Both events could number their participants at over 100,000, but they represented two very different faces of Ireland. The former suggested that the modernisation of Ireland might be linked to a new set of politics based on class division, while the latter indicated the continuing strength of traditional Catholicism.[1] For many left-wing writers of the time, there was little doubt that the conservative reaction would win out. According to Bew and Patterson, for example: 'A traditionalism which presents itself as based on deep communal values and concerns as opposed to an unrepresentative and liberal "cosmopolitan elite" can hope to mobilise working class support.'[2] It was an unduly pessimistic assessment which failed to capture the growing contradictions under the surface of Irish society. Despite temporary victories in the 1980s, the hold of Fianna Fáil and the bishops was being weakened in a way that would allow no return again to the values of the 1950s.

Recovering from Coalition

At first, the period seemed to augur well for Fianna Fáil. The 1973–77 Labour–Fine Gael coalition once again severely disillusioned labour supporters. An affinity of political interest became apparent between key union leaders and Fianna Fáil in two broad areas. The first concerned the repercussions of events in Northern Ireland. From 1975 onwards, Fianna Fáil took a more nationalist view, calling, for example, for 'an ordered withdrawal' by Britain. The coalition by contrast, embarked on a vigorous anti-republican campaign which ranged from championing revisionist interpretations of Irish history to the direct accumulation of repressive laws. In response to a supposed subversive threat to the South, seven-day detention orders were introduced, a state of emergency was declared and a strict regime of censorship was enforced on RTE. These repressive measures provoked considerable unease among workers, with the ICTU condemning the state of emergency. Other unions such as the ITGWU went further and adopted a more traditional nationalist position that was close to Fianna Fáil's. It argued that the Labour Party was trying to develop in people a 'sense of guilt about their nationality' and claimed that the 'ideas which held the state and nation together were being chopped or removed'.[3]

The second area of growing common concern was the economy. Unemployment had risen dramatically under the coalition government and demands for wage restraint remained the order of the day. In opposition, Fianna Fáil concentrated on presenting itself as the party of 'expansion'. It produced a manifesto on the first day of the 1977 general election campaign, disclaiming Charles Haughey's previous charges that manifestos 'had a Marxian ring about them'.[4] The manifesto promised to create 25,000 jobs a year, when the previous average had been around 4,000, as well as to introduce significant tax cuts. As if this was not enough, the party also promised to abolish rates and road tax, and to provide £1,000 grants for new home owners.

In one sense, Fianna Fáil was continuing an older tradition of national development, but it was doing so under very different conditions to the past. The coalition had been shaken by the first serious postwar recession which seemed to announce a new period of instability for world capitalism. Ireland's misfortune was to have integrated itself into the world economy just when the postwar boom was coming to a close. What Fianna Fáil's manifesto offered, therefore, was a much more 'consumer orientated' programme – one that was more opportunistically geared to the voter and less in tune with the realities of economic stagnation, which had returned to haunt the large economies of the world. However, it certainly worked. The voting figures for skilled workers show the degree of shift to Fianna Fáil. In 1969, 40 per cent of skilled workers voted Fianna Fáil and 26 per cent voted Labour. By 1977, the gap widened to 54 per cent voting Fianna Fáil while Labour's vote slumped to only 11 per cent.[5] It helped the party to win a landslide victory.

When it returned to office, Fianna Fáil resorted to classic Keynesian methods in the hope of fulfilling its promise of expansion. Two government papers, respectively titled *National Development 1977–1980* and *Development of Full Employment*, spelt out the details of the party's strategy. It proposed to seek a growth rate of 7 per cent per annum by cutting interest rates and taxation. Foreign borrowing was to make up any shortfall in government spending in order to give the economy an added stimulus. After 1979, however, public spending was to be cut back and private enterprise was to become the main source of investment. The aim of this economic strategy was nothing less than the achievement of full employment by the early 1980s. The party warned, however, that for this strategy to work, wage increases had to be severely limited. It believed that this could be achieved by a five-year period of social partnership with the unions.

In order to attract the union leaders into this longer-term arrangement, Fianna Fáil proposed a new form of collaboration which was based on the concept of a 'political exchange'. Here the union leaders were to be consulted on a range of political issues as a trade-off for enforcing pay moderation. The ICTU leaders found the proposal extremely attractive as they felt it offered a variant of social democracy at one remove. Because of the political weakness of the Labour Party, the leaders believed it fell to the ICTU to develop an industrial coalition with Fianna Fáil whereby, instead of simply making representations to government, they could enter into negotiations on what government policy actually was. The ICTU leaders believed that there were two sides to Fianna Fáil. As *Liberty* put it, Fianna Fáil could never decide whether it was a party 'representing men with open-necked shirts' or 'a party of TACA' (the business support group).[6] The dual nature of Fianna Fáil, vacillating between being a populist party and a supporter of the rich, made such an industrial coalition all the more necessary. It was only by entering a form of social partnership between the unions, the employers and Fianna Fáil that the party's populism could be strengthened – and, it was hoped, triumph.

The negotiation on the first National Understanding involved a broad politicisation of the process of collective bargaining. Working parties were established between the ICTU and the government on education, workers' participation, taxation, employment and health. Key ICTU leaders were given access to confidential Department of Finance files which contained details on the taxation of certain categories of people. The unions demanded that the government underwrite job targets where there was a shortfall from the private sector, and Fianna Fáil agreed that the state would create up to 5,000 new jobs if this sector failed to meet the annual target of 25,000 jobs. A National Enterprise Agency was created for the state to exploit commercial opportunities and so enter areas normally designated for private enterprise. The only requirement in exchange for all this amalgam of social democratic reforms was wage restraint.

To the union leaders it seemed like manna – or, more precisely, that Swedish-style reformism had arrived. They had risen beyond mere 'economic' concerns to play a role in directing state policy itself. Social partnership had reached the heights where they had more say in government policy than the junior partners in a coalition government. John Carroll expressed the sense of achievement in the ITGWU:

The breakthrough we had achieved was historic in that for the
first time in this country and indeed in any country and I
include the Socialist countries, we now had an acknowledge-
ment that the trade union movement not alone had a voice to
be listened to but had to be brought into the circles where
decisions are made.[7]

Problems

However, behind all the hopes for a bright future for social
partnership, there was a stumbling block: Fianna Fáil was in no
position to repeat the 1958 turn that had restored its image as the
party of national development. That had occurred during a sustained
boom within capitalism – what now faced the party were far more
bleak and unstable conditions.

The party's key strategist was Martin O'Donoghue, an economics
lecturer in Trinity College. Although much derided afterwards, he
sought to pursue a form of textbook Keynesianism to reflate the
economy and instil a new confidence in private enterprise. It was
a strategy which many newly industrialising countries (NICs) were
engaged in at the time. The huge growth in oil prices meant that
many wealthy producers had invested their surplus earnings in the
Western banking system, and so interest rates had fallen. Countries
as diverse as Poland, Brazil and Ireland all decided to take advantage
of this cheaper money by borrowing heavily in order to improve
their level of investment and infrastructure. With increased rates
of growth, they could reasonably expect to pay back the debt from
an expansion of their exports.

In a different period of capitalist growth this might have been
the case. However, O'Donoghue was unfortunate to take on the
inappropriately named Department of Economic Planning and
Development in a period when no real planning was possible. The
ironic logic of the free market dictates that what might be a useful
strategy for one competitor, can become a nightmare when adopted
by several. The fact that many NICs were all engaged in borrowing
to boost production meant that they could not all expect to
experience phenomenal rates of growth in their exports. Moreover,
as each of them took out huge loans, this in turn pushed up interest
rates. They had to pay back more than expected with less resources
than they had hoped for.

As if this was not bad enough, the plan for full employment
eventually coincided with the onset of the second major recession
of 1980–81. In Britain, which was Ireland's largest recipient of
exports, up to a quarter of manufacturing industry was simply
wiped out as Thatcher used the occasion to impose the new

discipline of the market. Ideologically, the apologists for capitalism explained this particular recession by the high levels of public spending which Western governments had engaged in. By urging this state spending, Keynesianism itself had become the mechanism by which rigidities were introduced into an otherwise perfect market economy – that, at least, was the view of the new guru of monetarism, Milton Friedman. Here, then, was O'Donoghue promoting a robust form of Keynesianism in the midst of a growing recession, where this particular form of economics was held up as the scapegoat for the failures of capitalism. As the level of public sector borrowing mounted – to nearly 15 per cent of GNP in 1981 – Fianna Fáil's profligate policies lost the allegiance of a section of bourgeois commentators.

The opposition to Fianna Fáil in elite circles was not compensated by a generosity among workers. Initially, the party's injection of borrowing into the Irish economy led to the creation of 60,000 extra jobs in two years and trade union membership rose to 60 per cent of the workforce, the third highest in Europe. Once again, this led to a renewed confidence and militancy at the base of the unions as workers sought to recover from defeats inflicted by the coalition. Strikes occurred in Aer Lingus and the telephone exchanges, and 1978 went down as another year where Ireland topped the European strike league. The *Irish Times* commented that it was a year 'when the lid blew off the kettle when just about every group from nurses to gardai to milkmen and postmen either went on strike or threatened to do so'.[8]

In two incidents the strikes led to sharp confrontation between workers and the forces of law and order. In Waterford, widespread anger developed after the National Board and Paper Mills announced a major redundancy programme. Workers occupied the plant to demand its nationalisation and announced that they would conduct a sit-down on the main bridge entering the city. As they arrived to do so, they were met by fully armed soldiers of the Irish army, who had been called out to block them. Instead of the troops causing fear, their presence only provoked more outrage, with other workers coming out to join in the protest. According to one shop steward: 'We were all expecting to make a dash for the bridge. The workers were going to throw the soldiers in the river.'[9] Confrontation was averted at the last moment, but later a two-hour general strike occurred in the town, with over 10,000 marching in support of the mill workers.

The second key strike was in the post office. In January 1979, a special conference of the Post Office Workers Union voted to pursue a claim for a 37 per cent wage increase, and a national strike began on 18 February. The ICTU, who were now seeking partnership with Fianna Fáil, accused the union of breaching agreed procedure and this emboldened Fianna Fáil to stiffen their resistance to the strike. Strikers were threatened with suspension, and attempts by postal workers to close down deliveries were met by a sustained gardai presence. Frequent baton charges and clashes occurred in the main sorting office in Dublin. After a 19-week strike the Fianna Fáil government wore down the workers and they were forced back to work. The defeat of the strike was later to have powerful repercussions in dampening public sector militancy and convinced many to look again at the option of social partnership.

The PAYE Revolt

Before this realisation sunk home, however, Fianna Fáil was confronted with yet another difficulty with a revolt of PAYE workers over tax. As discussed in a previous chapter, the costs of Ireland's industrialisation programme was mainly borne by PAYE workers and the burden on this sector had grown steadily in the 1970s. In 1975, for example, PAYE accounted for 71 per cent of all income tax revenue but by 1978 it had risen to 87 per cent.[10] Matters came to a head when Fianna Fáil was seen to retreat on a special 2 per cent levy on farm produce which was imposed in the 1979 budget. After a series of protests from the Irish Farmers Association and lobbying from within the parliamentary party, the tax was simply dropped. On the day that this was announced, 250 workers at CA Parsons Engineering in Howth stopped work in a spontaneous display of anger. The next day, representatives of 32 unions in Dublin Airport came together to plan a demonstration. The protest took on a more organised focus when craft unions officially called on the Dublin Trades Council to organise a strike in the city on 20 March. The workers' tax revolt had begun.

The ICTU leaders were now caught in a dilemma. If they supported the spontaneous revolt they would endanger the new form of social partnership that was opened to them – if they refused to back it, they could be outflanked by more militant rank-and-file representatives. The more astute wing of the union bureaucracy in the ITGWU decided to take the initiative by calling a demonstration outside working hours, in the hope of heading off a demand for strike action. The ICTU promptly backed this suggestion and on 11 March, 50,000 people marched through the streets of Dublin in one of the largest protests ever seen in the city.

This action had the opposite effect to that envisaged by the union leadership as its very size confirmed the degree of anger and strengthened the call for a general strike. The ICTU resolutely opposed this action, and in justifying this stance, its general secretary, Ruaidhri Roberts, argued the classic social democratic case for separating industrial and political action:

> By the constitution we are committed to support the democratic system of government ... we draw a clear distinction between strikes against government departments or state companies and strikes against the state itself or its democratic institutions ... Protest strikes are characteristically resorted to in countries where the trade union movement lacks real bargaining power. We do not lack real bargaining power.[11]

Because of the ICTU's refusal to organise strike action, local trades councils stepped into the breach and became the focus for rank-and-file militancy. Key figures of the ICTU representing, for example, telephone engineers and local government workers, saw their advice completely overturned in their own unions. Right up to the last moment, however, the ICTU kept up the pressure on the Dublin Council of Trade Unions to desist from organising strike, but eventually, when it came to a vote, it was decided to go ahead with a stoppage on 20 March. Thereafter, unions such as the ITGWU that initially opposed the strike action were forced to back it. According to the *Irish Times*: 'The urge for action came from the rank and file and swept the leadership along with it.'[12]

The first PAYE strike was phenomenal. As many as 150,000 people took to the streets of Dublin and 40,000 marched in Cork. It dwarfed any other action the workers' movement had taken and was the first general strike in the history of the Republic of Ireland. On the eve of the protest the Minister for Finance, George Colley, who had given in to the farmers, disparaged the action as unproductive. On the morning after the strike, the *Irish Times* rather prophetically noted that an obvious casualty of the day was Colley's leadership ambitions in Fianna Fáil.[13] The PAYE protests clearly contained a potential for a deeply politicising effect.

That was not how the Labour Party saw matters. Like the leaders of the ICTU, they accepted the notion that politics had to be reserved for the quiet debating chambers of Dáil Eireann. They regarded the desire for people power on the streets as nothing less than an attempt to undermine democracy as we know it. On the day of the strike, Barry Desmond demonstrated the deep antipathy which most Labour TDs held for this type of mass industrial action when he said:

> I have never supported and will never support as long as I am in public life the idea, concept or practice of a political one day strike. I believe in the ballot box ... The power of democracy should reside ... in the Houses of Oireachtas [parliament] and

the democratic exercise of power must remain at that level and not on the street.[14]

The scale of the protests and the accompanying strikes was also highly disorientating for Fianna Fáil. Four days after the protest, Jack Lynch attacked the 'plethora of protests, strikes, go slows and demands for large income increases'.[15] Sean Moore, a prominent Fianna Fáil speaker on labour affairs, said that 'it is baffling why there is so much hatred towards the state. The old order of unjust employers has almost disappeared.'[16] The Minister for Labour, Gene Fitzgerald, said: 'I wish to God at times like these that I had some magic formula which would once and for all remove from our country the hardship and damage caused by strikes. Unfortunately, I have no magic formula.'[17]

He could, however, count on the distaste that the union leaders felt for this type of action. After the first stoppage, ICTU stepped up their campaign against the tax protests, with the ICTU president, Harold O'Sullivan, claiming that 'taxation is fundamentally a job for parliament and government and I don't accept that mass democracy on the streets is the answer to our problems'.[18] Despite these strictures, another stoppage was called on 1 May by the Dublin Council of Trade Unions. This time, the ITGWU decided to stand firm against it and even threatened to discipline branches that backed it. Despite the more blatant opposition from the union bureaucracy, 30,000 people turned up to back the second major tax strike.

The militancy on the streets meant that the Fianna Fáil government had to pay even closer attention to the concerns of the union leaders. The National Understanding – which was negotiated while the tax strikes were taking place – came with extensive political promises on jobs, health and housing. It was comparable to pacts which other governments entered into at this time in Europe – the British Social Contract and the Moncloa Pact between the Spanish government and the unions are examples. These were all based on a political exchange where the union leaders were promised partnership in return for discouraging militancy. Later, however, it seemed that the agreements were only holding operations, while key sections of the ruling class readied themselves for a more headlong confrontation with workers.

Enter the Strong Man

While the National Understanding of 1979 helped temporarily to diffuse the tax protests, the rise in working-class militancy also had repercussions for Fianna Fáil. From the end of 1979, the party entered a period of intense factional struggle that was eventually to see Charles J. Haughey assume the leadership. Most accounts of Fianna Fáil's factionalism, both academic and popular, tend to ignore or play down this context of social unrest. Garvin's article on 'The growth of faction in the Fianna Fáil Party 1966–1980' is a typical example. Here Haughey's victory is presented as the result of a system of internal clientelism. He is supposed to have used his role as a minister to grant favours to backbench TDs in order to make them beholden to him for solving their constituents' problems. Little attention is paid to the tax protests and the danger they posed for the erosion of Fianna Fáil's electoral base.[19]

This perspective emerges from an approach which both ignores the reality of class struggle in Irish society and believes that 'catch-all parties' like Fianna Fáil are simply immune to the pressures placed on them by the activities of the working class. Throughout this book it has often been noted that when there is a significant rise in class struggle it has often brought electoral problems for Fianna Fáil. The tax protests and the general militancy of 1979 conform to this pattern. In June 1979, the Fianna Fáil vote in the European elections fell to 35 per cent – its lowest level of electoral support since the 1920s. In Dublin, the Labour Party vote grew from 18 per cent in the general election of 1977 to 30 per cent in the European election. A similar pattern manifested itself in the Cork by-elections at the end of the year. In November, the Fianna Fáil vote in one Cork city constituency fell from 59 per cent of the vote in the previous election to 36 per cent. These electoral disasters were the stimulus to the formation of the first organised factional grouping in Fianna Fáil. After the June electoral defeat, 30 TDs held a caucus meeting and, of these, 29 would later vote for Charles J. Haughey as leader of the party.

The factional struggle in Fianna Fáil was certainly conducted at one remove from the issue of workers' unrest, with its principle focus being Jack Lynch's conduct of Northern policy. A backbench revolt on the question of British army overflights seemed to be at the heart of the disagreement between the party establishment and the Haughey grouping, but the matter was more complex than this. Vincent Browne, who has produced the most detailed inside information on the faction fight, has argued that 'the issues on which the revolt was built were diverse and related more to the economy than to Northern Ireland'.[20] Fianna Fáil backbenchers were looking for solutions to the growing unrest in the South and its detrimental effects on their electoral survival. One of their key reflexes was to try to play the green card, which allowed them to engage in nationalist rhetoric about the border while doing little in practice to destabilise the existing arrangements of partition. Moreover, as the level of debate on party strategy was quite low, the key issue revolved around who could reinvigorate and lead.

After Haughey was elected leader, one of his chief supporters, Sile de Valera, explained that 'we've got what we needed, a strong man able to handle the political and economic challenges'.[21] Haughey's image as a 'strong man' had been carefully cultivated over decades. He was the man of action who had scaled the gates of Trinity College as a student to tear down a Union Jack. In the 1960s he typified the brash rich who had benefited from property speculation and had no embarrassment about flaunting their wealth. Alongside others in a secret cabinet committee he had been willing to intervene in the IRA with the promise of material help as a way of defeating the left-wing elements. His vindication by the courts after the arms trial added to his air of charisma and strength. Above all, Haughey presented himself as almost part of a natural aristocracy, surrounding himself with great cultural icons and even coming to own an island off the coast of Kerry. His long-time opponent, Conor Cruise O'Brien, probably best described the image:

> An aristocrat in the proper sense of the word – not a nobleman or even a gentleman but one who believed in the right of the best people to rule and that he himself was the best of the best people.[22]

Fianna Fáil needed a strong man because its economic strategy was antagonising a section of the bourgeoisie and winning little response from workers. Haughey's project aimed at nothing less than to replace the rhetoric of national expansion with a harsh form of monetarism. Instead of the dream of Lemass that the state and private enterprise could cooperate to break the chains of under-development, Haughey was charged with switching to the language of sacrifice and cutbacks. His rise coincided with the 'crisis of Keynesianism' which affected many European countries and made it impossible to continue Lemass's strategy of high levels of state intervention that had historically helped to maintain working-class support. Haughey hoped to combine monetarism with a heightened republican rhetoric in order to garner popular support. Quite simply, in a situation of social unrest the call for financial stringency had to be accompanied by a stronger assertion of Fianna Fáil's traditional values.

Haughey's first public address to the nation as Taoiseach began by stating baldly that 'as a community we are living beyond our means ... we have been living at a rate which is simply not justified by the amount of goods and services we are producing'.[23] In his first cabinet he sacked Martin O'Donoghue and scrapped the Department of Economic Planning and Development, thus removing the ambitious planning mechanisms which were supposed to accompany a statist strategy. The Fianna Fáil Ard Fheis in February

1980 revealed the full extent of Haughey's change of direction. In his presidential address, he once again returned to the theme of financial stringency, but this time accompanied it with a reassertion of Fianna Fáil's republican values. He looked forward to a day where Ireland was 'without British presence but with active British good will'.[24] In many ways the real significance of Haughey's message was not in the content of the speech but in the props which surrounded it. Haughey was led into the hall by the ITGWU band to the strains of 'A Nation Once Again'! The Ard Fheis summarised Haughey's programme for Fianna Fáil: financial stringency, traditional republicanism and a friendly relationship with the ITGWU.

Vacillation

Ultimately, Haughey was to fail. The strong man called to rescue Fianna Fáil from the crisis of Keynesianism adopted the most contradictory of policies. His party split over issues it later came to endorse and became riven with factions. The failure of Haughey was not, however, an individual failing. His complex manoeuvres all revolved around one central problem: the conditions which had built Fianna Fáil as a national movement rather than 'a mere political party' were disappearing.

The immediate problem Haughey faced was the continued resilience of working-class militancy. Just two weeks after his television address to the country, the ICTU called its first national general strike on tax. At its conference the previous year the leadership came under sustained attack for its refusal to back political strikes and the ICTU was forced into calling action on 20 January 1980. Some 700,000 people came out on strike in 37 centres and a staggering 300,000 took part in the street demonstration in Dublin alone. In some of the smallest provincial towns there was a re-emergence of trade union activity that had not been seen since the 1920s. In Abbeyfeale in West Limerick, for example, 3,000 people marched to the home of the Fianna Fáil minister Gerry Collins. The BBC described the event as the 'largest peaceful protest in postwar Europe', which was probably an exaggeration in absolute terms but made some sense in terms of the small size of the Irish population.[25] The *Irish Times* struck a more ominous note, claiming that 'the numbers demonstrated the strength of the trade unions and of the PAYE taxpayer – it may also have demonstrated the vulnerability of this small state'.[26]

It was a message that Haughey simply could not ignore. Other politicians who sought to dismantle the welfare state, such as Reagan and Thatcher, had begun by an all-out assault on militant trade unionism. In Thatcher's case, she benefited from the confusion and demoralisation that had already emerged under a previous Labour government. Haughey, however, faced a trade union movement which had just organised an extraordinarily popular general strike. Moreover, the ideology of Fianna Fáil, which built itself on the basis of a partnership for national development and even claimed to be a friend of the 'plain people', meant that it was ill-prepared for the depth of the struggle that a full-scale assault would have entailed. Haughey had little option but to do a complete about-turn. This had little to do with his shiftiness or his 'flawed pedigree'[27] and everything to do with the new contradictions in which Fianna Fáil found itself.

In the middle of 1980, after calling for cutbacks some months previously, Haughey announced his conversion. He began negotiations for a second National Understanding on the basis of rejecting 'the orthodox, rigid, and inflexible attitude of other European countries'.[28] He promised the ICTU that he would continue the policy of borrowing to 'set the target for infrastructure development as high as possible'.[29] He renewed the commitment to increased job targets and even promised to double social welfare payments at Christmas. A significant minority of the employers' organisation, the FUE, expressed their public disapproval of these events, and it took an unscheduled and unprecedented visit by Haughey to their headquarters to get that organisation to agree to the National Understanding.

The sight of the employers being reluctantly dragooned into a second National Understanding did Haughey's reputation with union leaders no harm. After it was concluded, union leaders like John Carroll of the ITGWU were fulsome in their praise, claiming that 'if the trade union movement were told tomorrow "you take over", the type of programme they would seek to implement would be almost line for line, set out in proposals for a second National Understanding'.[30] This was short-sighted in the extreme. Haughey only embarked on this form of social partnership as a way of buying time against union militancy. He was willing to promise all sorts of short-term advantages to workers so long as the unions were capable of delivering massive opposition on the streets. Once the militancy at the base had been defeated, however, there was no reason why Fianna Fáil should not align itself with the more vocal propagandists for the free market and implement the type of cuts that were needed.

That mood of demoralisation among workers, however, really only started to emerge after 1982. In his first period of office Haughey was still stuck in the position of making concession after concession to avoid a frontal assault on the unions. Two cases in particular highlighted Haughey's weakness and became a symbol of disgust for the more impatient representatives of the bourgeoisie. The first was in Clondalkin Paper Mills, where workers occupied the plant after its closure. The occupation was accompanied by a variety of tactics, ranging from hunger strikes to sit-downs on main roads to the lobbying of politicians and received widespread support from trade unionists throughout Ireland. To help diffuse the situation – and also to help gain short-term electoral advantage – Haughey promised to find new owners or, failing that, to nationalise the plant. The promise was never kept, but for his critics in the party it was another alarming retreat.

The second case involved a strike of 90 workers in the Talbot plant. This began over redundancies and then seemed to escalate when the ATGWU regional secretary, Matt Merrigan, was threatened with imprisonment for breaking a court injunction which forbade any attempt to block Talbot cars being into imported into Ireland. Haughey intervened personally in the dispute which occurred in his own constituency, brokering an agreement whereby the IDA agreed to find alternative jobs for the car workers at their equivalent wages. If such jobs were not secured by October 1981, the government itself agreed to maintain the average earnings of the workers. The Talbot deal was held up as a classic Fianna Fáil 'stroke' by the Labour Party, which increasingly saw the main issue in Irish politics as being one of 'integrity' versus the shifty manoeuvring of Fianna Fáil. Yet while there were some electoral considerations involved, Haughey's excuse, that he agreed to the proposal to 'obviate the most serious confrontation in industrial relations the country has ever seen', had a certain validity.[31] Matt Merrigan also claimed that if Haughey had not agreed to the Talbot deal, Fianna Fáil would have faced the same chaos they faced with the ESB (Special Provisions) Act in 1966.[32]

All of this severely damaged the political trust which the Irish upper class had in Haughey's leadership of Fianna Fáil. Inside his own party, factionalism re-emerged when the Club of 22 seized on issues such as the Talbot deal as an example of his unwillingness to adopt tough economic measures. This was a premature assessment, as Haughey would adopt the policy of cutbacks at the end of 1982 . However, he needed to buy time in order to subvert workers' militancy by wrapping up the union leaders into social partnership arrangements. But there was also something deeper involved: the basis of Fianna Fáil's appeal to workers was that it was the party of expansion, of national development. In an era when this was no longer possible to any significant degree, it was inevitable that the whole political structure would undergo an acute political crisis before there could be a restabilisation of normal politics.

The Green Card

Haughey originally hoped to restore Fianna Fáil's popularity by playing the green card, and his rhetoric on the North was probably the strongest since de Valera in his heyday. As Fianna Fáil's promise of economic expansion was fading, he hoped that the party faithful would be inspired by a rejuvenated republican rhetoric.

Yet here again the options were narrowing for Fianna Fáil. Every other leader had been able to turn on the republican rhetoric knowing that it was purely of symbolic value and that their words would never be put to the test of practice. Haughey's misfortune was to try to play the green card when the republican struggle was growing in the North. Within a year of his arrival in office, prisoners in the H Blocks began a hunger strike in pursuit of their demand for political status. The British government removed the special category status, which had been granted to republican prisoners in the 1970s, in order to portray them as criminals rather than political activists. Initially, a small support campaign was begun by a Relatives Action Committee, but it gained little support. After the hunger strike began, however, a solidarity movement developed throughout the whole island. On 6 December 1980, for example, 60,000 people marched to the British embassy.

Here, then, was an opportunity for Haughey to match his green rhetoric with a declaration of open support for the hunger strikers and a condemnation of Britain. Indeed, he could have gone further and taken small symbolic gestures such as expelling the British ambassador. This is certainly what the republicans hoped for. The genesis of their pan-nationalist strategy dated from this point where they hoped to construct a nationalist consensus comprising the SDLP, Fianna Fáil and sections of the Church hierarchy into an ill-defined alliance to pressurise Britain. However, Haughey proved a complete disappointment to the republicans.

On 8 December, an Anglo-Irish summit took place in Dublin where Ireland's reborn rebel presented Margaret Thatcher with a silver teapot. No disagreement was expressed over the British response to the hunger strike. Instead, Haughey claimed that great significance attached to a joint statement issued by both governments in which they promised to examine the 'totality of relationships' on the island. The claim to a historic achievement, however, was later deflated when the Secretary of State for Northern Ireland, Humphrey Atkins, argued that this examination did not mean that anyone other than the British government could interfere in the 'internal affairs' of Northern Ireland. When the second hunger strike began on 1 March 1981, this time led by Bobby Sands, Haughey concentrated his efforts on trying to pressurise the families to persuade the prisoners to give it up. After ten men died in this struggle, Haughey's green credentials were severely shaken. He failed to win a majority government in the election of 1981, partially because two seats went to H Block prisoners. At one point, the former Fianna Fáil minister Kevin Boland, who resigned in solidarity with Haughey during the arms crisis, caustically remarked that 'it's Garret Fitzgerald [the Fine Gael leader] that is leading Fianna Fáil and not Charles Haughey'.[33]

One of the outcomes of the H Block crisis was that both the British and Irish governments were forced seriously to examine possible solutions to end 'alienation' of the nationalist community in the North. When the Fine Gael leader Garret Fitzgerald came to power in 1983, he was particularly concerned with the threat which Sinn Féin posed electorally to the SDLP in the North and the implications that this might have for the stability of Southern politics.[34] One of the purposes of the New Ireland forum which he established in 1983 was to debate and redefine the parameters of constitutional nationalism. He hoped to explore areas like power-sharing or joint sovereignty which would help to co-opt the growing Catholic middle class into the structures of the Northern state. Throughout all these discussions, Haughey's response was highly traditional: he dismissed notions of federalism or joint authority and insisted that only a unitary Irish state could bring peace to the island.

The culmination of Fitzgerald's campaign was the Anglo-Irish Agreement which was signed in 1985. This represented an important milestone on the road to a possible solution to the Northern crisis. It established a joint Anglo-Irish secretariat in Maryfield in Stormont and recognised that henceforth the Irish government had the right to be consulted on the 'internal affairs' of Northern Ireland. In effect, a division of labour was set up whereby the Southern government acted as a guarantor for the interests of the Catholic middle class while the British played an equivalent role for Protestants. Far from removing sectarianism, this was designed to institutionalise existing structures and allow communal politicians a forum where they could continue to represent 'their side'. In return for these changes the Southern government formally acknowledged that unity in Ireland could only be established by consent.

Haughey's response was to make an even greater play for a reputation as a militant nationalist. He denounced the Anglo-Irish agreement in the following terms:

> In effect what is being proposed in this Agreement is that the Irish government, accepting British sovereignty over part of Ireland, will involve itself in assisting and advising the British government

to rule that part of Ireland more effectively to help make it more amenable to the authority of the British government.[35]

This was certainly the raw meat of republican rhetoric and it put Haughey significantly at odds with key sections of the Southern establishment. But it was rhetoric nonetheless. Fianna Fáil had greater scope to engage in this language when the Southern elite effectively turned its back on the North and concentrated on building their own state. However, the H Block crisis and the potential destabilising effects it had on the South, meant that they had to start devising practical strategies for the normalising conflict in the North. Haughey's dilemma was that his opposition to the new schemes of the British and Irish establishment aligned him more closely to the unconstitutional republicans. If he continued on this road, he would have to match his militant nationalist rhetoric with action.

Neither Haughey nor Fianna Fáil had the slightest intention of going this far. Instinctively, they knew that republican rhetoric was for ceremonial occasions and for when they were in opposition to a Fine Gael-led government. More than anyone, they knew the limits. After all, it was Fianna Fáil which had been willing to intern and hang republicans in the past. When he returned to power in 1987, Haughey carried out yet another U-turn. He decided to implement the Anglo-Irish Agreement and dropped all criticisms of the document. He also carried through its security provisions as effectively as any Fine Gaeler. In opposition he had opposed an Extradition Act which proposed to hand over republicans to the British authorities. A moratorium of one year had been placed on the Act, and it fell to the new Taoiseach to decide if it was to go ahead. Despite some fiery republican denunciations from the Fianna Fáil backbenches, the party voted unanimously to accept extradition with some minor safeguards. Within a short period of time, IRA members were handed over to Britain, courtesy of Fianna Fáil, the republican party.

The distance between Haughey and the practical strategies of the Southern establishment was closed with his acceptance of the Anglo-Irish Agreement, but there was a price to be paid. The ideological space to engage in green rhetoric was closed off. Fianna Fáil was finding that it simply could not repeat the techniques of the past.

Family Values

Fianna Fáil has traditionally turned to the Church when it has needed compensation for its failure to deliver on republican rhetoric. If the fourth green field was not available, at least there was comfort to be had from the fact that in the other three the Vatican flag flew high. Although Haughey's own life in the 1960s has been described as a trifle unconventional, he had little difficulty in picking up on this tradition – this time under the guise of defending 'family values'. In doing so, he made a vital contribution to the resurgence of the Catholic right.

In 1981, the then Taoiseach Garret Fitzgerald made a startling admission when he declared: 'If I were a Northern Protestant today, I cannot see how I could be attracted to being involved with a state which is itself sectarian.'[36] He promised to launch a constitutional crusade for far-reaching changes. It proved a damp squib, as Fitzgerald decided to adapt to the very sectarian structures he pointed to. However, for Fianna Fáil, Fitzgerald's outburst provided a heaven-sent opportunity to don the mantle of the Church militant. Haughey denounced Fitzgerald's 'colonial mentality' which caused him to impute 'inferiority and sectarianism' to the 26 counties. The Fianna Fáil leader's own vision of the new Ireland where Green and Orange were united was eloquently simple. Fianna Fáil wanted 'partnership where neither side should seek to absolve or change the other'.[37] Haughey's credentials as a defender of Catholic values had already been established. As Minister for Health in 1978 he introduced a Bill which demanded that those seeking condoms should first produce a prescription and then prove that its use was for 'bona fide family planning'. Appropriately enough, he coined the label 'an Irish solution for an Irish problem' for this measure.[38]

As the conservative groups began to promote a backlash against even the small openings in Irish society, they found Haughey and Fianna Fáil ready to cooperate. In 1981, he gave an assurance to the pro-life lobby that he would introduce a constitutional amendment to outlaw abortion. Fitzgerald gave the same assurance but then dithered about the wording. It fell to Fianna Fáil to introduce the exact constitutional clause which equated the life of a mother with that of a day-old fertilised egg. In 1985, after the Virgin Megastore faced a fine for selling condoms, the Fine Gael/Labour Government introduced a Bill to liberalise the law on contraception. Fianna Fáil opposed the measure, claiming that it would make contraceptives freely available to teenagers and ruin the moral fabric of society. In 1986, the party officially took a neutral stance on divorce, but at grass-roots level it worked closely with the Anti-Divorce Campaign to defeat the measure. Haughey gave the signal for this cooperation when he argued that they approached the issue 'from the point of view of the family' and claimed that divorce would create many problems, not least 'major financial implications for the Exchequer'.[39]

This alliance between Fianna Fáil and the fundamentalist right gave a considerable impetus to the backlash. In effect, small elite lobby groups found an inside track into the parliamentary power structures. Fianna Fáil TDs were regularly briefed by 'the masterminds of the right' and there is even some indication that they directly helped to frame laws such as the constitutional amendment on abortion.[40] Yet the championship of 'family values' and Catholic triumphalism did not help the party overcome its own problems.

For one thing, there was an air of fantasy and depression about the backlash of the 1980s. Many were uncertain that Ireland could really be rescued from the tidal wave of cosmopolitan liberalism. The older grass-roots supporters of the Catholic right held to a nostalgic image of the 1950s where 'the family that prayed together, stayed together'. But even at the height of their success, they found that many of their own sons and daughters had joined the liberal opposition, who had mustered one-third of the vote against them on divorce and abortion. One extraordinary manifestation of both the strength and deep uncertainty of the conservative reaction was the craze for 'moving statues' which swept the country in 1984. It was so widespread in rural areas that one local wit in Portlaoise went about the town placing 'Out of Order' signs on the religious icons. One writer at the time, Eamonn McCann, attempted to identify the social causes:

> Growing numbers of people in the 26 counties are no longer able to accept the authority of the Church with blind faith. And in that situation there are bound to be many who, having nothing *but* their religion to comfort them in a cruel world, yearn deep down for a sign that there *is* a supernatural authority which can be relied on. Such a sign, by definition, has to be irrational. Sudden movement by a stone statue of God's virginal mother fits the bill exactly.[41]

This mood of uncertainty had a real basis. Even as Irish liberalism succumbed to demoralisation, there was evidence that the institutional power of the Church had started to crumble. The urbanisation and modernisation of Ireland had eaten away at its foundations. Priests reported that in some Dublin working-class areas, only 10 per cent of the people attended Sunday mass.[42] Vocations to the priesthood were also falling rapidly, with a drop of 29 per cent between 1970 and 1986. By the end of the 1980s a mere 3 per cent of Ireland's 15,634-strong clergy were under the age of 30, although the country was known as having the youngest population in Europe.[43]

All of this meant that Fianna Fáil could no longer paper over the growing cracks in its power base by an appeal to Catholic nationalism. The great irony for the party was that while it created space for the fundamentalist right to emerge, its association with them did not rebound to its electoral benefit. Throughout the decade, Fianna Fáil never achieved a majority government – even though they helped to decisively beat the liberals on divorce and abortion. The days when the Vatican coat of arms could hide the fading of the green flag were ending.

The Split

Fianna Fáil's failures in the 1980s grew from the fact that it was no longer seen as the party of national development. The party's attempt to restore its hegemony by a stronger republican rhetoric brought it into dangerous waters, while its alliance with the Catholic fundamentalists had produced few benefits. Haughey had become a 'political adventurer', striking out in new and uncertain directions in a vain bid to restore past glory. These shifts and changes had dire consequences inside the party.

Haughey's own record during the arms trial guaranteed him a degree of hostility from the party's establishment. Key figures such as George Colley and Desmond O'Malley, who had supported the former leader, Jack Lynch, viewed him with unconcealed disdain. However, contrary to much Irish political commentary, it is facile to see these conflicts solely in personality terms. Of the degree of mutual loathing there is little doubt, but far more was involved. Haughey had come to power in the social crisis of 1979 when expectations raised by Fianna Fáil's new 'consumer led' political programme eventually rebounded against the party. His image as a 'strong, charismatic' figure was severely dented when he had to retreat before the workers' movement. This in turn gave his erstwhile opponents the confidence to regroup.

The omen for the future was set when George Colley, the defeated candidate for the Fianna Fáil leadership in 1979, made it clear that Haughey could not expect his full loyalty. Haughey exacerbated the problem by, unusually, taking full control of the party fund-raising activities from Des Hanafin, an old Lynch loyalist. The key issue in the growing factionalism was Haughey's rhetorical rejection of monetarism and his attempt to present a more green Catholic image. His willingness to engage in 'strokes' such as the Gregory deal – which guaranteed him a majority in the Dáil in return for investment in the inner city – added to his image as a political adventurer. Within a short space of time Haughey was confronted by an unofficial Club of 22, a grouping led by McCreevy and O'Malley who argued for greater 'responsibility' and for their party to move to a programme of cuts in public spending quickly.

Between 1982 and 1983, Haughey had to face down three 'heaves' from this group which sought his removal from office.

The issue which eventually shattered the fragile unity of the party was as unexpected as it was decisive. In February 1985, O'Malley abstained on a Fianna Fáil assault on a government measure to liberalise the sale of condoms and was duly expelled from the party. O'Malley had hardly an outstanding record as a liberal in Irish politics. He vigorously opposed a law on contraception in 1974, claiming that the duty of the Dáil deputy was 'to deter fornication and promiscuity; to promote public morality and to prevent insofar as we can – there are of course clear limitations on the practicality of that – public immorality'.[44] Although his views mellowed somewhat, neither O'Malley nor the party he founded, the Progressive Democrats, had any intention of fighting for sexual freedom or attacking the overall role of the Catholic Church in Ireland. Later attempts by some members of the Progressive Democrats to remove references to the Holy Trinity in the preamble to the Irish Constitution, for example, were quickly quashed, while TDs who opposed the legalisation of homosexuality were tolerated. The primary concern of the Progressive Democrats lay with the stability and legitimacy of the Irish state.[45]

They believed that the economic recession of the early 1980s was introducing new tensions into Irish society and that only a policy of tax cuts and privatisation could provide the ideological weapons to sustain support for capitalism. They regarded Haughey's initial refusal to openly espouse the emerging bourgeois consensus for imposing joint sovereignty on the North as dangerous. They also saw that the alliance with the fundamentalists could be counter-productive as it led many to regard the political establishment with disdain. In addition, O'Malley was also concerned with the type of lobbying tactics which the clericalist right were exerting on the TDs in the Dáil. In that sense, therefore, his liberalism was relatively limited: it was about preserving the traditional autonomy and stability of the state.

Fianna Fáil tried to turn the split to their advantage by presenting the Progressive Democrats as the real right wing of Irish politics. Lenihan, for example, warned that frustration among the middle class about jobs and education for their children had given rise to the right-wing radicalism, but that:

> The only end product of right wing radicalism is the destabilisation of the political system, leading to class antagonism, which we have never had here. It's based on extreme laissez faire, selfish materialism which takes no cognisance of the weak, deprived and less well-off in our society.[46]

The claim that class antagonism never existed in Ireland before this point probably rivalled the claim that sex did not exist before television. But this type of speech helped to create a new myth among the union leaders and sections of the left that Fianna Fáil were once again moving to a more progressive and populist role. Many attacked 'Thatcherism' as a code word not only for right-wing politics, but also as an alien ideology that moved beyond the Irish consensus.

The Progressive Democrats did not contribute a significant new element to Irish politics. They only added another variant to the conservative ideas which had been dominant for so long. Instead of being the 'real Thatcherite right', they were simply the harbingers of a new consensus to which all parties eventually agreed. They owe their origins primarily to the fact that Fianna Fáil had temporarily diverged from mainstream bourgeois opinion as it searched for a new route out of its difficulties. Once this adventure came to a close, there was little of fundamental difference between Fianna Fáil and the Progressive Democrats. The irony was that Haughey eventually took on board the political positions of O'Malley on most of the main issues. He dropped his republican rhetoric and implemented the Anglo-Irish Agreement; he embarked on a campaign of massive public spending cuts; and even on the liberal agenda, the man who had O'Malley expelled for allowing the free sale of condoms, eventually argued for the legalising of homosexuality. The political basis for a Fianna Fáil–Progressive Democrat coalition had been established just a few short years after the split.

Back to Normal?

There was one area, however, where Fianna Fáil achieved a notable success. Haughey described an agreement he concluded with the union leaders in 1987, the Programme for National Recovery, as a 'national pearl of great price'.[47] It was certainly the crowning achievement of his period of office as it restored the type of stable social partnership bargaining that brought considerable benefits for Irish capitalism.

The relationship between the millionaire leader of Fianna Fáil and the top officials of unions such as the ITGWU was often extremely close. Haughey had long cultivated this link, but it really blossomed during the period when he was the leader of the Opposition in the mid-1980s. He regularly denounced the monetarist policies of the Fine Gael–Labour government, claiming that they were 'not an indigenous but entirely imported product' which would cause 'widespread alienation and social unrest'.[48] He supported calls from the union leaders for a return to the social partnership agreements from which the employers had withdrawn in 1982. He pledged that if Fianna Fáil returned to power, it would not privatise any of the commercial semi-state industry.[49] All of these overtures were put on a more formal basis after 1986, when a newly organised Fianna Fáil Trade Union Committee began a series of meetings with key figures in the unions to lay the basis for a future agreement with the party.

When Fianna Fáil returned to office in 1987, the union leaders believed that this would put a stop to the growth of the 'New Right' who were dominating the economic policies of the Progressive Democrats and Fine Gael. Their argument in support of the Programme for National Recovery, which was concluded in October 1987, was that it was a way of preventing Ireland going down the Thatcherite road where the unions had been excluded from power. The union leaders' belief that Fianna Fáil was more 'progressive' meant that they urged workers to accept measures that a government of the 'New Right' would not have got away with. While workers were tied to very small wage increases over a three-year period, Fianna Fáil was given a free hand to implement major cuts in public spending. Just after the agreement was signed, Haughey announced a cuts package of £485 million which amazed the opposition with its sheer scale and daring. The slogans that Fianna Fáil used during the election campaign, such as 'Health cuts hurt the old, the poor and the handicapped', were quietly dropped. Fine Gael was so impressed that it devised a Tallaght strategy – so called after the venue where the new party leader Alan Dukes delivered a speech – to support Fianna Fáil from the opposition benches. One biographer of Haughey explained the scale of the achievement:

> Any other government would have found it difficult, if not impossible, to proceed with two apparently contradictory policies. One that involved huge cuts in public spending and the other that involved doing a deal with the trade unions designed to effectively tie them into the process of government. Haughey managed to follow both roads simultaneously.[50]

The achievement was all the more singular because even after the huge programme of cuts was announced, Fianna Fáil continued to make inroads into the unions. Its Trade Union Committee continued to meet senior trade union leaders, and in May 1989, the party organised its first ever trade union conference, with 300 party members in attendance. Afterwards, each constituency organisation was instructed to appoint a trade union coordinator to liaise with unions in their area.[51] These overtures from Fianna Fáil produced some direct results. In the run-up to the 1989 general election, John Carroll of the ITGWU claimed that none of the opposition parties could talk to the unions as well as Fianna

Fáil. According to the *Industrial Relations News*: 'This was perhaps the closest that any union leader could come to suggesting which of the two immediate alternatives [Fianna Fáil or a Fine Gael–Labour coalition] could be the preferred option from this perspective.'[52]

How were such developments possible? The reality was that the militancy which had characterised the workers' movement in the early 1980s had run out. The recession of 1980–81 led to a dramatic growth in unemployment and emigration. It is estimated, for example, that nearly 200,000 people left the country in this decade because of the depth of the economic crisis. Those who remained at work often found themselves the victims of an employers' offensive that began after 1982 when a Federated Union of Employers document called for a more 'hard headed' approach to bargaining.[53] Unofficial strikes became a comparative rarity and the rank-and-file activity which was so much a feature of the late 1960s faded. In this situation, the union leaders once again found themselves with a relatively free hand to pursue the type of social partnership arrangements that they had long desired. They argued that the defeat of the British miners in 1985 was the result of their own militancy rather than the lack of solidarity given by the TUC, and saw it as an omen of a terrible future unless they cemented their alliance with Fianna Fáil.

The Programme for National Recovery, like many of its predecessors, was not simply an agreement on wages and conditions – it involved an understanding about what type of trade union movement was most desirable. Soon after it was concluded there was a shift in policy towards a more open espousal of a 'new realism'. 'New realism' can be described as a full acceptance of the need for workers and employers to form a partnership to compete in a market economy. It defined itself in opposition to older forms of 'adversarial' trade unionism that recognised, to some degree at least, the reality of class conflict. Thus the Irish Congress of Trade Unions dropped its opposition to outright privatisation and claimed that it was not 'opposed to the declared aim of a share holding democracy'.[54] Increasingly, it presented Germany as a country where its image of a social market economy was best realised. It also claimed that unions had to move towards providing services for their members – ranging from bulk buying, to travel concessions, and even 'social tourism' – as an alternative to trade union struggle.[55]

This shift in policy was accompanied by a series of mergers which reduced the number of unions from 95 in 1970 to 68 in 1990. These mergers became the occasion for major changes to union rule books, usually to the detriment of democratic participation. The most prominent merger was the formation of the Services, Industrial Professional and Technical Union in 1990 from the old rivals, the ITGWU and the WUI. The new organisation received a grant of over £700,000 from the Department of Labour, which believed that larger and more disciplined unions were an important component of social partnership. The merger led to extensive internal changes, with union conferences becoming more infrequent and leaders occupying unelected positions for longer than before and with higher salaries.

Decisive legal changes also facilitated the growing power of the union officials over their organisations. In 1990 the Industrial Relations Act was introduced after union leaders committed themselves to change during negotiations on the Programme for National Recovery. Under this Act, political strikes were no longer deemed legitimate trade disputes. Picketing over cases which involved one worker was defined as illegal, raising difficulties over cases relating to victimisation. Only direct employees of individual firms were given the right to picket and their numbers were limited. Secret ballots were required from all who might possibly be affected by strike action. With the exception of proposals for an outright ban on unofficial strikes, the provisions of the Industrial Relations Act represented a fulfilment of Fianna's Fáil programme of reform that was first mooted in 1966.

The great irony of Charles J. Haughey was that while he presided over the decline of Fianna Fáil as a party, he restored the old social partnership mechanisms which his predecessor Lemass had started. Moreover, he achieved this in far more unfavourable circumstances than those which faced Lemass. In doing so, he helped to usher in a new period of stability for Irish capitalism. Nevertheless, even this important success had its limitations for Fianna Fáil. It established centralised bargaining as the principal model by which wages in Ireland were to be regulated, and the Thatcherite model of encouraging individual employers to launch frontal assaults on union organisations was dropped. This became the position of all the main parties and this particular strategy was no longer specific to Fianna Fáil. The union leaders found that they could as easily promote the same sort of arrangements with Fine Gael or Labour as with Fianna Fáil.

Nor did the new form of social partnership mean that Fianna Fáil could simply restore the type of hegemony it exercised over labour in the past. Then, there was a real feeling that the party had a strategy for overcoming backwardness and bringing about substantial economic development. The social partnership arrangements of the 1980s mainly grew out of defeats and demoralisation. Haughey had been able to push through substantial cuts and still keep the union leaders on board because there was little organised rank-and-file opposition. Yet compliance in the new arrangements should not be confused with acceptance of Fianna Fáil's ideological project. The party had exhausted its specific role as a champion of national development and had been forced to seek other political substitutes, which only increased its difficulties. Increasingly, the various programmes which followed the Programme for National Recovery were seen mainly as mechanisms for wage restraint because the sacrifices of workers did not seem to translate into new jobs.

Inevitably, this will set the stage for a new round of struggle. When it happens, workers will enter the fight having less ties with or hopes in Fianna Fáil.

Conclusion

In 1992, Charles Haughey was forced to resign from office when a ghost from the past came back to haunt him. A former supporter, Sean Doherty, claimed that he had been ordered as Minister for Justice to organise the bugging of the telephones of two prominent journalists. The incident had occurred ten years before, but its refusal to go away was symbolic of the fact that Haughey never managed to resolve the tensions and divisions that persisted in Fianna Fáil.

Haughey had always the air of a political adventurer lashing out in one direction, then another, ever willing to bend the rules when it suited him. The decision of backbench TDs to hand him the leadership in 1979 arose from the fact that the party found itself in a very new situation. On the one hand, it could no longer promise a regime of expansion and growth after its programme of Keynesian economics came crashing down. Yet historically it was this promise of growth which had partially explained its success. On the other hand, the tax protests of that same year contained very ominous signs for the future as they were of a fundamentally different character to tax protests in other countries. They arose from a growing sense of class consciousness and raised fundamental questions about why the costs of Ireland's industrialisation programme was mainly carried by PAYE workers.

Haughey's mission was to effect a change to the new language of austerity and cutbacks, while waving the green card and championing family values. For much of his early period as leader of Fianna Fáil, he failed miserably. The militancy of workers forced him on to the defensive to such an extent that he lost the confidence of the upper class. His nationalist rhetoric clashed with the need for a serious bourgeois strategy to integrate the Catholic middle class into Northern society. He won Pyrrhic victories on divorce and abortion, but even while he was holding back the winds of change, the power of the Catholic Church was already being eroded. All of this meant that Fianna Fáil remained divided and faction-ridden to such an extent that his successor as leader of Fianna

Fáil, Albert Reynolds, once told a parliamentary party meeting that his house was being watched by a white Hiace van, the traditional mode of transport of the undercover police!

Haughey only succeeded in fully imposing a programme of cuts after workers had experienced significant defeats. When he returned to office in 1987, rank-and-file militancy had virtually disappeared. He was able to establish a strong form of social partnership that outlived his period in office, and which, in the process, strengthened the hand of the union bureaucracy over their own organisations. Some writers have claimed that this type of agreement, often termed corporatism, is normally associated with quite advanced industrial countries where there are social democratic governments.[56] Yet if we forgo the assumption that these agreements benefit both sides and see them as a strategy for domination, it is quite clear why they developed in Ireland: both the union leaders and Fianna Fáil had an interest in quelling the powerful militancy they had witnessed.

Haughey's success with the union leaders did not save him. He had established a relatively successful model through which Irish capitalism could manage its industrial relations, but he had not restored the basis of Fianna Fáil hegemony. This had rested on the sense of a national community growing and developing so that all sections prospered in the process. When he left office, the signs of decline were clearly visible. As another of his original supporters, Charlie McCreevy, put it:

> No more than a decade ago, the accolade of the greatest political organisation in the democratic free world was commonly ascribed to the party by friend and foe alike. Now, not even the diehard of the diehard Fianna Fáiler believes such a description to be accurate.[57]

Conclusion

Fianna Fáil has never been satisfied to relate to its supporters as isolated voters. Throughout its history the party has had a clear strategy of seeking to influence social groups such as the organised labour movement. The party understood from an early stage that this was a comparatively strong movement and sought to develop a close relationship with its leaders. In this, it was highly perceptive. The nationalist ethos of Southern Ireland has often been based on a denial of class conflict and Fianna Fáil has done more than its share to perpetuate this myth. Yet this never meant that it ignored the importance of organised workers or the necessity for a political struggle to win their support for its policies.

It is impossible to understand Fianna Fáil's dominance over the labour movement if no account is taken of Ireland's experience as a former colony of the British Empire. This led to considerable underdevelopment and a distorted economy whose key function was to supply primary produce and labour to the British market. Throughout the nineteenth century there emerged an indigenous Irish elite who initially reaped some benefit from this state of affairs. They had, after all, found a niche in the largest market in the world and this was often sufficient to compensate for the slightly lower status that befell them as 'natives'. But there were also considerable tensions. As comparatively late arrivals on the stage of capitalism, some of them saw the advantage that having their own state might bring in promoting industrial development – but they also feared the social unrest that would follow any forcible attempt to establish it. It was only reluctantly and with a good deal of hesitation that the majority of the Irish bourgeoisie embarked on the path of national independence after the 1916 rebellion and the crisis produced by the First World War.

Yet the struggle for independence did not remove the legacy of division within the nationalist elite. Garvin has shown how the post-1918 Sinn Féin movement was, in fact, an amalgam of factions from the Home Rule tradition and the republican revolutionaries.[1] Superimposed upon these divisions were others which grew from the very process of revolution itself. Some wanted to settle quickly with the Empire in order to restore stability and end the social conflict that had unleashed land seizures and even 'soviets', or, more

175

precisely, workplace occupations.[2] Others were more determined to win full national freedom and, while not approving of actions which interfered with private property, were willing to take risks in order to extract the maximum degree of independence. These matters were only settled in a bloody fashion by a conservative victory in the Irish Civil War.

It has often been argued that Irish political debate was focused on a replay of Civil War issues and irrational hatreds that were passed on through generations. This, however, is to ignore the real material consequences that followed from the Civil War settlement. The victory of Cumman na nGaedheal meant that considerable restrictions were accepted on Irish sovereignty and that the economy slipped neatly back into the groove of a supplier of primary produce. The Cumman na nGaedheal economic policy consisted mainly of supporting large farmers to supply the British market with Irish livestock and associated products at the cheapest price. Taxation of farm incomes was kept to a minimum and the state performed only the classical function assigned to it by liberal economics: it was the 'nightwatchman' who patrolled the perimeter of society to establish security and never interfered in production. As a result, there were few state supports for industry, even though no large economy, advanced or backward, has ever established a regime of capital accumulation without such support. Free trade and fiscal rectitude were the main slogans of a government who worked to bolster the big farmers and the commercial sectors that benefited from the neocolonial arrangements.

Here, there were some similarities between Ireland and other former colonies in Latin America, such as Argentina or Brazil. In these countries, an anti-establishment elite argued that there was a need to break from neocolonialism to pursue the path of national industrial development. In order to win political power, however, they had to mobilise the lower classes on their side. In Ireland, the structures of parliamentary democracy and the tradition of election machines had been established prior to independence, and so working-class support was essential. In Latin America, the new elite often won political power through military coups. The officer corps in the army provided a framework within which a middle-class intelligentsia could debate ideas and cultivate ambitions to remove the chains of backwardness that hung on their countries. But even if they won power through a coup, they still needed some degree of popular mobilisation to sustain themselves against a deeply entrenched landed oligarchy. The ideological vehicle by which these mobilisations occurred in both Ireland and Latin America we have referred to as populism.

Populist movements generally claim to represent the needs of the 'real' people who come from the poorer sections of society, but deny that they are a direct expression of specific class interests. They display a wide scope for radical rhetoric which is anti-establishment and full of promise of change, but the alternative is often an idealised picture of capitalism. Typically, it is the capitalism of the small producer who is free to ascend in a world where the banks do not have a grip on finance, where big companies are compelled to act fairly, and where the state does not rob you of your hard labour. The imagery of populist movements is often drawn from a rural past where people are working for themselves in social harmony, and where the alien body which is the cause of all division is removed. Yet the basis by which the ideology garners support is by pointing to the need for a remedy to the real problems that stem from underdevelopment and neocolonialism. At the core of populist ideology is a desire to create a unity between producers – an industrial bloc that will pursue a strategy of national development and leave behind the insults of backwardness.

This is the essence of Fianna Fáil's early politics. Although it emerged from the militant wing of republicanism which opposed the political aspects of the settlement with Britain, the party always leant more heavily on the 'social and economic' side to win a base. It used a radical rhetoric which often included attacks on the 'rich' and professed an open sympathy for labour. Yet on closer examination, the target of these attacks were not the wealthy in general, but only that 'parasitic' unproductive element which was associated with the imperialists. Fianna Fáil argued that neocolonialism rather than capitalism was the cause of economic misery for the poor and focused on popular targets that were associated with imperial rule – overpaid civil servants, symbols of British pomp such as the office of Governor General, and even the standing army, which it claimed was a product of colonisation. Fianna Fáil's promise was that the political and economic freedom of the 26 counties would improve the conditions of everyone. In all of this rhetoric, Fianna Fáil never disguised its view that the building of a native capitalist class was the key to breaking out of underdevelopment. It simply claimed that it would behave humanely and fairly to the workers of its own community.

This raises the question of why workers supported this project – having, after all, experienced the tender mercies of this class during the 1913 lockout. A number of factors were involved. First, a series of defeats in the 1920s undermined the militant syndicalist tradition which stressed the industrial strength of workers. Surrounded by fairly large pools of unemployment and already fairly enthusiastic about the republican cause, many workers came to believe protectionism was a necessary pre-condition for advance.

When the Wall Street crash occurred in 1929 and impacted on economies all over the world, Fianna Fáil's radical economic nationalism became the outlet for much of the anger at poverty and deprivation.

Secondly, after Fianna Fáil came to power in 1932 it was able to produce some gains for workers. Sometimes this was highly symbolic, as in the case where cheap beef appeared on the tables of many urban dwellers as the big farmers were forced to enter a subsidised slaughter scheme. On other occasions, there were small but more tangible gains. Under the first Fianna Fáil governments there was an increase in employment, a substantial house-building programme, and some welfare legislation. These gains were certainly paid for by continued high levels of emigration and a regime of intensified exploitation in the factories under the nationalist employers. But to a working class that had not recovered its full strength, there was a difference between the grasping employer who took on more juveniles for higher profits and a Fianna Fáil government who built new houses from their taxes, even if that same government was also concerned with the drive for profit. Although Fianna Fáil was initially seen as radical, its economic strategy was quite commonplace in the 1930s: it used Keynesian methods to expand the home market and create an infrastructure for native capitalism. Just as Roosevelt's Democrats won a reputation among workers because of the New Deal, Fianna Fáil's minor changes stood in sharp contrast to the experience under Cumman na nGaedheal.

Thirdly, the labour movement's support for Fianna Fáil was re-enforced by the formation of the Blueshirts. This was an explicitly fascist movement that grew out of the divisions which existed within elite circles. The large farmers believed that the control of the state gained by Fianna Fáil represented a direct threat to their economic links with Britain. They were unwilling to have these matters settled within the parliament. They looked to the model of European fascism and made it clear that they would not tolerate free trade unionism. The strategy of the union leaders was to oppose fascism by relying on the state rather than street confrontations, and this brought them closer to Fianna Fáil. Historians who play down the fascist threat of the Blueshirts are simply reading back the subsequent harmony that was established within the Irish bourgeoisie for ideological purposes. They wish to present a picture of tremendous stability in parliamentary institutions in the belief that change always occurs slowly and gradually.

Finally, there was the abject failure of the Labour Party. After the formation of the Irish state its leaders discarded any of the revolutionary rhetoric they had picked up from Connolly and shifted to a cautious form of economic nationalism which stressed items such as state development and a national economic council.

In brief, a programme that was hardly distinguishable from Fianna Fáil. The problem, however, was that their respect for the 'institutions of the state' made them appear more timid and inconsistent than their rivals. So, for example, when Fianna Fáil was whipping up a vigorous campaign against the land annuities, the Labour Party was urging payment out of respect for law. After it was beaten in the polls, the Labour Party compounded its problems by arguing that Fianna Fáil was a 'progressive' force that might even challenge capitalism. Its own view that 'socialism' implied only state ownership of industry meant that it could only celebrate the strides Fianna Fáil made in this direction in the 1930s. By turning its back on class struggle, Labour missed hitting Fianna Fáil on its weak spot. As Lemass stated, Labour was politically marginalised not because it was too radical, but because it was not radical enough.

All of this enabled Fianna Fáil to win a certain hegemony over the labour movement from an early stage. There were certainly differences and conflicts between the unions and Fianna Fáil governments, but the politics of the official organisations of the working class operated on the same tracks that Fianna Fáil opened up. National development and support of the 26-county state became their abiding concerns and industrial conflict was relegated to the category of a 'breakdown in industrial relations'. The links between Fianna Fáil and the unions operated primarily on an ideological level and through close personal ties with its official leaders. There was no attempt to formalise any institutional links between the party and the official labour movement, as occurred in Latin American countries. In part, this had to do with the particular division of labour that is set up within the framework of a parliamentary democracy. Normally, there is a rigid distinction between the 'political' and 'industrial' spheres, and a collapse of both areas into one another is thought to have dangerous consequences. This is why, for example, economic strikes are regarded as undesirable but relatively normal, whereas political strikes threaten democracy itself. As Fianna Fáil made the journey from the physical force tradition to normal politics, it accepted these basic ground rules.

In addition, while there was serious conflict within the ruling elite caused by the attempted break from neocolonialism, the social base of Fianna Fáil's opponents was far weaker than their equivalents in Latin America. It was the difference between large farmers who had edged out the older British aristocracy and a landed oligarchy who controlled vast clientelist networks. When Peron was overthrown in 1945, he needed direct physical mobilisation of the 'descamisados' (the shirtless) or, as one writer put it, 'Argentina's sans cullottes' to regain his position.[3] When de Valera faced the Blueshirts in 1933, he could rely on the state machinery itself and even had the luxury of cracking down on his left-wing opponents at the same time. The relative weakness of the pro-British lobby meant that no real mobilisations were required, and so few direct institutional links between de Valera and mass organisations were needed. While there were Peronist unions in Argentina, there was never a possibility of a de Valeraist union in Ireland.

While populism gave rise to the initial relationship between Fianna Fáil and the labour movement, by the end of the 1930s there was also a broader identification with the 26-county state and Catholic nationalism. The threats from both Nazism and the arch imperialist Churchill created mass support for the policy of neutrality, which was tied to an assertion of sovereignty. During the Emergency, Fianna Fáil pressed for a more intense identification with the 26-county state as the primary unit of loyalty, and they found a willing response from the leaders of organised labour. The ITGWU leaders became the centre of a right-wing axis which was formed to expel British-based unions, defend neutrality and launch an anti-communist campaign. Instead of sorting out the issue of Irish versus British-based unions by means of debate and democratic decisions, the ITGWU turned to Fianna Fáil to have these unions expelled. Both organisations claimed that British unions were more militant in their 'experiments' in Ireland because they owed no allegiance to the state. In effect, an alliance was formed between Fianna Fáil and the ITGWU leaders to demand that the labour movement restructure itself to mirror and display a loyalty to the 26-county state.

A suitable cover for this alliance was found in the anti-communist witch-hunt which split both the Labour Party and the unions in the 1940s. This was directly comparable in scale and in consequence to the McCarthyite witch-hunts in America. One of the effects of McCarthyism was to destroy the networks of radicalism that had been built up by socialists in the mass unionisation drives in the 1930s. Similarly, the anti-communist campaign promoted by Fianna Fáil, the *Catholic Standard* and the ITGWU obliterated the small Connolly tradition that had survived from the 1920s. Anti-communist rhetoric was directed at all who did not subscribe to the idea that Catholic social teaching should dominate the 26 counties. In brief, it was the means by which an unashamed Catholic nationalism came to dominate the labour movement.

It did not last. When the top of the labour movement is politically co-opted as it was in this era, it can seem as though the domination of conservative forces is complete. Yet even though nationalism and pride in Catholicism are powerful emotions they could never guarantee Fianna Fáil a lasting base. Nationalism is not a form of magic that removes all the contradictions in the society. It is not a drug that, once taken, leads to permanent addiction. Workers with deeply held nationalist and religious ideas still have to face questions about poverty and emigration and why they occur. The secret of Fianna Fáil's success had always been to move beyond the ephemeral nationalism of feeling to point to real gains. The argument throughout this book has been that the party has been most successful when its economic nationalism caused a tide to flow that seemed to lift all boats. When that tide ebbed, the party was in trouble. The depression that Ireland suffered in the 1950s showed that the protectionism had come to a dead end.

Fianna Fáil's about-turn in 1958 both offered a way out for Irish capitalism and created new conditions whereby it could restore its domination over the labour movement. Far from being a 'sell-out' or a new form of neocolonialism, the integration of Ireland into the wider world economy created a situation where there was a loosening of the ties with Britain. US, German and Japanese factories appeared in the new industrial estates. Trade, which had been solely directed at the British market, began to diversify. Even in the area of finance capital the bonds with sterling were eventually broken.[4] The primary beneficiary of the 1958 turn was the Irish capitalist class, who were given new opportunities for investment by a dynamic economy. The fact that Ireland was used as an export platform for goods entering the European market meant that there was little competition on the home markets. Much of the cost of the industrialisation programme was paid through increased tax levels on workers. But once again, it was Fianna Fáil who seemed to deliver real improvements from expansion as the economy took off in the 1960s, and that did much to restore its base.

After 1958, however, there was also a change in the relationship between Fianna Fáil and the labour movement that is best characterised as a shift from populism to social partnership. Under the populist mode, neither the party nor the state machine was open to direct institutional links with the unions. The unions were sometimes consulted on legislation but it was quite spasmodic, and the level of discussion was entirely at the discretion of the individual Fianna Fáil ministers. They were not even given a voice on state agencies or semi-state boards, but were only appointed to these positions in a personal rather than representative capacity.

All of this meant that the day-to-day contacts between Fianna Fáil and organised labour were based primarily on informal arrangements. When the party collaborated with the ITGWU leader William O'Brien on the Trade Union Act of 1941, it did so by virtual cloak-and-dagger methods, whereby decisions were arrived at in secret meetings. These informal arrangements were possible because the ITGWU shared a similar set of ideas to Fianna Fáil. It articulated positions on partition, the Church and foreign unions which simply dovetailed with Fianna Fáil's. The ITGWU, for example, could indulge in militant republican rhetoric about the North, but like Fianna Fáil, it sought to avoid being embroiled in any fight on the issue. Both organisations used partition as a symbol of a national wrong to help bind the Southern community together.

In the new era after 1958, there were some continuities in the relationship between the unions and Fianna Fáil governments, but it was organised in quite a different way. Two factors stimulated the emergence of links which bound the unions into close institutional ties with the state. The first was a shift to free-trade conditions in the early 1960s, which started with the removal of tariffs between Ireland and Britain but also paved the way for a wider entry into the world economy. This entailed considerable intervention by the state to restructure the Irish economy in order to boost productivity. Lemass concluded that these adjustments could not be made unless the unions were involved at both national and industry level in discussing the details of the process. As a result, through the formation of tripartite agencies such as the Commission on Industrial Organisation and the National Industrial and Economic Council, the unions won a voice in industrial policy. The older forms of populist nationalism were now transmuted into a wider concern to help advance the interests of the Irish economy on the world stage. The shared concern of both the labour leaders and Fianna Fáil no longer centred on easing the stranglehold that Britain had on the Irish economy, but rather on making advances on the world stage. Instead of rivalry with the 'old enemy', there was to be a partnership to enter the super-league.

The second factor which stimulated the development of a formal social partnership was working-class militancy. With the upturn in the economy in the 1960s, a mood of confidence returned to the union grass-roots. Rank-and-file organisations, breakaway unions, and unofficial strikes all characterised an explosion of militancy as major battles took place over pay and the 40-hour week. For both the union leaders and Fianna Fáil this was an extremely worrying development, which they put down to 'indiscipline'. Fianna Fáil's strategy was to bind the union leaders ever closer to the state in the hope that this would encourage them to face down the militants. The party no longer relied on shared ideas to maintain its relationship with labour, but needed direct institutional links between unions and government to enforce the message of productivity, orderly industrial relations, and social partnership. Unions were given rights to sit on various quasi-state agencies, but the trade-off was that they were pressed into accepting more responsibilities for the national economy. Greater state regulation was imposed on their activities through ever more restrictive industrial relations' legislation, and pressure was exerted for a more bureaucratic hierarchy to discipline members. There were many attractions in these arrangements for the union leaders. It enabled them to advance beyond 'mere' economic matters to the sphere of political exchange. It allowed them to gloss over the anarchy of the free market with talk of planning and state regulation. Above all, it seemed to provide a stability that removed the discomforts that come with constant struggle, endless debate and democracy.

Ever since the 1960s there has been a progressive development of these arrangements. In the early 1960s, the unions won access to the limited area of industrial policy. The attempts at establishing a stable incomes policy tended to be sporadic and haphazard. By the end of the 1970s, a much stronger variety of social partnership had emerged. Union leaders were consulted on a range of issues as diverse as health and education, where detailed targets were often agreed. Taxation policies were often linked directly to wage agreements as a form of political exchange developed. A near permanent incomes policy brought with it new institutions which involved the social partners in increasingly closer relations. Today, the great irony is that in the name of 'flexibility' union members face ever greater attacks on the slightest vestige of control they exercise over their jobs, while in the name of 'social partnership' their leaders claim that they can be consulted on almost every item of government.

Other governments were in office while these arrangements existed, but it was Fianna Fáil who pioneered this approach. In the 1980s, for example, an extraordinary close relationship developed once again between the ITGWU and the millionaire leader of Fianna Fáil, Charles Haughey, after he helped to restore centralised bargaining. The pragmatism of Fianna Fáil meant that it had less qualms about ceding areas of decision making that were supposed to reside in parliament to the social partners. Its own tradition of informal links with the union leaders made this all the easier to achieve.

For their part, the union leaders were always attracted to an offer of social partnership. In modern unions there is a bureaucracy that operates as a stratum which has different interests to those of the rank-and-file membership. Of its very nature, it is two-faced, balancing as it does between employers and workers. The bureaucracy is compelled to defend the basic sinews of union organisation, otherwise its own position would be undermined. On the other hand, it wants the stability that comes with respect for the norms of collective baragaining and regards strikes as disruptive. It fears that the privileges that come with office in terms of pay and job security might be swept away in a grass-roots-led militant movement. All of this means that the bureaucracy is always attracted to long-term arrangements with government and employers which promise social peace.

However, social partnership can no longer guarantee Fianna Fáil a base like it did in the past. For one thing, it has no particular copyright – Fine Gael and Labour Parties can adopt these structures once they are established. More importantly, these arrangements tend to be based on what one writer called a 'growth coalition'.[5] There is an assumption that the economy will expand, and so a 'positive sum' game applies where all gain something. However, this prospect of steady expansion is by no means what capitalism entails today. Periods of growth tend to be more short-lived and do not exhibit the levels of expansion that occurred in the 1960s. Recessions are more frequent, longer and more general throughout the Western economies. In this situation, the very centralised arrangements that have been forged to ensure social peace can politicise the bargaining process, raising questions not only about individual employers but also about governments themselves. Moreover, as union leaders adapt to an economy that has less to offer by encouraging even greater moderation, they face the prospect of rank-and-file revolts. Even where they are not facing a rank-and-file rebellion, union leaders can come under great pressure to call national action to resist programmes of cutbacks. All of this means that Fianna Fáil and Irish Governments generally enter a much more uncertain period than ever before.

A Mere Political Party – No Longer a National Movement

The Fianna Fáil organisation is already in decline. The party has not won an overall majority in parliament for over 15 years. At base, its roots are also starting to wither. At the 60th conference of the party in 1993, the general secretary claimed that it had 30,000 members.[6] This is a major decline on previous decades when the party claimed a membership of nearly 90,000.[7] However, even this smaller figure seems to contain some exaggeration, as membership figures are often inflated to give aspiring candidates for office additional voting strength at party conventions. A more serious indicator of the decline is the fall-off in the national collection. In the past, the party prided itself on its ability to raise funds from the 'plain people of Ireland' through its national church-gate collection. While the party raised £496,000 in 1983, it raised only £345,000 in 1991 despite the fact that inflation had increased by 47 per cent.[8]

Alongside this decline, the party is viewed by many as a supporter of big business after a series of scandals in recent years. The most prominent of these occurred in the beef industry, where Fianna Fáil gave grants and insurance cover, with unprecedented generosity, to the Goodman group of companies, even though these companies were later found to have engaged in tax evasion and fraud. Goodman was an active contributor to the party and seemed to have immediate and direct access to the Fianna Fáil leaders, Haughey and Reynolds.[9] Despite the party's stated concern for law and order, it inaugurated a number of tax amnesties which became an opportune occasion for laundering the proceeds of crime. It was also revealed that businessmen who bought property cheaply sought large returns on their investments by using Fianna Fáil connections to persuade the state to buy back sites from them. Most blatantly, while political refugees found it difficult to enter Ireland, one wealthy family had no difficulty gaining a passport after they invested in the firm of the Irish Taoiseach, Albert Reynolds.

Moreover, the party has difficulties responding to the changes that are occurring in Irish society. After helping to inflict big defeats on the liberal camp in the 1980s, it was left reeling by events that followed the infamous X case. Here the Fianna Fáil appointee to the office of Attorney General, Harry Whelehan, a former member of the Catholic Marriage Advisory Board, tried to prevent a 14-year-old rape victim going to Britain for an abortion. After the High Court attempted to ratify his decision, 14,000 people took to the streets of Dublin and forced the Supreme Court to overturn the decision and allow the girl to have an abortion. After this, the flood gates began to open as information on abortion, divorce and homosexuality became fully legal. In response to the changes, the party has tried to project a more liberal image, but this has only added to the tensions in its ranks as others hark back to the good old days of Catholic power.[10]

All of this means that the era when Fianna Fáil could claim – with some justification – to be a 'national movement' is over. At the root of its difficulty is the fact that catch-all politics that claim to stand above class divisions no longer have the same appeal. The myth that everyone has to pull together to promote national development is fading. The dominance of Fianna Fáil in the past was linked to the experience of economic backwardness. It grew on the promise that a particular form of national capitalism could deliver, and when this disappointed, it offered the comfort of a Catholic ethos. Fianna Fáil and the bishops were the lynchpins of conservatism in the South and now, as a new working-class generation emerges in the cities, they are often objects of contempt.

This, however, does not mean that Fianna Fáil is doomed to move to the sidelines. Far from it. The party can still function as a relatively standard right-wing party that seeks to make gains by playing on divisions between workers. It need only learn from the other models of right-wing politics on tax, law and order, and social welfare that have been pioneered elsewhere. There are already signs that it will move in this direction. The party's championship of law and order, for example, is almost always directed at inner-city youth, drug addicts and the poor – rather than, for example, at the building bosses whose sheer negligence of safety rules has led to thirteen deaths on sites in 1996 alone.[11] In the past, Fianna Fáil boasted how it extended social welfare and, in this sense, was a party of 'practical socialism'.[12] Today, its representatives often try to direct the frustrations of employed workers at social welfare recipients, rather than, say, at 'the spongers' of the beef industry who cost the country over £60 million in a European Union fine. The degree to which Fianna Fáil succeeds or fails in this approach is very much dependent on the alternatives that are on offer.

One alternative is the Labour Party, but this party has constantly thrown away opportunities to challenge Fianna Fáil. Its discomfort with being a minority party has never outweighed its fear of being labelled a radical force. There are ample indications that this pattern is being repeated in the 1990s. After it trebled its vote in 1992 with attacks on the 'golden circle' that linked Fianna Fáil to big business, it then proceeded to join the same party in coalition. When Labour withdrew from this particular coalition to join Fine Gael and the Democratic Left, little changed in society at large. It only indicated that virtually any combination of parties could form an Irish government. Whether or not Fianna Fáil was in government, the old policy that what was best for business was best for Ireland was pursued.

Even if Fianna Fáil can no longer restore the hegemony of the past, the cynicism created by Labour's betrayals can give it a boost in the future. In a sense, this simply repeats a pattern that is evident in countries as diverse as Spain, France and Australia, where right-wing parties grew out of the disillusionment created by Labour Parties among their supporters. But there is also a peculiar weakness associated with the Irish Labour Party evident in the fact that it has only ever managed to garner one-fifth of the popular vote. Despite the fact that social democratic parties often claim that a hundred votes is worth a thousand strikes, the irony of history is that most other Labour Parties owe their origins to a growth in consciousness that emerged from class struggle in decades gone by. As we have shown, the Irish Labour Party missed those opportunities in the past, and, as likely as not, will be on the other side of the fence in future workers' struggles.

As a result, the Labour Party will most probably remain a small social democratic party whose ambition rises no higher than to become a participant in future coalitions with right-wing parties.

Sometimes it will justify its choice of Fianna Fáil as partner by pointing to the party's populist record and its use of the state to expand Irish capitalism. At other times, it will claim that Fianna Fáil is built on a peculiar culture of secrecy and corruption, and so the more clean-cut Fine Gael is required as a partner. Yet revelations that a Fine Gael Minister was the recipient of large donations from the Dunnes empire, show that Fianna Fáil do not have a monopoly on this culture.

The other alternative that is available to Irish workers is the smaller tradition of radical republicanism. This, however, has a far more ambiguous relationship with Fianna Fáil than even the Labour Party. Although republicans have often suffered at the hands of Fianna Fáil governments, they remain impressed by its occasional anti-British rhetoric. Ever since the H Block crisis, republicans have worked on a strategy of constructing a pan-nationalist alliance that stretches from Irish America to the local Fianna Fáil branch. This has meant that they now disavow any intention of undermining the Southern state. Looking at Irish society exclusively from the point of view of political rhetoric used about the North, they tend to see Fianna Fáil as the more 'progressive' of the main parties. As they seek to make their peace with the system, it is likely that republicans will look to Fianna Fáil as their gatekeeper into the establishment.

What is needed in Ireland is a very different type of left-wing force which can oppose the conservative legacy that Fianna Fáil helped to create. Marxism has often been regarded as an irrelevant, alien and certainly un-Irish approach by the political establishment. They have been able to celebrate the fact that those who stood up for left-wing ideas in the past were often crushed by the sheer difficulty of the task or the dominance of the Catholic Church. However, today there is a new Ireland. The working class is stronger and more aware of itself than ever. The sheer contrast between the new wealth that has emerged in the South and the stark poverty in many working-class suburbs leads many to look for fundamental change. The challenge facing Marxists is to build a force that combines the militancy of workers with the type of socialist politics which can oppose the state that was fashioned by Fianna Fáil from the partition settlement. It is a challenge that can be met.

Notes

Introduction

1. M. Manning, *Irish Political Parties* (Dublin: Gill and Macmillan, 1972), p. 60.
2. O. Ianni, 'Political process and economic development in Brazil', *New Left Review*, No. 25 (1964), p. 57.
3. R. Hindley, *The Death of the Irish Language* (London: Routledge, 1990), pp. 34–5.
4. K. Boland, *Up Dev* (Dublin: Boland, 1978), p. 26.
5. J. Whyte, 'Ireland: politics without social bases', in R. Rose, *Electoral Behaviour: A Comparative Handbook* (New York: Free Press, 1974), pp. 619–52.
6. D. Walsh, *The Party: Inside Fianna Fáil* (Dublin: Gill and Macmillan, 1986), pp. 32, 42.
7. J.P. O'Carroll, 'Eamon de Valera, charisma and political development', in J.P. O'Carroll and J.A. Murphy (eds), *De Valera and His Times* (Cork: Cork University Press, 1983), p. 33.
8. J. Praeger, *Building Democracy in Ireland: Political Order and Cultural Integration in a Newly Independent Nation* (Cambridge: Cambridge University Press, 1986), p. 208.
9. Quoted in M. Hechter, *Internal Colonialism: The Celtic Fringe in British National Development 1536–1966* (London: Routledge and Kegan Paul, 1978), p. 127.
10. B. Chubb, 'Going about persecuting civil servants', *Political Studies*, Vol. 11, No. 3 (1963), pp. 513–640; id., *The Government and Politics of Ireland* (London: Longman, 1982), pp. 3–24.
11. T. Garvin, 'Political cleavages, party politics and urbanisation in Ireland: the case of a periphery dominated centre', *European Journal of Political Research*, Vol. 2 (1974), pp. 307–27.
12. M. Bax, *Harpstrings and Confessions* (Assen: Von Gorcum, 1976); P. Sacks, *The Donegal Mafia* (New Haven: Yale University Press, 1976).
13. P. Gibbon and M.D. Higgins, 'Patronage, tradition and modernisation: the case of the Irish gombeenman', *Economic and Social Review*, Vol. 6, No. 1 (1974), pp. 27–44.
14. L. Komito, 'Irish clientelism: a re-appraisal', *Economic and Social Review*, Vol. 15, No. 3 (1984), p. 180.
15. P. Bew and H. Patterson, *The Dynamics of Irish Politics* (London: Lawrence and Wishart, 1989); H. Patterson, 'Fianna Fáil and the working class: the origins of an enigmatic relationship', *Saothar*, No. 13 (1988), pp. 81–8; R. Dunphy, *The Making of Fianna Fáil*

Power in Ireland 1923–1948 (Oxford: Oxford University Press, 1995).

16. Dunphy, *The Making of Fianna Fáil*, p. 321.
17. M. Gallagher, *The Irish Labour Party in Transition, 1957–82* (Manchester: Manchester University Press, 1982) p. 262.
18. C. Kostick, *Revolution in Ireland: Popular Militancy 1917–1923* (London: Pluto Press, 1996), Ch. 2.
19. Gallagher, *Irish Labour Party*, p. 262.
20. See C. Harman, 'The return of the national question', *International Socialism*, Vol. 2, No. 59 (1992), pp. 3–63.
21. I. Roxborough, *Theories of Underdevelopment* (London: Macmillan, 1979), p. 110.
22. T.S. di Tella, 'Populism and reform in Latin America', in C. Veliz (ed.), *Obstacles to Change in Latin America* (Oxford: University Press, 1965), p. 47.
23. M. Weber, *Economy and Society*, Vol. 1 (New York: Bedminister Press, 1968), p. 216.
24. This description of populist movements is actually used by M.P. Troncoso and B.G. Burnett, 'Labour and politics: problems and Prospects', in J.D. Martz (ed.), *The Dynamics of Change in Latin American Politics* (Englewood Cliffs, NJ: Prentice Hall, 1965), pp. 252–3.
25. Ianni, 'Political process in Brazil' pp. 10–11.
26. T. Skidmore and P.H. Smith, *Modern Latin America* (Oxford: Oxford University Press, 1989), p. 56.
27. J. Petras, *Politics and Social Structure in Latin America* (New York: Monthly Review, 1970), p. 83.
28. N. Hardiman, *Pay, Politics and Economic Performance in Ireland 1970–1987* (Oxford: Clarendon Press, 1988).
29. W. Streeck, 'Organisational consequences of neo-corporatism in West German labour unions', in G. Lehmbruch and P. Schmitter (eds), *Patterns of Corporatist Policy Making* (London: Sage, 1982), p. 70.

1   Fianna Fáil: The Radical Years, 1926–1932

1. T. Ryle Dwyer, *De Valera: The Man and the Myth* (Dublin: Poolbeg, 1991) p. 139.
2. *An Phoblacht*, 30 May 1925.
3. *Sinn Féin*, 30 August 1924.
4. N. Manseragh (ed.), *Speeches and Statements by Eamon de Valera 1917–1973* (Dublin: Gill and Macmillan, 1980), p. 140.
5. *Irish Times*, 26 October 1927.
6. De Valera, *Speeches*, p. 140.
7. Fianna Fáil, *Coiriu Fianna Fáil* (Dublin: n.d.).
8. Fianna Fáil, *Founding Document and Constitution*, in Sean McEntee papers, P 67/90/1, UCD Archives.
9. Ibid.
10. De Valera speech to Fianna Fáil Ard Fheis, in de Valera Papers, File 366.

11. Fianna Fáil, *Founding Document.*
12. Fianna Fáil, *Coiriu.*
13. *Dáil Debates,* Vol. 21, Col. 818, 3 November 1927.
14. *Dáil Debates,* Vol. 22, Col. 1522, 21 March 1928.
15. Fianna Fáil, *Clar of the First Ard Fheis,* Resolution 42.
16. Ibid., Resolution 38.
17. Fianna Fáil, *Clar of the Second Ard Fheis,* Resolutions 5,19,6.
18. S. Cronin, *For Whom the Hangman's Rope was Spun: Wolfe Tone and the United Irishmen* (Dublin: Repsol, 1991), pp. 21–2.
19. J. Smyth, *The Men of No Property* (Dublin: Gill and Macmillan, 1991), pp. 140–1.
20. M. Elliot, *Partners in Revolution: The United Irishmen and France* (New Haven and London: Yale University Press, 1982), p. xvii.
21. F.S.L. Lyons, *Ireland Since the Famine* (London: Collins/Fontana, 1982), p. 257.
22. *The Harp,* June 1908.
23. P. Lynch, 'The social revolution that never was', in T. Desmond Williams, *The Irish Struggle 1916–1966* (London: Routledge and Kegan Paul, 1966), pp. 41–54.
24. C.D. Greaves, *Liam Mellows and the Irish Revolution* (London: Lawrence and Wishart, 1971), p. 364.
25. Ibid., pp. 364–5.
26. Ibid., p. 188.
27. De Valera to Ruttledge (n.d.); quoted in Ryle Dwyer, *De Valera,* p. 134.
28. Ibid.
29. Quoted in R. Fanning, *Independent Ireland* (Dublin: Helicon, 1983), p. 96.
30. Quoted in J. Praeger, *Building Democracy in Ireland* (Cambridge: Cambridge University Press, 1986), p. 88.
31. See M. Moore, *British Plunder and Irish Blunder* (Dublin: Gaelic Press, n.d.); A. Mitchell and P.O. Snodaigh, *Irish Political Documents 1916–1949* (Dublin: Irish Academy Press, 1985), pp. 173–4.
32. Moore, *British Plunder,* p. 6.
33. *Dáil Debates,* Vol. 25, Col. 478, 12 July 1928.
34. K.A. Kennedy, T. Giblin and D. McHugh, *The Economic Development of Ireland in the 20th Century* (London: Routledge, 1988), p. 38.
35. Department of Industry and Commerce, *Trade and Shipping Statistics 1926,* Vol. 111, No. 4, p. vi.
36. Ibid.
37. R. Dunphy, *The Making of Fianna Fáil Power in Ireland 1923–1948* (Oxford: Oxford University Press, 1995), p. 28.
38. D. Johnson, *The Inter-War Economy in Ireland* (Dublin: Economic and Social History Society, 1985), p. 28.
39. C. McCormack, 'Policy making in a small open economy: some aspects of the Irish experience', *Central Bank Quarterly,* Winter 1979.
40. K. Daniel, 'Griffith on his noble head: the determinants of Cumman na nGaedheal economic policy 1922–1932', *Irish Economic and Social History,* Vol. 3 (1976), pp. 58–9.

41. *Dáil Debates*, Vol. 31, Col. 397, 26 October 1927.
42. *The Nation*, 16 April 1927.
43. *The Nation*, 27 August 1927.
44. *The Nation*, 5 October 1929.
45. Sean McEntee papers, P 67/350/10, UCD Archives.
46. *The Nation*, 30 April 1927.
47. *Irish Times*, 2 February 1931.
48. *The Nation*, 30 April 1927.
49. *Dáil Debates*, Vol. 22, Col. 1417, 20 March 1928.
50. Fianna Fáil, *North Dublin Election Leaflet 1928*, O'Brien Collection, National Library of Ireland.
51. *Dáil Debates*, Vol. 25, Col. 476, 12 July 1928.
52. *Dáil Debates*, Vol. 25, Col. 498, 13 July 1928.
53. Sean McEntee papers, P 67/344 (2), UCD Archives.
54. Minutes of Standing Committee of Fianna Fáil, 16 April 1928.
55. *Dáil Debates*, Vol. 30, Col. 2067, 28 June 1929.
56. *Dáil Debates*, Vol. 30, Col. 2066, 28 June 1929.
57. *Clare Champion*, 26 December 1931.
58. *Dáil Debates*, Vol. 22, Col. 1651, 22 March 1928.
59. Minutes of Standing Committee of Fianna Fáil, 30 October 1928.
60. *Irish Independent*, 5 October 1931.
61. *Irish Independent*, 5 January 1931.
62. *The Nation*, 31 January 1931.
63. Ibid.
64. *Dáil Debates*, Vol. 41, Col. 913, 29 April 1932.
65. *Irish Independent*, 24 October 1931.
66. Sean McEntee papers, P 67/346.
67. *The Nation*, 9 July 1929.
68. *Dáil Debates*, Vol. 41, Col. 907, 29 April 1932.
69. *The Nation*, 2 April 1927.
70. *The Nation*, 3 August 1929.
71. *Dáil Debates*, Vol. 21, Cols 718–9, 3 November 1927.
72. *The Nation*, 24 August 1929.
73. Minutes of Standing Committee of Fianna Fáil, 26 June 1931.
74. *The Nation*, 28 January 1928.
75. *The Nation*, 14 January 1928.
76. A. Gramsci, 'Soviets in Italy', *New Left Review*, Vol. 51, pp. 35–7.
77. Department of Industry and Commerce, *Statistical Abstract* (1932), p. 162.
78. Department of Industry and Commerce, *Census of Industrial Production* (1931), p. xvii.
79. Discussion document of Erskine Childers Fianna Fáil Cumman (n.d.), McGilligan papers, P 35c/165, UCD Archives.
80. K. Allen, *The Politics of James Connolly* (London: Pluto Press, 1990), pp. 163–9.
81. E. O'Connor, *Syndicalism in Ireland* (Cork: Cork University Press, 1988), p. 109.
82. C. McCarthy, *Trade Unions in Ireland 1894–1960* (Dublin: IPA, 1977), p. 96.

83. Johnson to ITUC Executive, 5 July 1925, Tom Johnson collection National Library of Ireland, Ms 17230.
84. Ibid.
85. Ibid.
86. Gramsci, 'Soviets in Italy', p. 39.
87. Johnson memo, 13 March 1926, ITUC files, National Archives.
88. Labour Party Manifesto to Electors of North Dublin June 1927, O'Brien Collection, National Library of Ireland.
89. *The Irishman*, 19 November 1927.
90. *The Irishman*, 19 January 1927.
91. Ibid.
92. *The Irishman*, 23 November 1929.
93. *The Watchword*, 21 November 1928.
94. Labour Party, *First Annual Report* (1931), p. 53.
95. Moore to Johnson, 12 December 1925, Johnson papers, National Library, Ms 17242.
96. *The Irishman*, 25 August 1928.
97. *The Irishman*, 8 August 1928.
98. A. Gaughan, *Tom Johnson* (Dublin: Kingdom, 1980), p. 327.
99. *Dáil Debates*, Vol. 21, Col. 699, 2 November 1927.
100. *Dáil Debates*, Vol. 34, Col. 318, 2 April 1930.
101. T. Cliff, *Deflected Permanent Revolution* (London: Bookmarks, 1990).
102. *Dáil Debates*, Vol. 21, Col. 694, 2 November 1927.
103. *The Nation*, 12 April 1930.
104. *Irish Independent*, 16 September 1929.
105. *The Nation*, 18 April 1931.

2   The Triumph of Fianna Fáil, 1932–1939

1. McEntee papers, UCD Archives, P 67/350/7.
2. Oscar Traynor election leaflet 1932 and Fianna Fáil North Dublin leaflet, in William O'Brien Collection, National Library of Ireland.
3. Secretary of Cork Flour Millers section ITGWU to ITUC, 27 May 1928, ITUC files, National Archives.
4. Secretary of Cork Flour Millers section ITGWU to ITUC (n.d.), ITUC files, National Archives.
5. Ibid.
6. *The Watchword*, 5 February 1932.
7. R. Fanning, 'The rule of order: Eamon de Valera and the IRA 1923–1940', in J.P. Carroll and J.A. Murphy (eds), *De Valera and his Times* (Cork: Cork University Press, 1983), p. 163.
8. D. Johnson, *The Inter-War Economy in Ireland* (Dublin: Economic and Social History Society, 1984) p. 28.
9. L. Longford and T.P. O'Neill, *Eamon de Valera* (London: Hutchinson, 1970), p. 282.
10. *Dáil Debates*, Vol. 42, Col. 1525, 16 June 1932 and Vol. 44, Col. 1618, 15 November 1932.
11. D. Nevin, 'Labour and political revolution', in F. McManus (ed.), *The Year of the Great Test* (Cork: Mercier Press, 1967), p. 61.

12. *Dáil Debates*, Vol. 41, Col. 1931, 18 may 1932.
13. *Dáil Debates*, Vol. 41, Col. 738, 28 April 1932.
14. *Dáil Debates*, Vol. 42, Col. 1434, 15 June 1932.
15. Ibid.
16. ITUC, *Annual Report and Conference Proceedings* (1932), p. 25.
17. *Irish Press*, 13 May 1932.
18. Sean O'Faoilean, quoted in R. English, *Radicals and the Republic* (Oxford: Clarendon Press, 1994), p. 167.
19. *Dáil Debates*, Vol. 42, Col. 262, 1 June 1932.
20. M. Daly, 'An Irish Ireland for business', *Irish Historical Studies*, Vol. 24, (1984), pp. 266–72.
21. *Dáil Debates*, Vol. 42, Col. 1252, 14 June 1932.
22. Department of Industry and Commerce, *Census of Industrial Production 1932–1935* (Dublin: Stationery Office, 1937), pp. 2–3.
23. Department of Industry and Commerce, *Census of Industrial Production 1936* (Dublin: Stationery Office, 1938), p. x.
24. Ibid., p. xxii.
25. Ibid.
26. Department of Industry and Commerce, *Statistical Abstract* (1939).
27. J.A. Murphy, *Ireland in the Twentieth Century* (Cork: Mercier, 1981), p. 86.
28. R. Dunphy, *The Making of Fianna Fáil Power in Ireland 1923–48* (Oxford: Oxford University Press, 1995), p. 170.
29. F. Munger, *The Legitimacy of Opposition* (London: Sage, 1975).
30. Minutes of Fianna Fáil Parliamentary Party Meeting, 7 July 1932.
31. Ibid., 14 July 1932.
32. Ibid., 11 May 1933.
33. Moss Twomey papers, UCD Archives, P 67/52.
34. Minutes of Fianna Fáil parliamentary party meeting, 10 January 1934.
35. Ibid., 11 April 1935.
36. Ibid., 22 June 1933.
37. J. Lee, *Ireland 1912–1985* (Cambridge, Cambridge University Press, 1989), p. 161.
38. J.H. Whyte, *Church and State in Modern Ireland 1923–1979* (Dublin: Gill and Macmillan, 1980), pp. 45–6.
39. Ibid., p. 48.
40. Ibid.
41. McQuaid to de Valera, 19 November 1934, in de Valera papers, file 1440.
42. McQuaid to de Valera, 9 November 1934, in de Valera papers, file 1440/2.
43. McQuaid to de Valera, 26 November 1934, in de Valera papers, file 1440/3.
44. De Valera to papal nuncio, 9 July 1933, in de Valera papers, file 1280/11.
45. Dunphy, *The Making of Fianna Fáil*, p. 134.
46. McQuaid to de Valera, 17 March 1943, in de Valera papers, file 1280/1.
47. ITGWU, *Annual Report and Conference Proceedings* (1933), p. 19.

48. ITUC, *Annual Report and Conference Proceedings* (1933), p. 109.

49. *Fianna Fáil Bulletin*, May 1936.

50. *Dáil Debates*, Vol. 56, Cols 1264 and 1275, 17 May 1935.

51. ITUC, *Annual Report and Conference Proceedings* (1933), p. 115 and ITUC, *Annual Report and Conference Proceedings* (1934), pp. 159–60.

52. *Dáil Debates*, Vol. 48, Col. 917, 21 June 1933.

53. *Dáil Debates*, Vol. 48, Cols 951–2, 21 June 1933.

54. ITGWU, *Annual Report and Conference Proceedings* (1934), pp. 159–60.

55. *Irish Times*, 30 March 1935.

56. ITGWU, *Annual Report and Conference Proceedings* (1936), p. 7.

57. *Irish Press*, 8 March 1934.

58. *Republican Congress*, 5 May 1934.

59. English, *Radicals and the Republic*, p. 208.

60. *Republican Congress*, 13 October 1934.

61. Ibid.

62. A. Orridge, 'The Blueshirts and the Economic War', *Political Studies*, Vol. 31, No. 3 (1983), pp. 351–69.

63. M. Manning, *The Blueshirts* (Dublin: Gill and Macmillan, 1987), p. 44.

64. Dunphy, *The Making of Fianna Fáil*, p. 195.

65. Manning, *The Blueshirts*, p. 57.

66. *Irish Times*, 11 August 1933.

67. Manning, *The Blueshirts*, Ch. 14.

68. J. Lee, *Ireland 1912–1985* (Cambridge: Cambridge University Press, 1989), pp. 181–4.

69. *Dáil Debates*, Vol. 50, Col. 2237, 28 February 1934.

70. ITUC, *Annual Report and Conference Proceedings* (1934), p. 39.

71. Ibid., p. 27.

72. Manning, *The Blueshirts*, p. 74.

73. S. Cronin, *The McGarrity papers* (Tralee: Anvil, 1972), p. 157.

74. Labour Party, *Annual Report* (1933), p. 63.

75. Ibid., p. 66.

76. Ibid., p. 61.

77. *Republican Congress*, November 1934.

78. M. Milotte, *Communism in Modern Ireland* (Dublin: Gill and Macmillan, 1984) p. 117.

79. *Irish Press*, 1 February 1932.

80. Labour Party, *Annual Report* (1931), pp. 60–1.

81. Labour Party, *Annual Report* (1933), p. 65 and *Annual Report* (1943), p. 118.

82. Milotte, *Communism*, p. 170.

83. De Valera, *Speeches and Statements of Eamon de Valera*, ed. M. Manseragh, (Dublin: Gill and Macmillan, 1980), p. 288.

84. ITUC, *Annual Report and Conference Procedings* (1936), p. 27.

85. Labour Party, *Annual Report* (1937) p. 113.

86. Labour Party, *Annual Report* (1938) p. 193.

87. *Dáil Debates*, Vol. 56, Col. 2150, 4 June 1935.

88. Milotte, *Communism*, p. 170.

89. *Connaught Sentinel*, 6 October 1936.

90. ITUC Reply to National Joint Labour Committee for Spanish Relief, 7 March 1938, ITUC files, National Archives.
91. E. O'Connor, *A Labour History of Waterford* (Waterford: Waterford Trades Council, 1989), p. 241.
92. ITGWU, *Annual Report and Conference Proceedings* (1935), p. 30.
93. ITUC, *Annual Report and Conference Proceedings* (1935), p. 145.
94. Ibid.
95. Irish Women Workers Union, *The Right to Work but not for Women*, William O'Brien collection, National Library of Ireland.
96. Ibid.
97. ITGWU, *Three Men and Three Days* (Dublin: ITGWU, 1934).
98. *Cork Examiner*, 19 March 1934.
99. File 91, ITUC files, National Archives.
100. C. McCarthy, *Trade Unions in Ireland 1894–1960* (Dublin: IPA, 1977), p. 133.
101. Minutes of the Special Conference of Enquiry into Trade Union Organisation, 5 February 1937, file 91, ITUC files, National Archives.

3 Tying the Knot: Fianna Fáil and Irish Labour, 1939–1945

1. F.S.L. Lyons, *Ireland Since the Famine* (London: Collins/Fontana, 1982), p. 557.
2. See R. Fisk, *In Time of War* (London: Deutsch, 1983); J.T. Carroll, *Ireland in the War Years* (Newton Abbot: David and Chambers, 1975); B. Share, *The Emergency: Neutral Ireland 1939–45* (Dublin: Gill and Macmillan, 1978).
3. Fisk, *In Time of War*, p. 145.
4. T.P. Coogan, *Ireland Since the Rising* (London: Pall Mall Press, 1966), p. 88.
5. Ibid.
6. T. Brown, *Ireland: A Social and Cultural History 1922–1985* (London: Fontana, 1985), pp. 215–16.
7. Quoted in J. Swift, 'Report on the Commission on Vocational Organisation', *Saothar*, No. 1 (1975).
8. Share, *The Emergency*, p. 18.
9. McQuaid to de Valera, 8 May 1943, in de Valera papers, file 1400/5.
10. Minutes of Fianna Fáil parliamentary party meeting, 19 October 1944.
11. Carroll, *Ireland in the War Years*, p. 86.
12. S.T. O'Kelly, 'Budget speech', 8 November 1939, file 7128, ITUC collection, National Archives.
13. *Dáil Debates*, Vol. 83, Col. 365, 14 May 1941.
14. ITGWU, *Fifty Years of Liberty Hall* (Dublin: ITGWU, 1959), p. 89.
15. *The Torch*, November 1939 to February 1940.

16. Congress of Irish Unions, *Annual Report and Conference Proceedings* (1945), p. 54.
17. *Cork Examiner*, 20 February 1940.
18. Ibid.
19. *Dáil Debates*, Vol. 78, Col. 947, 5 December 1939.
20. Federation of Irish Manufacturers, *Report for Seventh Annual General Meeting* (1941), National Archives.
21. Ibid., pp. 4–5.
22. *Commission on Vocational Organisation*, Evidence No. 16, 18 June 1940, p. 2.
23. Ibid.
24. Office of Public Works document on labour camps, S10 927, National Archives.
25. Ibid.
26. Ibid.
27. Ibid.
28. *The Torch*, 4 May 1940.
29. Office of Public Works document on labour camps, S10 927, National Archives.
30. *The Torch*, 30 November 1940.
31. National Executive ITUC minutes, 31 May 1940.
32. Minutes of interview with de Valera, 29 August 1940, ITUC file 6100, National Archives.
33. ITUC circular, 10 October 1940, ITUC files, National Archives.
34. Dublin Constituency Council of Labour Party circular (n.d.), ITUC files, National Archives.
35. *Cork Echo*, 15 May 1941.
36. Eamon de Valera to ITUC, 14 May 1941, ITUC file 6100, National Archives.
37. Share, *The Emergency*, pp. 91–2.
38. Ibid., p. 92.
39. Cabinet minutes, 26 January 1940, National Archives.
40. State Papers Office, file S11 616A, National Archives.
41. S. Redmond, *The Irish Municipal Employees Trade Union* (Dublin: IMETU, 1983), p. 104.
42. Cabinet minutes, 8 March 1940, National Archives.
43. McEntee to Secretary, Department of Industry and Commerce, 17 March 1940, McEntee papers, P 67/229, UCD Archives.
44. Ibid.
45. Ibid.
46. Ibid.
47. State Papers Office, file S11 750, National Archives.
48. Lemass to McEntee, 23 May 1940, in SPO file S11 750, National Archives.
49. ITGWU *Conference Proceedings* (1940), p. 24.
50. M. Merrigan, *Eagle or Cuckoo?* (Dublin: Matmer Publications, 1989), p. 100.
51. Labour Party, *Annual Report* (1942), p. 186.
52. ITUC, *Annual Report and Conference Proceedings* (1942), p. 157.
53. ITGWU, *Conference Proceedings* (1940), p. 20.

54. Ibid., p. 21.
55. *The Torch*, 2 September 1939.
56. Labour Party, *Conference Proceedings* (1941), p. 109.
57. Minutes of National Executive of ITUC, 28 August 1942.
58. Minutes of National Executive of ITUC, 25 September 1942.
59. Memo, Department of Industry and Commerce, 22 August 1940, Department of Labour files, TIW 766, National Archives.
60. Meeting of Secretary of Department of Industry and Commerce with William O'Brien, 23 September 1940, Department of Labour file TIW 766, National Archives.
61. Ibid.
62. Ibid.
63. Memo, Department of Industry and Commerce, 28 April 1941, SPO file S11 750, National Archives.
64. For full details of the Trade Union Act 1941 see B. Shillman, *Trade Unionism and Trade Disputes in Ireland* (Dublin: Dublin Press, 1960), pp. 58–9.
65. *Senate Report*, Vol. 25, Col. 2279, 7 August 1941.
66. *Dáil Debates*, Vol. 83, Col. 1631, 5 June 1941.
67. Memo, Department of Industry and Commerce, 30 January 1941, SPO file S11 750, National Archives.
68. Memo, Department of Industry and Commerce, 20 July 1940, SPO file, S11 750, National Archives.
69. Minutes of National Executive of ITUC, 16 May 1941.
70. *Dáil Debates*, Vol. 84, Cols 553–4, 1 July 1941.
71. Police report on demonstration against Trade Union Bill, 22 June 1941, Department of Labour file TIW 766, National Archives.
72. ITGWU, *Annual Report and Conference Proceedings* (1941), p. 32.
73. Minutes, National Executive of ITUC, 16 May 1941.
74. Council of Irish Unions circular, Desmond papers, P 56/330, UCD Archives.
75. Report on Special Delegate Conference of ITUC on Trade Union Act, P. 29 in Desmond papers, UCD Archives.
76. ITUC *Annual Report and Conference Proceedings* (1942), p. 121.
77. ITGWU, *Conference Proceedings* (1942), p. 29.
78. Minutes of meeting between Department of Industry and Commerce and ITUC, 11 March 1942, ITUC file 3411, National Archives.
79. ITUC, *Annual Report and Conference Proceedings* (1948), p. 32.
80. SPO, file S13 029, National Archives.
81. T.D. Williams 'Ireland and the war', in K.B. Nowlan and T.D. Williams (eds), *Ireland and the War Years and After* (Dublin: Gill and Macmillan, 1969), p. 21.
82. SPO, file S13 029, National Archives.
83. Labour Party, *Annual Report* (1942) and *Annual Report* (1943).
84. *The Torch*, 2 August 1942.
85. Dublin Township Constituency, Fianna Fáil leaflet (1943), McEntee papers, P 67/362, UCD Archives.
86. McEntee speech, 4 June 1943, McEntee papers, P 67/364, UCD Archives.

87. Letter from Lemass to McEntee (n.d), in McEntee papers, P 67/363, UCD Archives.
88. McEntee to de Valera, 28 June 1943, McEntee papers, P 67/366, UCD Archives.
89. Ibid.
90. M. Milotte, *Communism in Modern Ireland* (Dublin: Gill and Macmillan, 1984), p. 197.
91. ITGWU reply to Labour Party, attempting to explain why the ITGWU disaffiliated, Tom Johnson papers, Ms. 17197, National Library of Ireland.
92. Milotte, *Communism in Ireland*, p. 198.
93. McCrory to de Valera, 29 September 1942, de Valera papers, file 1280/4.
94. McEntee papers, P 67/535, UCD Archives.
95. Ibid.
96. J.P. Patterson to W. O'Brien, 12 February 1944, O'Brien papers, Ms. 13960, National Library of Ireland.
97. P.J. O'Brien to W. O'Brien, 21 February 1941, O'Brien papers, Ms. 13960, National Library of Ireland.
98. Report of Commission into Communism in the Labour Party in Tom Johnson papers, Ms. 17267, National Library of Ireland.
99. A. Gaughan, *Tom Johnson* (Dublin: Kingdom, 1980), p. 379.
100. O'Rahilly to O'Brien, 14 February 1944, O'Brien papers, Ms. 13960, National Library of Ireland.
101. Report on Commission on Vocational Organisation, para. 583.
102. Labour Party, *Annual Report* (1941), pp. 106–7.
103. ITUC, *Annual Report and Conference Proceedings* (1942), p. 157.
104. Congress of Irish Unions, *Special Conference Proceedings* (1945), p. 4.
105. Ibid., p. 10.
106. Ibid., p. 17.
107. Ibid.
108. Minister for Industry and Commerce Instructions to all Departments, 23 May 1945, Department of Labour files, W 63, National Archives.

4 Fianna Fáil's Failure, 1945–1958

1. J. Lee, *Ireland 1912–1985: Politics and Society* (Cambridge: Cambridge University Press, 1989), p. 226.
2. Aiken to de Valera, 24 February 1942, SPO file S131018, National Archives.
3. S. Lemass, memo on Labour Policy, June 1942, SPO file S12882A, National Archives.
4. Ibid.
5. Memo on Full Employment Policy from Minister for Industry and Commerce, McEntee papers, P 67/264 (4), UCD Archives.
6. Ibid.
7. ITGWU, *Annual Report and Conference Proceedings* (1945), p. 5.
8. R. Roberts, 'Trade union organisation in Ireland', *Journal of Social Inquiry Society of Ireland*, Vol. 20 (1959), p. 95.
9. ITGWU, *Annual Report and Conference Proceedings* (1946), p. 38.

10. Lemass to FUE and ITUC, 19 December 1945, Department of Labour file IR 19, National Archives.
11. Memo from Department of Local Government, 18 April 1946, Department of Labour file 9, National Archives.
12. ITUC, *Annual Report and Conference Proceedings* (1947) p. 78.
13. *Irish Press*, 21 March 1946.
14. T. Derrig to INTO, 8 May 1946, ITUC file 4211, National Archives.
15. D. Bradley, *Farm Labourers: Irish Struggle 1900–1976* (Belfast: Athol Books, 1988), p. 82.
16. Ibid., p. 83.
17. Ibid., p. 85.
18. ITGWU, *Annual Report and Conference Proceedings* (1948), p. 14.
19. Memo, McMullen to CIU Central Council, 19 May 1947, CIU files, National Archives.
20. Cabinet minutes, 16 May 1947, file 4/258, National Archives; SPO, file S11 750B National Archives.
21. Minutes of meeting between de Valera and CIU, 20 May 1947, SPO file S11 750 B , National Archives.
22. *Irish Press*, 15 February 1946.
23. Ibid.
24. Minutes of CIU Central Council Special Meeting, 18 July 1947.
25. Irish Railwaymen's Union to CIU, 18 September 1947, CIU files, National Archives.
26. Cork Council of Trade Unions to CIU 18 September CIU files, National Archives.
27. *Irish Times*, 10 September 1947.
28. *Irish Press*, 15 September 1947.
29. Ibid.
30. *Irish Press*, 29 October 1947.
31. *Irish Press*, 13 October 1947.
32. Ibid.
33. *Irish Press*, 13 October 1947.
34. Minutes of Special Conference of CIU, 17 October 1947, p. 11, CIU files, National Archives.
35. Draft Heads of Industrial Emergency Bill 1947, Department of Labour file IR 33, National Archives.
36. CIU Statement on Re-establishment of Comintern in Europe, CIU files, National Archives.
37. CIU press statement, 21 January 1948, CIU Files, National Archives.
38. Lee, *Ireland,* p. 283.
39. CIU, *Annual Report and Conference Proceedings* (1950), p. 37.
40. Labour Party, *Labour's Constructive Programme* (Dublin: Labour Party, 1952).
41. N. Browne, *Against the Tide* (Dublin: Gill and Macmillan, 1986), p. 191.
42. Revd E.J. Hegarty, 'The principle against state welfare schemes, *Christus Rex*, Vol. 4, No. 4 (1950), p. 315.
43. CIU, *Annual Report and Conference Proceedings* (1951), pp. 37–8.

44. Ibid., p. 126.
45. Ibid., pp. 126–7.
46. ITUC, *Annual Report* (1951), p. 37.
47. ITUC, *Annual Report and Conference Proceedings* (1951), pp. 76–7.
48. Labour Party, *Annual Report* (1951–52), p. 15.
49. Browne, *Against the Tide*, p. 190.
50. CIU, *Annual Report and Conference Proceedings* (1949), p. 91.
51. ITGWU, *Annual Report and Conference Proceedings* (1950), p. 15.
52. ITUC to British TUC, 6 July 1945, CIU file 38, National Archives.
53. See ITUC, *Annual Report and Conference Proceedings* (1949).
54. ITUC, *Annual Report and Conference Proceedings* (1950), pp. 100–4; minutes of Central Council of CIU 29, December 1950.
55. See R. Roberts, 'Trade union organisation in Ireland', *Journal of Statistical and Social Inquiry Society of Ireland*, Vol. 20, No. 2 (1959), pp. 95; and B. Hillery and A. Kelly, 'Aspects of trade union membership', *Management*, Vol. 21 (4 April 1974).
56. Minutes of the Central Council of CIU, 25 August 1950.
57. Minutes of the Central Council of CIU, 26 October 1951.
58. A. O'Rahilly, 'Trade union leadership today', *Christus Rex*, Vol. 3, No. 1 (1949), p. 67.
59. F.S.L. Lyons, *Ireland Since the Famine* (London: Fontana, 1982), p. 624.
60. *Dáil Debates*, Vol. 133, Cols 1830–1, 24 July 1952.
61. *Dáil Debates*, Vol. 126, Col. 53, 13 June 1951.
62. ITUC Statement on the Budget, *Trade Union Information*, Vol. 6 (1952), pp. 32–3.
63. P. Bew, E. Hazelhorn, and H. Patterson, *The Dynamics of Irish Politics* (London: Lawrence and Wishart, 1989), p. 83.
64. ITGWU, *Annual Report and Conference Proceedings* (1952), p. 49.
65. *Dáil Debates*, Vol. 127, Col. 402, 7 November 1951.
66. *Dáil Debates*, Vol. 134, Col. 855, 31 October 1952.
67. *Dáil Debates*, Vol. 134, Col. 861, 31 October 1952.
68. CIU, *Annual Report and Conference Proceedings* (1953), p. 97.
69. *Irish Times*, 7 March 1953.
70. *Irish Times*, 10 April 1953.

5 State Intervention, Social Partnership, and Rank-and-File Militancy, 1958–1965

1. Whitaker memo to Minister for Finance; repr. in *Economic Development* (Dublin: Stationery Office, 1958), p. 227.
2. *Economic Development*, p. 2.
3. P. Bew and H. Patterson, *Sean Lemass* (Dublin: Gill and Macmillan, 1982).
4. R. Breen, D.F. Hannan, D. Rottman, and C. Whelan, *Understanding Contemporary Ireland* (Dublin: Gill and Macmillan, 1990), p. 39.
5. See G. Adams, *The Politics of Irish Freedom* (Dingle: Brandon, 1986) and R. Crotty, *Ireland in Crisis: A study in Capitalist Colonial Undevelopment* (Dingle: Brandon, 1986).

6. P. Lynch, 'The economics of independence: some unsettled questions of Irish economics', in B. Chubb and P. Lynch (eds), *Economic Development and Planning* (Dublin: IPA, 1969), p. 143.

7. *Dáil Debates*, Vol. 199, Col. 1002, 5 February 1963.

8. E. O'Malley, *Industry and Economic Development* (Dublin: Gill and Macmillan, 1990), p. 79.

9. R. Fanning, *The Irish Department of Finance 1922–1958* (Dublin: IPA, 1978), p. 514.

10. *Irish Press*, 18 January 1957.

11. National Economic and Social Council, *A Review of Industrial Policy (Telesis Report)* (Dublin: NESC, 1982), pp. 187–8.

12. O'Malley, *Industry and Economic Development*, p. 104.

13. For a more extensive discussion see K. Allen, *Is Southern Ireland a Neo-Colony?* (Dublin: Bookmarks, 1990), pp. 21–4.

14. *Irish Press*, 11 November 1959.

15. *Irish Press*, 9 November 1960.

16. ICTU, *Annual Report and Conference Proceedings* (1961), p. 211; and *Liberty*, April 1960.

17. *Trade Union Information*, August 1962.

18. ITGWU, *Annual Report and Conference Proceedings* (1962), p. 95.

19. ICTU statement in *Trade Union Information*, August 1962.

20. *Cork Examiner*, 6 February 1959.

21. *Liberty*, July 1961.

22. ICTU Executive Committee minutes, 15 July 1960.

23. ICTU, *Annual Report and Conference Proceedings* (1961), p. 266.

24. *Irish Press*, 9 November 1960.

25. F. Tobin, *The Best of Decades* (Dublin: Gill and Macmillan, 1984), pp. 72–3.

26. *Liberty*, February and March 1962.

27. Tobin, *Best of Decades*, p. 60.

28. *Irish Press*, 23 August 1961.

29. *Irish Press*, 24 August 1961.

30. Ibid.

31. *Dáil Debates*, Vol. 191, Col. 2870, 1 September 1961.

32. *Dáil Debates*, Vol. 191, Col. 2889, 1 September 1961.

33. *Irish Press*, 3 May 1962.

34. Ibid.

35. L. Panitch, 'Trade unions and the state', *New Left Review*, No. 125 (1981), p. 24.

36. J. Lee, 'Workers and society since 1945', in D. Nevin, *Trade Unions and Change in Irish Society* (Cork: Mercier, 1980), p. 20.

37. Bew and Patterson, *Sean Lemass*, p. 187.

38. Ibid., p. 164.

39. G. Fitzgerald, *Planning in Ireland* (Dublin: IPA. 1968), pp. 38–9.

40. J. O'Connor, *The Fiscal Crisis of the State* (New York: St Martin's Press, 1973), Chs 4 and 5.

41. ICTU, *Annual Report and Conference Proceedings* (1965), p. 263.

42. Ibid.

43. *Dáil Debates*, Vol. 202, Col. 305, 24 April 1963.

44. Ibid.

45. ITGWU, *Annual Report and Conference Proceedings* (1963), p. 122.
46. Ibid., pp. 119–20.
47. *Liberty*, May 1964.
48. Tobin, *The Best of Decades*, p. 77.
49. Quoted in C. McCarthy, *Decade of Upheaval* (Dublin: IPA, 1973), p. 62.
50. ITGWU, *Annual Report and Conference Proceedings* (1963), p. 91.
51. Ibid., p. 99.
52. ICTU, *Annual Report and Conference Proceedings* (1964), pp. 364–5.
53. *Irish Press*, 31 August 1964.
54. B. Farrell, *Chairman or Chief* (Dublin: Gill and Macmillan, 1971), p. 66.

6   *The Fire Last Time, 1965–1973*

1. J. Wickham, 'The politics of dependent capitalism', in A. Morgan and B. Purdie (eds), *Ireland: Divided Nation, Divided Class* (London: Inklinks, 1980), pp. 53–74.
2. E. Hazelhorn, 'Class, clientelism and political process in the Republic of Ireland', in P. Clancy, S. Drudy, K. Lynch and L. O'Dowd, *Ireland: A Sociological Profile* (Dublin: IPA, 1986), pp. 326–44.
3. E. O'Connor, *A Labour History of Waterford* (Waterford: Waterford Trades Council, 1989), p. 313.
4. Central Statistics Office, *National Income and Expenditure* (Dublin: Stationery Office, various years).
5. J. Rafferty, 'Patterns of taxation and public expenditure: towards a corporatist approach', in M. Kelly (ed.), *Power, Conflict and Inequality* (Dublin: Turoe, 1982), p. 133.
6. F. Kennedy, *Public Social Expenditure in Ireland* (Dublin: ESRI Broadsheet No. 11, 1975), p. 37.
7. W.K. Roche and J. Larragy, 'The trend of unionisation in the Republic of Ireland', in Department of Industrial Relations, UCD (eds), *Industrial Relations in Ireland* (Dublin: UCD, 1987), p. 22.
8. A. Kelly and T. Brannick, 'Strikes in Ireland: measurement, incidence and trends', in Department of Industrial Relations *Industrial Relations*, p. 157.
9. L. German, *A Question of Class* (London: Bookmarks, 1996), p. 19.
10. P. Ginsborg, *A History of Contemporary Italy: Society and Politics 1943–1988* (Harmondsworth: Penguin, 1990), pp. 315–16.
11. *Irish Press*, 30 January 1969.
12. Script of speech by Sean Lemass to Dublin Fianna Fáil, 1 March 1966, in ICTU files, National Archives.
13. Labour Court, *Nineteenth Annual Report* (1965), p. 3.
14. *Irish Press*, 29 October 1965.
15. *Irish Press*, 5 November 1965.
16. *Irish Press*, 4 April 1966.
17. *Liberty*, April 1966.
18. *Liberty*, January 1967.
19. *Irish Press*, 29 March 1968.

20. *Clare Champion*, 13 April 1968.
21. Script of P. Hillery's speech at Fianna Fáil function at Ballinsloe, 29 April 1968, in Department of Labour files.
22. *Dáil Debates*, Vol. 233, Col. 1054, 26 March 1968.
23. *Dáil Debates*, Vol. 235, Col. 732, 6 June 1968.
24. *Dáil Debates*, Vol. 253, Col. 1943, 19 May 1971.
25. *Dáil Debates*, Vol. 223, Col. 93, 7 June 1966.
26. *Dáil Debates*, Vol. 223, Col. 235, 8 June 1966.
27. C. McCarthy, *Decade of Upheaval* (Dublin: Gill and Macmillan, 1984), p. 115.
28. *Irish Press*, 1 April 1968.
29. Proposal for amendment of the Industrial Relations Acts and Trade Union Act (49-Point Memorandum), in ICTU file 2103, National Archives; and also in ICTU, *Annual Report and Conference Proceedings* (1966), pp. 66–8.
30. Script of P Hillery's speech to ITGWU Conference, 4 May 1967, in Department of Labour files.
31. Report of Working Party meeting, ICTU file 2103, National Archives.
32. Script of P. Hillery's speech, 19 February 1969, in Department of Labour files.
33. J. Kelly, *Trade Unions and Socialist Politics* (London: Verso, 1988), pp. 82–125.
34. Script of P. Hillery's speech to NUJ, 14 September 1966, in Department of Labour files.
35. M. Gallagher, *Labour in Transition 1958–1973* (Manchester: Manchester University Press, 1982), p. 69.
36. Ibid., p. 67.
37. Labour Party, *Outline Policy Document for 1969 Conference*, pp. 31–2.
38. Gallagher, *Labour in Transition*, p. 93.
39. *Irish Times*, 29 January 1969.
40. *Irish Press*, 22 November 1967.
41. *Dáil Debate*, Vol. 238, Col. 1802, 26 February 1969.
42. *Dáil Debates*, Vol. 234, Col. 1638, 21 May 1968.
43. *Dáil Debates*, Vol. 238, Col. 228, 4 February 1969.
44. T.P. Coogan, *Disillusioned Decades* (Dublin: Gill and Macmillan, 1987), p. 18.
45. T. Ryle Dwyer, *Charlie* (Dublin: Gill and Macmillan, 1987), p. 67.
46. See e.g. E. McCann, *War and an Irish Town* (London: Pluto Press, 1993); or K. Kelley, *The Longest War* (Dingle: Brandon, 1982).
47. Labour Party, *Annual Report* (1969), p. 54.
48. *Dáil Debates*, Vol. 241, Cols 1425–6, 22 October 1969.
49. *Dáil Debates*, Vol. 241, Col. 1430, 22 October 1969.
50. *Dáil Debates*, Vol. 241, Col. 1550, 23 October 1969.
51. *Dáil Debates*, Vol. 241, Col. 1553, 23 October 1969.
52. *Dáil Debates*, Vol. 246, Cols 1536–7, 14 May 1970.
53. Labour Party, *Annual Report* (1971), p. 31.
54. N.I. Committee of ICTU statement, 10 August 1971, in minutes of ICTU Executive, 18 August 1971.

55. Gallagher, *Labour in Transition*, p. 172.
56. *Dáil Debates*, Vol. 256, Col. 191, 21 October 1971.
57. Gallagher, *Labour in Transition*, p. 172.
58. *Dáil Debates*, Vol. 246, Col. 1506, 13 May 1970.
59. Labour Party, *Annual Report* (1970), p. 13.
60. *Dáil Debates*, Vol. 258, Cols 1009–10, 3 February 1972.
61. ICTU, *Annual Report and Conference Proceedings* (1969), p. 271.
62. Script of P. Hillery's speech, 9 February 1969, in Department of Labour files.
63. ICTU, *Annual Report and Conference Proceedings* (1969), p. 327.
64. ICTU, *Conference Proceedings* (1970), p. 333.
65. *Dáil debates*, Vol. 251, Col. 116, 27 January 1972.
66. *Liberty*, November 1970.
67. Hazelhorn, 'Class, clientelism and political process', pp. 334–5.

7   The Rise and Fall of Charles J. Haughey, 1973–1990

1. L. Gibbons, 'Coming out of hibernation: the myth of modernization in Irish culture', in R. Kearney (ed.), *Across the Frontier* (Dublin: Wolfhound Press, 1988), pp. 217–18.
2. P. Bew and H. Patterson, 'Ireland in the 1990s – North and South', in Kearney (ed.), *Across the Frontier*, p. 87.
3. ITGWU, *Annual Report and Conference Proceedings* (1977), pp. 24, 35.
4. C.J. Haughey, *Spirit of the Nation* (Cork: Mercier, 1986) p. 109.
5. R. Sinnot, 'Patterns of policy support: social class', in P. Mair, M. Laver and R. Sinnot, *How Ireland Voted* (Dublin: Poolbeg, 1987), p. 102.
6. *Liberty*, April 1977.
7. ICTU, *Annual Report and Conference Proceedings* (1979), p. 668.
8. *Irish Times, Annual Review* (1978).
9. E. O'Connor, *A Labour History of Waterford* (Waterford: Waterford Trades Council, 1989), p. 349.
10. *Magill* (April 1979).
11. ICTU, *Annual Report and Conference Proceedings* (1979), pp. 271–2.
12. *Irish Times*, 15 March 1979.
13. *Irish Times*, 21 March 1979.
14. *Dáil Debates*, Vol. 312, Cols 1605–6, 15 March 1979.
15. *Irish Times*, 24 March 1979.
16. *Dáil Debates*, Vol. 313, Col. 2094, 15 March 1979.
17. *Irish Times*, 7 April 1979.
18. *Irish Times*, 2 April 1979.
19. T. Garvin, 'The growth of faction in the Fianna Fáil Party 1966–1980', *Parliamentary Affairs*, Vol. 34 (1981), pp. 110–22.
20. V. Browne, 'The making of a Taoiseach', *Magill* (January 1980).
21. Quoted in J. Lee, *Ireland 1912–1985* (Cambridge: Cambridge University Press, 1989), p. 500.
22. Quoted in S. Collins, *The Haughey File* (Dublin: O'Brien Press, 1992), p. 19.

23. Haughey, *Spirit of the Nation*, p. 324.
24. Ibid., p. 325.
25. Quoted in S. Cody, *Parliament of Labour* (Dublin: Council of Trade Unions, 1986,) p. 237.
26. *Irish Times*, 23 January 1980.
27. G. Fitzgerald, *All in a Life: An Autobiography* (Dublin: Gill and Macmillan, 1991), p. 340.
28. ICTU, *Annual Report and Conference Proceedings* (1981), p. 120.
29. Ibid., p. 121.
30. Ibid., p. 240.
31. *Dáil Debates*, Vol. 336, Col. 462, 10 June 1982.
32. M. Merrigan, *Eagle or Cuckoo* (Dublin: Matmer Publications, 1989), p. 267.
33. Quoted in V. Browne, 'The chickens come home to Roost', *Magill* (August 1980).
34. Fitzgerald, *All in a Life*, p. 463.
35. Haughey, *Spirit of the Nation*, p. 1015.
36. Quoted in H. Penniman and B. Farrell, *Ireland at the Polls: A Study of Four General Elections* (Durham, NC: Duke University Press, 1987), p. 12.
37. Haughey, *Spirit of the Nation*, p. 525.
38. T. Ryle Dwyer, *Charlie* (Dublin: Gill and Macmillan, 1987), p. 122.
39. Haughey, *Spirit of the Nation*, pp. 1122–3.
40. E. O'Reilly, *Masterminds of the Right* (Dublin: Attic Press, 1988).
41. E. McCann, 'A most impressive scene to behold', in C. Toibin (ed.), *Seeing is Believing* (Mountrath: Pilgrim Press, 1985), p. 35.
42. P. Kirby, *Is Irish Catholicism Dying* (Cork: Mercier Press, 1984), p. 37.
43. G. Hussey, *Ireland Today* (Dublin: Townhouse, 1993), p. 373.
44. D. Walsh, *Des O'Malley: A Political Profile* (Dingle: Brandon, 1986), p. 47.
45. T. Lyne, 'The progressive democrats 1985–1987', *Irish Political Studies*, Vol. 2 (1987).
46. Walsh, *O'Malley*, pp. 92–3.
47. *Industrial Relations News*, 12 April 1990.
48. Haughey, *Spirit of the Nation*, p. 870.
49. ICTU, *Annual Report and Conference Proceedings* (1987), p. 209.
50. Collins, *The Haughey File*, p. 128.
51. Fianna Fáil, *Annual Report* (1990).
52. *Industrial Relations News*, 8 June 1989.
53. M. Fogarty, D. Egan and W. Ryan, *Pay Policy for the 1980s* (Dublin: Federated Union of Employers, 1981), p. 72.
54. ICTU, *Public Enterprise and Economic Development* (Dublin: ICTU, n.d.), p. 3.
55. ICTU, *Trade Unions and Change* (Dublin: ICTU, 1989), p. 18.
56. See C. Mair, 'Pre-conditions for corporatism', in J. Goldthorpe (ed.), *Order and Conflict in Contemporary Capitalism* (Oxford: Clarendon Press, 1984), p. 49.
57. *Irish Times*, 31 October 1991.

Conclusion

1. T. Garvin, *The Evolution of Nationalist Politics* (Dublin: Gill and Macmillan, 1981).
2. E. O'Connor, *Syndicalism in Ireland* (Cork: Cork University Press, 1988).
3. R. Munck, *Argentina: From Anarchism to Peronism* (London: Zed, 1987), p. 129.
4. For wider argument see K. Allen, *Is Southern Ireland a Neo-Colony?*, (Dublin: Bookmarks, 1990).
5. A. Cawson, *Corporatism and Political Theory* (Oxford: Blackwell, 1986), p. 87.
6. F. Mockler, 'Organisation changes in Fianna Fáil and Fine Gael', *Irish Political Studies*, Vol. 9 (1994), pp. 165–71.
7. P. Mair, *The Changing Party System* (London: Pinter, 1987).
8. Mockler, 'Organisation changes', p. 166.
9. For full investigation see F. O'Toole, *Meanwhile Back at the Ranch* (London: Vintage, 1995).
10. K. Allen, 'What's changing in Ireland', *International Socialism*, No. 64 (Autumn 1994), pp. 65–105.
11. *Socialist Worker*, No. 33 (1966).
12. M. Gallagher, *Political Parties in the Republic of Ireland* (Manchester: Manchester University Press, 1985), p. 27.

Select Bibliography

Unpublished Manuscripts and Government Records

CIU deposit (National Archives).
CIU, minutes of National Executive (various years) (ICTU headquarters).
De Valera papers (Franciscan Library).
Fianna Fáil, minutes of parliamentary meetings (1926–47) (Fianna Fáil headquarters).
Fianna Fáil, scripts of speeches of Fianna Fáil Ministers of Labour (1966–90) (Department of Labour).
ICTU deposit (National Archives).
ICTU, minutes of National Executive (various years) (ICTU headquarters).
ITUC deposit (National Archives).
ITUC, minutes of National Executive, 1938–58 (ICTU headquarters).
Moss Twomey papers (National Library of Ireland)
Patrick McGilligan papers (National Library of Ireland).
Sean McEntee papers (UCD Archives).
State papers (National Archives).
Thomas Johnson papers (National Library of Ireland).
William O'Brien papers (National Library of Ireland).

Newspapers

Irish Press.
Irish Independent.
Irish Times.
Liberty.
The Torch.
The Irish Socialist.
Republican Congress.
Clare Champion.
Connaught Sentinel.
Cork Examiner.
The Irishman.
The Watchword.
The Nation.
Labour News.
Magill.
Industrial Relations News.

Miscellaneous

Dáil Debates (various years).

CIU, *Annual Reports* (various years).

CSO, *Census of Industrial Production* (various years).

CSO, *Statistical Abstracts* (various years).

Department of Industry and Commerce, *Statistical Abstracts* (various years).

Department of Labour, *Annual Reports* (1966–90).

Fianna Fáil *Ard Fheis Clar* (1926–90).

Fianna Fáil Bulletin (1936–39) (National Library of Ireland).

FUE, *Annual Reports* (1977–90)

IDA, *Annual Reports* (1970–90).

ITGWU, *Annual Reports* (various years).

ITUC, *Annual Reports* (various years).

Labour Court, *Annual Reports* (1947–90).

Labour Party, *Annual Reports* (1930–90).

Trade Union Information (1955–90) (National Library of Ireland).

Published Sources

Aiken, F., *A Call to Unity* (Dublin: Fodhla, 1926).

Allen, K., *Is Southern Ireland a Neo-Colony?* (London: Bookmarks, 1990).

Allen, K., *The Politics of James Connolly* (London: Pluto, 1990).

Allen, K. 'What is changing in Ireland', *International Socialism Journal*, No. 64 (August 1994).

Andrews, C.S., *A Man of No Property* (Cork: Mercier, 1982).

Arnold, B., *What Kind of Country?* (London: Cape, 1984).

Bax, M., *Harpstrings and Confessions* (Assen: Van Gorcum, 1976).

Bew, P. and Patterson, H., *Sean Lemass and the making of Modern Ireland 1945–64* (Dublin: Gill and Macmillan, 1982).

Boyer Bell, J., *The Secret Army: A History of the IRA* (Dublin: Academy Press, 1980).

Boland, K., *Up Dev* (Dublin: Boland, 1978).

Bradley, D., *Farm Labourers' Irish Struggle 1900–1976* (Belfast: Athol, 1988).

Brown, T., *Ireland: A Social and Cultural History* (London: Fontana, 1985).

Browne, N., *Against the Tide* (Dublin: Gill and Macmillan, 1986).

Busteed, M. and Mason, H., 'Irish Labour in the 1969 election', *Political Studies*, Vol. 18 (1970).

Carroll, J.P. and Murphy, J.A., *De Valera and His Times* (Cork: Cork University Press, 1983).

Carroll, J.T., *Ireland in the War Years 1939–45* (Newton Abbot: David and Charles, 1975).

Chubb, B., 'Going around persecuting civil servants: the role of the Irish Parliamentary Representative', *Political Studies*, Vol. 11 (1963).

Chubb, B., *The Government and Politics of Ireland* (London: Longman, 1982).

Coogan, T.P., *The IRA* (London: Pall Mall, 1971).

Coogan, T.P., *Disillusioned Decades* (Dublin: Gill and Macmillan, 1987).

Cronin, S., *The McGarritty Papers* (Tralee: Anvil, 1972).

Crotty, R., *Ireland in Crisis: A Study in Capitalist Colonial Undevelopment* (Dingle: Brandon, 1986).

Daly, M., 'An Irish Ireland for business: the Control of Manufacturers Acts 1932 and 1934', *Irish Historical Studies*, Vol. 24 (1984).

Daniel, T.K., 'Griffith on his noble head: the determinants of Cumman na nGaedheal economic policy 1922–1932', *Irish Economic and Social History*, Vol. 3 (1976).

Department of Industrial Relations, UCD (eds), *Industrial Relations in Ireland* (Dublin: UCD, 1987).

Dunphy, R., *The Making of Fianna Fáil Power in Ireland 1923–1948* (Oxford: Oxford University Press, 1995).

Fanning, R., *The Irish Department of Finance 1922–1958* (Dublin: Institute of Public Administration, 1978).

Fanning, R., *Independent Ireland* (Dublin: Helicon, 1983).

Farrell, B., 'Labour and the Irish political system: a suggested approach to analysis', *Economic and Social Review*, Vol. 1 (1970).

Farrell, B., *Chairman or Chief* (Dublin: Gill and Macmillan, 1971).

Farrell, B., *Sean Lemass* (Dublin: Gill and Macmillan, 1983).

Fisk, R., *In Time of War: Ireland, Ulster and the Price of Neutrality 1939–45* (London: Deutsch, 1983).

Gallagher, M., *The Irish Labour Party in Transition 1957–1982* (Manchester: Manchester University Press, 1982).

Gallagher, M., *Political Parties in the Republic of Ireland* (Manchester: Manchester University Press, 1985).

Garvin, T., 'Political cleavages, party politics and the urbanisation of Ireland: the case of a periphery dominated centre', *European Journal of Political Research*, Vol. 2 (1974).

Garvin, T., 'The growth of faction in the Fianna Fáil Party', *Parliamentary Affairs*, Vol. 34 (1981).

Garvin, T., *The Evolution of Nationalist Politics* (Dublin: Gill and Macmillan, 1981).

Gaughan, T., *Tom Johnson 1872–1963, First Leader of the Labour Party in Dáil Eireann* (Dublin: Kingdom, 1981).

Girvin, B., 'The dominance of Fianna Fáil and the nature of party adaptability in Ireland', *Political Studies*, Vol. 32 (1982).

Girvin, B., *Between Two Worlds* (Dublin: Gill and Macmillan, 1989).

Hardiman, N., *Pay, Politics and Economic Performance in Ireland 1970–1987* (Oxford: Clarendon Press, 1988).

Haughey, C.J., *The Spirit of the Nation* (Cork: Mercier, 1986).

Hutton, S. and Stewart, P., *Ireland's Histories* (London: Routledge, 1991).

ICTU, *Ireland 1990–2000* (Dublin: ICTU, n.d.).

ICTU, *Trade Unions and Change* (Dublin: ICTU, 1989).

Johnson, D., *The Inter-War Economy in Ireland* (Dublin: Economic and Social History Society, 1984).

Jones, M., *Those Obstreperous Lassies* (Dublin: Gill and Macmillan, 1988).

Kelley, K., *The Longest War* (Dingle: Brandon, 1982).

Laver, M., 'Ireland: politics with some social base', *Economic and Social Review*, Vol. 17 (1986).

Lee, J.(ed.), *Ireland 1945–1970* (Dublin: Gill and Macmillan, 1979).

Lee, J., *Ireland 1912–1985* (Cambridge: Cambridge University Press, 1989).

Lee. J. and O'Tuathaigh, G., *The Age of De Valera* (Dublin: Ward River Press, 1982).

Litton, F., *Unequal Achievement: The Irish Experience 1957–1982* (Dublin: IPA, 1982).

Longford, L. and O'Neill, T.P., *Eamon de Valera* (London: Hutchinson, 1970).

Lyons, F.S.L., *Ireland Since the Famine* (London: Collins/Fontana, 1982).

McCarthy, C., *Decade of Upheaval* (Dublin: IPA, 1973).

McCarthy, C., *Trade Unions in Ireland 1894–1960* (Dublin: IPA, 1977).

McMahon, D. *Republicans and Imperialists: Anglo-Irish Relations in the 1930s* (New Haven: Yale University Press, 1984).

McManus, F. (ed.), *The Years of the Great Test* (Cork: Mercier, 1967).

Mair, P., 'Ireland 1948–1981: issues, parties, strategies', in I. Budge, D. Robertson and D. Heart, *Ideology, Strategy and Party Change: Spatial Analysis of Post War Election Programmes in 19 Democracies* (Cambridge: Cambridge University Press, 1977).

Mair, P., *The Changing Irish Party System* (London: Pinter, 1987).

Manning, M., *Irish Political Parties* (Dublin: Gill and Macmillan, 1972).

Manning, M., *The Blueshirts* (Dublin: Gill and Macmillan, 1987).

Manseragh, N. (ed.), *Speeches and Statements of Eamon de Valera* (Dublin: Gill and Macmillan, 1980).

Meehan, J., *The Irish Economy since 1922* (Liverpool: Liverpool University Press, 1970).

Merrigan, M., *Eagle or Cuckoo* (Dublin: Matmer Publications, 1989).

Milotte, M., *Communism in Modern Ireland* (Dublin: Gill and Macmillan, 1984).

Mitchell, A. and O'Snodaigh, P., *Irish Political Documents 1916–1949* (Dublin: Irish Academy Press, 1985).

Mitchell, A., *Labour in Irish Politics* (New York: Barnes and Noble, 1974).

Morgan, A. and Purdie, B., *Ireland: Divided Nation, Divided Class* (London: Inklinks, 1980).

Morrissey, M., 'The politics of economic management in Ireland 1958–1970', *Irish Political Studies*, Vol. 1 (1986).

Moss, W., *Political Parties in the Irish Free State* (New York: AMS Press, 1968).

Moynihan, M. (ed.), *Speeches and Statements by Eamon de Valera 1917–1973* (Dublin: Gill and Macmillan, 1980).

Munger, F., *The Legitimacy of Opposition: The Change of Government of 1932* (London: Sage, 1975).

Murphy, J.A., *Ireland in the Twentieth Century* (Cork: Mercier, 1981).

Nevin, D., *Trade Unions and Change in Irish Society* (Cork: Mercier, 1980).

O'Connor, E., *Syndicalism in Ireland* (Cork: Cork University Press, 1988).

O'Connor Lysaght, D.R., *The Republic of Ireland* (Cork: Mercier, 1970).

O'Malley, E. *Industry and Economic Development: The Challenge of the Latecomer* (Dublin: Gill and Macmillan, 1989).

Orridge, A., 'The Blueshirts and the Economic War', *Political Studies*, Vol. 31 (1983).

Patterson, H., 'Fianna Fáil and the Irish working class: the origins of an enigmatic relationship', *Saothar*, Vol. 13 (1988).

Patterson, H., *The Politics of Illusion* (London: Hutchinson, 1989).

Praeger, J., *Building Democracy in Ireland* (Cambridge: Cambridge University Press, 1986).

Redmond, S., *The Irish Muncipal Employees Trade Union* (Dublin: IMETU, 1983).

Rumpf, E. and Hepburn, A.C., *Nationalism and Socialism in Twentieth Century Ireland* (Liverpool: Liverpool University Press, 1977).

Ryle Dwyer, T., *Charlie: The Political Biography of Charles J. Haughey* (Dublin: Gill and Macmillan, 1987).

Ryle Dwyer, T., *De Valera: The Man and the Myth* (Dublin: Poolbeg, 1992).

Sacks, P., *The Donegal Mafia* (New Haven: Yale University Press, 1976).

Swift, J., 'Report of the Commission on Vocational Organisation', *Saothar*, Vol. 1 (1975).

Tobin, F., *The Best of Decades* (Dublin: Gill and Macmillan, 1984).

Walsh, D., *The Party: Inside Fianna Fáil* (Dublin: Gill and Macmillan, 1986).

Whitaker, T.K., *Interests* (Dublin: IPA, 1983).

Whyte, J., 'Ireland: politics without social bases', in R. Rose, *Electoral Behaviour: A Comparative Handbook* (New York: Free Press, 1974).

Whyte, J., *Church and State in Modern Ireland 1923–1970* (Dublin: Gill and Macmillan, 1980).

Williams, T.D., *The Irish Struggle 1916–1966* (London: Routledge, 1966).

Index

Index by Judith Lavender